D1614904

SECRETS OF THE COLD WAR

US Army Europe's Intelligence and Counterintelligence activities against the Soviets during the Cold War

Leland C. McCaslin

Helion & Company Ltd

Helion & Company Limited
26 Willow Road
Solihull
West Midlands
B91 1UE
England
Tel. 0121 705 3393
Fax 0121 711 4075
Email: info@helion.co.uk
Website: www.helion.co.uk

Published by Helion & Company 2010

Designed and typeset by Farr out Publications, Wokingham, Berkshire
Cover designed by Bookcraft Ltd, Stroud, Gloucestershire
Printed by Gutenberg Press Limited, Tarxien, Malta

ISBN 978 1 906033 91 0

British Library Cataloguing-in-Publication Data.
A catalogue record for this book is available from the British Library.

For details of other military history titles published by Helion & Company Limited
contact the above address, or visit our website: http://www.helion.co.uk.

We always welcome receiving book proposals from prospective authors.

Dedication

Dick Hinderliter (March 9, 1929 – January 21, 2008), whom I did not personally know, but had the pleasure of communicating with, wrote his story and sent it to me, which has been included in Chapter 15: Border Patrol.

John E. Pendergast (October 2, 1930 – August 6, 2009), whom I did not personally know, wrote his story and sent it to me, which has been included in Chapter 2: Allied Military Liaison Missions Potsdam – Our Collectors in the East. "Slán agus beannacht leat – Farewell and blessings on you!"

Bernard (Bud) F. Hiller (December 29, 1931 – January 16, 2009) was my friend and known to most in the Army intelligence community as an expert in the Security arena and a colleague. He will be remembered as the "Grandfather of Security."

Gary Arrasmith (June 3, 1943 – January 19, 2010) was my friend and in charge of Personnel Security in the Security Branch. He was a security expert and was responsible for providing special clearances under combat conditions for troops moving to the Persian Gulf for Desert Shield/Desert Storm.

We note the passing of all who have served our great country with both sorrow and gratitude. With the publication of this book, I add my thanks for their dedication, numerous contributions and faithful labor that they have given throughout the years.

Map of Divided Germany

HEIDELBERG

★★★★

AMERICAN CINC

66th MI Group

ZOSSEN-WÜNSDORF

★★★★

SOVIET CINC

Contents

Preface

"What was the Cold War?" a young lad asked his dad. The father explained to his son and then later told me about the question.

The young boy's question pulled me into the memories of the Cold War. Faded images of spies, terrorists, and the Berlin Wall flashed through my mind. It was an era that reshaped the world and those who were tangled within its dangerous deceptions.

Being at the Army's Headquarters in Germany during the Cold War for those many years, I knew the command's secrets and inner workings.

I remembered it all started when the Nazis surrendered at the end of WWII and the Allied occupiers settled into Germany in 1945. The Cold War was over in the early 1990s when the Soviet Union dissolved.

Circa 1945: Campbell Barracks, the home of HQ USAREUE. (US Army)

Campbell Barracks in the snow. (Author's collection)

Generally, the French, English and American Allied occupiers were on one side and the Soviet occupiers (and Soviet dominated countries) were on the other side.

Specifically, it was a war of hostilities without bullets (usually, as we shall see) or a stand-off between the two superpowers, the United States and the USSR. The center of this simmering war was divided Germany where the US faced the Soviet Union on the ground with tanks and in the air with U-2s and smaller jets; this cold war could have turned hot and exploded into WW III.

It seems like only yesterday when I was in Heidelberg. Its cobble-stoned streets, the Neckar River, and its great castle make Heidelberg a special and romantic place.

The US Army Europe (USAREUR) or better known as Eisenhower's Army has been headquartered in Heidelberg since the end of World War II until the present day.

I would like to thank my guest writers from enlisted SP4 (Corporal) to General Officers from the US, British, and French militaries for entrusting me with their exciting, and in some cases, never-before-told true accounts of the Cold War.

Some events that happened were omitted because they are still classified and government officials have forbidden me from mentioning them. As I told one would-be contributor: "I guess your part of the war, however noble, must remain silent."

I conducted a modicum of general research while preparing this manuscript; but the main preparation was recalling that time and putting it on paper, finding guest writers with interesting and relevant topics and adding appropriate Cold War-era images to match the text.

If there are inaccuracies in this manuscript, they are unintentional; I take responsibility.

Military intelligence personnel are 'raised' to be careful about mentioning government secrets; therefore, it goes against my moral grain to say anything. Although acutely aware of and sensitive to the protection of classified information, I wrote this book for its historical value before those of us who were there during the Cold War pass on. I made sure to obtain exhaustive Federal Government security reviews prior to releasing this book to the public. This manuscript is not a comprehensive record of the Cold War but adds to the body of previously published accounts. I wrote it as a salute to those that served. You know who you are!

Foreword

Frederick James Kroesen, Jr. is the former Commander-in-Chief (CINC) of the US Army Europe from 1979 to 1983. He is a retired Army four star general.

Given the criticism, bad news and alleged malfeasances associated with our intelligence services during the past decade, it is most refreshing to find a book relating a far different story. The successes of our Cold War efforts to track, examine and thwart the intelligence systems of the Warsaw Pact nations, especially the Soviet Union, are interesting, educational and ought to be reassuring for Americans and their government who are still in dire need of reliable intelligence. This volume reflects what we can do when the mission is clear and the resources are committed.

Frederick J. Kroesen, General, USA-Ret

General Kroesen later describes how the Red Army Faction terrorist group fired a Russian rocket-propelled grenade (RPG-7) at the limo he and his wife were in - they survived. I obtained a picture of his destroyed RPGed limo from the *Stars & Stripes*. Upon my sending him a copy, he said, "Thanks for the reminder!"

Acknowledgements

Thanks to my literary agent, Al Longden, and to my publisher, Duncan Rogers at Helion & Company Ltd. Many thanks to my wife Charlotte for her encouragement and support! I must also express my appreciation to Louis Zammarella. He has worked for many premier US intelligence agencies, was a prior supervisor (leader), mentor and now I trust, good friend.

Thanks to GEN Frederick J. Kroesen former CINC USAREUR for the well thought-out Foreword and first-hand description of the Red Army Faction terrorist attack along with MG William F. Burns and MG James L. Dozier (kidnapped!). Many thanks to Francis Gary Powers, Jr., for his kind words. Thanks to COL Jack Hammond, former G2 USAREUR for the great sum-up and special historical insights! Thank you to many individuals for some of the beautiful images! Thanks to Scott O'Connell, a current national defense security expert who contributed and offered suggestions in writing this manuscript.

Sincere thanks to LTC Paul Harpin who also contributed and who was a tough consultant. I especially appreciate him for reviewing and making suggesting as to fact and style in the extensive Glossary. Thanks to my brother, LTC Jim McCaslin, for his Hotline chapter and the frequent German and Russian translation assists. Thanks Brigadier General Julia Kraus, a former work colleague, as of this date still on active duty and a research associate for this book; she opened many closed doors for me. Thanks to USAREUR Historian Bruce Siemon; he contributed to the book and provided other invaluable Army information. Also thanks to Frank R. Shirer, Chief, Historical Resources Branch, U.S. Army Center of Military History. Also my gratitude is due to Bob Stone, INSCOM Public Affairs Office and James Hill, Department of the Army Office of Chief of Public Affairs. And thank you DOD polygraph expert, Gordon Barland, PhD, for your advice, support and for being my friend.

Thanks, Pat Lezzer, for the wordsmith editing. She was a real trooper and friend. Thanks to Brenda Drake, who writes novels for young adults and middle grade, for the amazing edit job!! Her suggestions were invaluable. Thanks to graphic artist D.L. Keur (zentao.com) for producing an earlier cover design and whose work, although ultimately not used, is warmly appreciated.

Also thanks to SP4 Alberto "AJ" M. Juliachs, SP5 Conrad (Connie) Schornhorst, British RAF Frank Naylor and MG PG Williams, French Colonel Daniel Pasquier, U.S. LTC John Pendergast, LTC Charles Stiles, John Rademacher, Dr Julie Mehan, Arnie Hunter, LTC Ken Krantz, MG Lajoie, COL Ron Gambolati, Train Commander CPT Dani Smyer Wildason and her Train Commander cohorts, Robert Rynerson for his input and all the other contributors to the book. Thanks to Bob Bowles for his expert guidance. Thanks to the many paratroopers who contributed, such as SP4 Frank Brown and LTC Frank Tapparo. Thanks to Dr. /LTC Jim Holbrook, author of *Potsdam Mission*. Hats off to artist Andy bell (sic). Thanks to the guidance of a certain USMLM member. Thanks to Master Sergeant Dale Day (Ret) for his editing advice. Thanks to David Perk for his Cold War Super Car photo and the contributors who wrote about it. Also, many thanks to Richard A. Fisher and his USMLM-Potsdam website.

Thanks to Dr. Rhonda Parker, Professor of Communication Studies at Stanford University for all her guidance, expertise, and encouragement. It meant much to me! Also thanks to Dr. John Forde, head of the Communication Department at Mississippi State University (my BS Alma Mater) who helped me, as well as Bobby Harmous of the MSU Barnes & Noble. Also thanks to all the government pre-pub security professionals (and their staffs) who ensured it contained no classified material. Thank you Ann Griffin for your computer expertise and many and varied assists.

I give a 'hats off' to PhDs Dr. Rhonda Parker (again) and Dr. Leslie Epstein (BU English) for their review of the all-important proposal.

I wrote this true story and orchestrated guest-writer input after I suffered a paralyzing stroke. Thanks to all who cared for me in those dark days and today. Specifically, thanks to my wife, Charlotte; mother-in-law Margaret Shewmaker; Dr. Emily Riser, Neurologist; Dr. Lawrence Hawley, Internal Medicine; Dr Marion Buckley, PhD; Clinton Reeves; therapists like Anthony, Joanne, Ann, Kathy, Cheryl, Monica, Mandy and Mary Gwen (and all you others) and hospital ward caregivers, like Ros. All super caregivers!

If I forgot anyone, I apologize.

List of contributors

Pre-publication security reviews

This book was reviewed under the previous working title of *Collectors, Blockers & Memories*. Later the title was changed to *Secrets of the Cold War*.

Favorable/Approved security reviews were conducted by:

- HQ United States Army Europe (USAREUR) – ISR Directorate,
- National Security Agency (NSA),
- National Military Command Center (NMCC – J3) concerning the Hotline (MOLINK) chapter.

Specific approvals are on file.

1

The threat: seven case histories
(Terrorists and covert spies)

Short of all-out-war the greatest threats against US Army Europe (USAREUR) were spies and deadly terrorist attacks.

The major terrorist group which faced USAREUR was the **Red Army Faction** (RAF). They were violent, lethal and used bombings to try to intimidate USAREUR and our government. The Red Army Faction, also known as the Baader-Meinhof Gang, was one of the most dangerous terrorist groups in the Cold War. They launched approximately 24 anti-Western attacks (mostly bombings), killed about 30 people, and wounded from 65 to 70 people.

National defense expert Scott O'Connell says:

> The RAF did pin down scarce CI assets that we could have used more effectively used to root out spies. Even more curious, a lot of it tapered off and died down when the Berlin wall came down raising the credibility of those who felt the Communist east bloc of countries was behind or at least lent material support to them.

Another defense expert, LTC (Ret) Ken Krantz, former USAREUR Counterintelligence Chief of Analysis reports

> The relationship between the East German *Stasi* (Secret Police) and the RAF was confirmed after 1990. The *Stasi* gave financial and identity support as well as sanctuary to the RAF.

A different terrorist group was the **Red Brigades** (*Brigate Rosse)*. They were a Marxist-Leninist terrorist group in Italy in the 1970s and encouraged Italy's separation from NATO by kidnapping and murder. Italian law enforcement broke up the group in the 1980s.

General (Ret) Frederick Kroesen, Major General (Ret) William Burns and Major General (Ret) James Dozier tell their first-hand stories of battling the terrorist during the Cold War. Names, units and locations were not changed – they are factual.

Case 1
The terrorist attack on General Kroesen by the terrorist group the Red Army Faction (*Rote Armee Faktion*): Sedan shot by a rocket grenade!

General Kroesen tells us ...
On the morning of September 15, 1981 at about 7AM, my wife, Rowene, and I were *en route* from our quarters in Schlierbach to USAREUR headquarters in Heidelberg. We were

riding in a Baden-Wuerttemburg armored state police car because they, the police, had been warned that I was a terrorist target.

We were accompanied by a German police officer/driver and my American aide de camp, Major Phillip Bodine. We were led by another state police car and followed by Heidelberg police and US Army military police. At a routine traffic light stop, a Russian rocket-propelled grenade (RPG-7) was fired at the car from a hillside position approximately 100 meters to the left rear. The warhead penetrated the trunk and exited through the right rear fender. My wife and I were both injured by flying glass as the explosion destroyed the rear window. A second round landed in the street just behind the car and a machine gun strafed the left side.

Our driver was told to drive on if the car was still operable and he did so, but not before my wife observed an interested female pedestrian spectator who had not run for cover when all others scattered from the area. It was an important sighting as she was later able to identify one of the principal members of the Baader-Meinhof gang during the police investigation that followed.

The driver delivered us to the US Army 130th Station Hospital where our wounds were treated before we continued with our scheduled activities for the day.

The perpetrators had camped on the hillside for some time before they found the opportunity to attack, and they departed immediately, abandoning their camping equipment and a third RPG round. They were not apprehended for two or more years, but they were caught, tried and sentenced to long prison terms. One, the gunner, remains in jail today.

My subsequent travels on that day took me to a field maneuver headquarters where, at a hastily assembled news conference, I was able to assure my German friends that I assigned them no fault for the incident. I was also able to express appreciation that the gang members were not equipped with an American weapon and to remind everyone that it was not the first time a German had shot at me and missed.

FJK – Aug 2008

Case 2
The terrorist attack on the 42nd Field Artillery Brigade – *Rote Armee* Faktion terrorist group: depot attacked!

General Burns tells us...
In January 1977 I was a brigade commander as well as the Giessen-North Sub-community commander in Giessen, about thirty miles northwest of Frankfurt. At that time, there was an incident at the Giessen Army Depot during which there was a minor explosion and fire at a fuel storage tank adjacent to the Depot. This tank was used to store fuel under NATO control and was almost empty at the time. Apparently, a group of terrorists later identified as probably Red Army Faction attempted to destroy the tank, cause a major conflagration, and possibly damage the Giessen Depot. The depot housed the headquarters of the 42d Field Artillery Brigade, a major storage facility for the Army/Air Force Exchange System in Europe, the Giessen Sub-community headquarters, and some ancillary facilities.

The incident was a failure for the RAF for two reasons: first, the attack on the tank was based on the assumption that the tank was almost full, but the attackers misread the gauge and the explosive charge went off above the fuel level. Thus, the explosion was relatively minor, the tank did not rupture, and the fuel in the tank did not burn to any degree. Second, the response of the soldiers on guard was superb – detailed plans had been made to thwart just such an incident and coordination with the local German police had been planned. Several perpetrators were later arrested – I'm not sure whether the German police arrested any that night or the next day, however. Whether the RAF element intended only to destroy the fuel storage tanks or whether they also intended to damage the Giessen Army Depot proper is not clear. The fact that there was a classified facility within the Depot may or may not have been known to them. In any event, troops on security duty within the Depot responded to small arms fire; there was no hostile penetration of the Depot. The security plan called for reinforcements from the 3rd Armored Division located nearby, and these additional troops arrived well within the time limits specified, further securing the area. Interestingly, about two years later two alleged members of the RAF were on trial in Dusseldorf for terrorist acts including the Giessen incident. One of their defenses was that "small arms firing that night in Giessen was caused by US military police chasing US Army deserters in the woods near the Depot." I was asked to testify to the facts – units in Giessen had no deserters or soldiers absent without leave at the time in question. Because of the sensitive nature of the area and status of forces agreements that pertained, I was assured that the defense counsels for the accused would not be able to press the issue of what kind of facilities were located at Giessen – and they did not. (I don't even remember the names of the accused at this point.) During this period, terrorists had attacked several NATO/US facilities and individuals and the entire European Command was under heightened alert against this threat. It put a strain on already over-committed resources, but my command was able to accomplish its various missions throughout the period. Thus, if the RAF's objective was to reduce the US Army's combat effectiveness in Europe, it failed.

William F. Burns – 5 August 2008 Major General, US Army, Retired Former Commander (as Colonel, Field Artillery) 42d Field Artillery Brigade, Giessen, FRG

Case 3
The kidnapping of Major General James Dozier in Italy – Red Brigades: Kidnapped!

General Dozier is a graduate of the U. S. Military Academy, West Point, and the University of Arizona, with an MS degree in Aero Space Engineering. He has 35 years military service with the U. S Army and NATO in the United States, Europe and Asia, with two tours in the Pentagon on the Army Staff, specializing in Current Operations and Resource Management. He was awarded the Silver Star for heroism and the Purple Heart for wounds received in combat in Viet Nam. He currently serves as an anti-terrorism consultant to various government and private agencies as a result of his kidnapping by the Italian Red Brigades terrorists in Italy in 1981.

General Dozier tells us …
Purpose of the kidnapping

The purpose of my kidnapping was to help bring down the government of Italy and get Italy out of NATO. Collapsing the government and getting Italy out of NATO was plainly stated as a goal in their 1981-82 Fall Campaign Plan. They figured that if they could kidnap a senior American military officer, it would embarrass the Italian security services who had the security responsibility for the NATO HQ as well as the personnel assigned to the various HQs. If successful, they thought it would tend to destabilize the Italian government and lead to its collapse. As a left wing urban guerilla organization, the Red Brigades had been at war with the Italian government for about 10 years. They had thus far been unsuccessful, but for the 81-82 campaign they decided to make a final push. The code name for the operation was called *Winter of Fire*. I, of course, was not the only kidnapping target. A number of high Italian officials had also been targeted.

My experience

At the time of the kidnapping, I was assigned to a predominantly Italian NATO HQ in Verona, Italy known as LANDSOUTH, the land component of the Southern Command of NATO headquartered in Naples Italy. My title was the Deputy Chief of Staff for Administration and Logistics. As such, I was the senior US officer in the headquarters.

In addition to my NATO military duties, I was the community leader of the small American community in the Verona area, about 85 families, mostly USAF communicators. There was no US housing area in Verona, so all of us lived on the economy. My wife and I occupied the top floor and penthouse of a seven story high-rise apartment building in downtown Verona.

The American general assigned to LANDSOUTH had occupied the apartment for quite a few years. It was well-known as the American General's quarters. After I was rescued, we looked for a better place to house the American General and couldn't find one better suited, so we hardened up the apartment with a number of security measures.

I had come home early on the evening of 17 December in order to get ready for a Community Council meeting of our small American community. It was about 1730 on a Thursday evening. My wife and I were having a drink in the kitchen when the front doorbell of our apartment rang. That was unusual, because in our building, there were two doorbell systems. One was at the front entrance to the building, which allowed a person who wanted to visit a given apartment to ring a bell, and then talk to someone in the apartment via an intercom. If those in the apartment wanted to let them in, they could unlock the front door of the building electronically, or tell them to go away. *That bell had not rung prior to the bell ringing at our front door* and my wife was concerned about it. I told her not to worry, sort of "famous last words", and I went to the door and asked who was there. A voice answered in Italian saying that they were plumbers and that there was a leak in the apartment downstairs and that they wanted to check our apartment to see if that was where the leak had occurred. It sounded reasonable to me, the building was about 20 years old and things were always going wrong in it, so I opened the door.

There stood two young men. They looked like plumbers and they acted like plumbers, so I let them in. We checked the washroom and utility room for leaks, but couldn't find any. Then, one of the young men used a word in Italian that I didn't understand, so I told him that we needed to go to the kitchen where I kept an Italian-English dictionary so I could understand what he was saying. We all went back to the kitchen where my wife continued to fix dinner. As I was bending over the kitchen table looking up the word in the dictionary the fun began.

I was jumped from the rear, spun around and was looking down the barrels of two silenced pistols. A fight started which I very quickly began to lose. During the scuffle one of the young men rushed into the kitchen and grabbed my wife. I was soon hit on the head and knocked to the floor in the hallway outside of the kitchen. When I looked back into the kitchen, the young man who had grabbed my wife by this time had her on her knees with a pistol pointed at her head. That was when the fight was over. I was immediately handcuffed, blindfolded, and gagged. As I was further immobilized and my wife immobilized, they let two other individuals into the apartment who began to ransack it.

I was soon loaded into a steamer trunk, disguised as the packing carton for a small refrigerator. It was padded on the inside, but from my standpoint, it had one major design flaw – no air holes. When they closed the lid for more than a short period of time that caused some problems. The trunk was put into the building elevator, taken downstairs into a courtyard behind the apartment building, then loaded into a rented van. The van was driven to a basement-parking garage in another high rise apartment building where the trunk was transferred to Fiat hatchback sedan. The van was then abandoned in another part of town. I was driven, still in the trunk, for about an hour and a half enroute to Padova.

At this point, even though I did not know why they kidnapped me, or what, they intended to do with me, during the kidnapping itself and during the ride to Padova, I got some indications that they did not want to kill me right then. After I was knocked into the hallway of the apartment, I briefly feigned unconsciousness and one of them hastily checked my breathing and pulse. Later, during the ride to Padova (we took back roads), they would open the lid of the trunk after we had cleared a town and would check my pulse and breathing.

Also, during the ride to Padova, I managed to get a feel for the direction we were taking. On two of the main roads leading out of Verona there was a bakery followed by an oil refinery. I was able to smell each of them, so was sure that I was headed either South toward Modena or East toward Venice. I later figured out we had gone East when they provided me with Italian news magazines with Veneto advertisements in them.

When we arrived at another high-rise apartment building in Padova, they put the box into the building elevator, went up and down a few times to disorient me and then stopped on the second floor. I was taken into an apartment and dumped onto a metal bunk, inside of a cabana type tent erected in one of the apartment bedrooms. The area of the tent I was in was about 6 feet square. In addition to the metal bunk, which had a mattress and pillow, there was a chemical toilet and a light bulb which was changed periodically from white to blue to indicate day and night. My part of the tent was separated from the guard's part of the tent by a flap kept partially closed. Three men and one woman rotated guard duty. I was chained to the bunk by an arm and a leg. The wounds that I had suffered during the fight in Verona were taken care of and from that point on I was generally well treated, even though I was made to wear a headset through which recorded music was played almost continuously. At first it was hard rock and that was pretty awful, I complained and later they changed it to Gershwin, but it was a daily battle with the guards as they changed shifts over the volume. I was fed three meals a day – nothing great, but certainly adequate. At no time was I ever completely unhooked from the bunk, so in all the escape plans that I came up with, I had to consider that bunk. Anywhere I went it was going to go.

I later learned that the technique of erecting a tent inside of a structure to house kidnap victims was first used by Argentinean organizations in the early 1970s. It is designed to do a couple of key things. First, by separating the guard and the prisoner, they hoped to preclude the onset of the Stockholm Syndrome – the relationship that sometimes develops between a prisoner and a guard held in close proximity each other for extended periods.

Patty Hearst is a good example of how that might work. In my case one of the guards was somewhat affected – which worked to my benefit at the time of my rescue. The second thing it is designed to do is to allow the guards to completely control the environment in which they keep the prisoner. This was initially very successful. None of my senses could penetrate outside of that small confined area.

They made a concerted attempt to get me to understand what the Red Brigades were all about – I guess you could call it brainwashing. Sometime during the first week or so, they brought in a 12 page typewritten document on legal sized paper and told me to read it. It was in Italian, so I skimmed it and threw it under the bunk. A day or so later they gave me a quiz on it, which I flunked. So for the next several days one of them sat on the bunk with me and we translated that thing word for word using a Italian-English dictionary. It was a detailed treatise on the Red Brigades. It was filled with a lot of revolutionary rhetoric and difficult to understand. A lot of it was just illogical. When I told them that, they would get upset and redouble their efforts to get me to understand. At one point, they said that if they couldn't convert me, perhaps at least they could make me neutral.

To illustrate how bizarre some of their thinking was, there was this exchange: I asked why they kidnapped me. They replied that they wanted me to explain to the Italian people what the overall US plan was to subjugate Italy politically, economically and militarily. I laughed and told them that there was no such plan, and even if there was one, at the level I operate, I wouldn't know what it was. They answered that the US had done this before on Europe as a whole. When I asked what they talking about, they brought up the Marshall Plan, which they viewed as an attempt to subjugate Europe.

Even though I didn't realize it at the time, they put me on trial as a war criminal in what they called a People's Court. That consisted of one of them sitting on the floor in my part of the tent reading questions from notes on a ruled pad. It soon dawned on me that they were asking questions based on documents they had taken from the Verona apartment. I had kept nothing classified in the apartment, but they got hold of some award citations for my exploits in Viet Nam. They viewed these as *prima facie* evidence of me being a war criminal. I rued the day we inflated the prose associated with some of the write-ups for awards. Sure enough, they put the results of the interviews in their periodic communiqués. However, when shown the communiqués, my wife picked up on the fact that they were embellishing my comments as they saw fit, in that they included information that I had no way of knowing, but which was contained in some of the officer's wives' activity documents, for instance.

I was rescued after 42 days as the result of just good, plain police work on the part of the Italian authorities. They would get a lead, follow it to develop more leads and when they got the break they wanted (where I was), they came and got me.

During the past several years, my wife and I have gotten to know the folks (NOCS – national level police organization) who rescued me as well as the owner of the apartment I was held in. In the fall of 2006, my daughter and I went to Italy and spent several days with the NOCS. We visited their first class training facility and had several nice evenings with them reminiscing about their involvement. All are retired now, but they view my rescue as the highlight of their careers. After a couple of days in Rome, we all went to the apartment in Padova and they talked me through the rescue.

They had learned that the guards always watched the parking lot in front of the apartment building. So, on the morning of the rescue (28 January, 1982), the guards saw an air compressor and jackhammer arrive in the parking lot and began to dig it up. While that was going on, other elements of the rescue team secured the floor I was on and prepared to break in the door. Other elements, with the cooperation of the local police had secured the general apartment area. While the parking lot activity was going on, a two-man element of the team pulled up to the front of a supermarket just below the apartment I was held in. The two men, dressed in tight fitting clothes, wearing ski masks and carrying automatic weapons went into the supermarket. At first, the guards thought that this was an attempt to rob the supermarket, but as more security showed up, they realized that a rescue attempt was underway. The guards quickly decided not to resist. They took advantage of a law that the Italians had at the time, called the Penitents Law – which says that if you are a convicted terrorist, but cooperate with the authorities, whatever sentence you may receive, it is automatically cut in half.

I was first aware of something unusual going on that morning when, as I was sitting on the edge of the bunk reading, the walls of the tent billowed. This usually meant that someone was either coming in or going out of the room. As I looked out under the flap of the tent, I saw an arm reach through the outer flap of the tent handing my guard a silenced pistol. This was unusual, because the guards were never armed. Almost simultaneously, a man dressed in tight-fitting clothes burst through the outer tent flap and knocked the guard down. I jumped off the bunk and stood in one corner of my part of the tent. My first thoughts were that I was caught up in a jurisdictional dispute between rival elements of the Red Brigades. This had happened before and had led to the death of Aldo Moro who had been killed by some of the same folks who were involved with me. The man who knocked the guard down then pushed his way into my part of the tent. Somewhat naively and instinctively, I tried to push him out, even though he was calling me General and saying that he was a policeman. I finally felt his flak vest and it then dawned on me that he was who he said he was. The rescuers quickly cut off the chains and hustled me out of the building because they had been told it had been rigged for demolition. It wasn't, even though they found a lot of arms, ammunition and explosives in the apartment.

My wife's experience (written as she used to tell it – she died of Parkinson's in 2005)
I was fixing dinner when the doorbell rang. It was strange that the building entrance doorbell had not rung first, but I considered that it might be one of our neighbors in the building even though they usually called first. Nevertheless, I told Jim I was concerned about it and to be careful. Jim went to the door and I heard him talking in Italian. I was curious, so I looked out of the kitchen door, down the hall to our entrance foyer where I saw Jim talking to two young men. They were dressed in dark blue workmen's coveralls and were carrying little "kit bags". I also noticed that they looked very much alike – dark black moustaches, beards and hair.

I later learned that this was stage makeup. Jim told me they were plumbers and that they wanted to check our apartment for leaks into the apartment downstairs. While he showed them the washroom and utility room, I went back to fixing dinner. It then occurred to me that I had used the washing machine earlier in the day, so I went to the washroom to tell them that.

When I got to the washroom, the two men were standing side by side, blocking the door, while Jim was on his hands and knees looking for leaks around the washing machine. I think I surprised them when I showed up. I later learned that they had been considering grabbing Jim while he was on the floor. They then used a word in Italian ('Caldaia') that we didn't know and we went back to the kitchen to check the dictionary. I went back to fixing dinner again while Jim looked up the word in the dictionary. The two young men (one I called the big guy and the other the little guy) were standing in the door. When I looked up toward the door, I saw that of they were beginning to take something shiny out of their kitbags. At first I thought the shiny objects were tools, but what I was focusing on were the silencers on their pistols. It then it dawned on me that they were holding pistols.

The big guy jumped on Jim's back and spun him around. While he and Jim were scuffling, the little guy, pointing his pistol, came toward me. I wasn't sure what was going on, so I dropped to my knees. When the little guy reached me, he pointed the pistol at my head and said in English "shut up or we will kill your husband". That was the only English spoken. Soon, Jim was knocked to the floor in the hallway outside of the kitchen and I could see that he was bleeding from his nose. I watched them handcuff and blindfold Jim. They then took chains out of their kitbags and began to chain me up. They wrapped one chain around my ankles, then another around my wrists behind my back, plus another that ran between the wrist and ankle chains. All were secured with small padlocks.

Although I was still not sure what was going on, about this time a calm came over me and I began to have rational thoughts. One of my first thoughts was "don't scream". I thought that I might get one out and the neighbors would hear it, but I would probably get hurt and if another didn't follow, the neighbors would go on about their business. While I was lying there in the kitchen, I began to get some clues as to what was going on. The two young men told me several times that they were members of the Red Brigades. I guess they wanted me to tell the authorities who were responsible for all this so they could be sure to get the credit in case someone else tried to do the same. I also heard them ask each other if Jim was breathing. This was while he was feigning unconsciousness. This assured me that they didn't want Jim dead right away. I also discovered that the locks securing my chains had keys in them, so I figured that at some point they wanted me to be able get loose. While I was lying on the floor in the kitchen, I saw them place the trunk next to Jim in the hallway and was later able to describe it to the authorities. They also began to rifle through a lot of mail on the kitchen table that had been collecting while Jim had been on TDY. At this point, I didn't know that others had been let into the apartment and were searching it. At one point, one of them came into the kitchen holding the holster to Jim's General Officer Pistol and asked where the pistol was. I told them it was probably in the safe at his HQ office – which it was.

I was soon blindfolded and dragged out of the kitchen. I didn't initially know where they were taking me, but I knew that by this time, Jim was gone or else they could not have moved me out of the kitchen into the hall. While they were dragging me down the hall, the blindfold caught on the floor carpet and came down over my nose making breathing difficult. They noticed my breathing difficulty and a hand reached down and pulled the blindfold back up. They pulled me into a room and shut the door. I thought about checking the keys in the locks, but decided that now was not the time. By this time, I knew that I was in either the washroom or the utility room and that they were still in the apartment because I could hear room indicators ring as they were going through the apartment. The room indicator switches looked like light switches. The apartment was designed with a servant's area (small bedroom, washroom, utility room with toilet and basin). In the servants' area there were lighted room indicators with bells the owners could use to call household help when needed. We had no household help, but the devices were still operative.

Several times, I could hear the door open as they checked on me. About the third or fourth time, when they came in they did something different. They brought in a small radio and turned it to an all music station. They then put a pillow under my head and unzipped my skirt. I thought "now what?" They then closed the door and left. I figured that they had left for good, so I started to fiddle with the keys and locks. The key in the first lock that I tried wouldn't work. It turned out to have been the wrong key. The second key I tried opened the lock, but did not release a chain.

I kept moving around and finally the chain that ran from the wrist to the ankle chains came loose. I now had mobility. I was able to rub my head on the pillow so that the blindfold came up on my forehead. I then spotted the pilot light in our hot water heater. I now knew where I was in the apartment.

I wiggled around and was able to get my feet up and turn on turn on the light. Then I went over to the washing machine and started to beat on it with my shoulders and knees. I tried to put this into a rhythm (three bangs and three cries for help in Italian) so that the downstairs neighbors wouldn't think I was simply working in the apartment. It turns out that our downstairs neighbors heard the noise, but thought we were working in the apartment, so they went down to the other end of their apartment to watch a TV special.

After about an hour, the daughter came back to use the bathroom and heard the noise continuing. They figured something was wrong and reported the noise to a neighbor who knew us better than they. They called the police while the husband went up to the penthouse level, broke into a bathroom window and began to check the apartment. By this time, the police had arrived at our front door and they found me in the washroom – the only room with a light on.

Once the military authorities were notified, I was moved into a small guest apartment at the NATO HQ and stayed there until my children arrived. At this time, our daughter was a USAF 2LT stationed at Rhine Main AFB. She was flown down the next day on a medevac plane. Our son was in college in the states, but the USAF immediately flew him to Italy under an assumed name.

During these initial several days, I worked very hard with the police and was able to identify several members of the Red Brigades from mug shots, to include two of the kidnappers and several others who had come to the apartment door in the weeks before the kidnapping posing as pollsters and sales people.

The Italian authorities also asked me to publicly appeal to the kidnappers to release my husband on Italian National TV, which I did. After that appeal, US authorities began to decide what I should and should not do regarding the media.

Initially, the media were one of my biggest problems. During the several days in the HQ apartment they didn't have access to us other than the one media event. Once the children arrived, I insisted that we go back to our apartment. By this time a wonderful support and security system had been put together by the men and women in Jim's office, the Italian authorities, our embassy and the American military.

One of the first problems we addressed was how to deal with the media, as Army Public Affairs suggested we pool all of our interviews. We realized that the media had a job to do so we thought it best to help them do that job, but do it on our terms. For instance, when we first left the HQ apartment, the media swarmed us, even while we were travelling in official sedans. We couldn't even go to church without a crowd of reporters and cameras. They were all over our apartment building, bothering our neighbors. So we worked out a protocol that was a win-win for both of us. With the help of Italian security, we arranged for them to set up their cameras under trees across the street from our apartment. When we would plan to leave the apartment, a member of our support group would go downstairs and tell the folks gathered there, what the Doziers were going to do and ask them to respect our privacy. That way, they didn't have to chase us. In addition, we would alert the media several times a day that we would appear on our upstairs balcony so that they could get their visuals. This system worked very well. Soon we established a trusting, cordial relationship.

Support system (as written by my wife)
My support system was put together by the personnel in Jim's office as well as by the American and Italian communities. Both the Italian and American governments were involved. Our embassy was very active. Of course, the Italians were mortified that something like this had happened in their country. Our neighbors were wonderful. They bent over backwards to help in any way that they could.

Since my parents lived in Washington, DC, the Army assigned an officer to keep them informed of developments. This worked very well. They in turn took on the responsibility of keeping the rest of our stateside friends in the loop. In Italy, a member of Jim's office staff screened our phone calls and mail. We received calls and letters from all over the world expressing outrage and support. We learned of prayer vigils taking place in various parts of world. After Jim was rescued, we answered every letter and card that we had received.

After about 4 weeks in Verona after the kidnapping, I decided that I had helped the authorities all that I could and that it would be better for me to stay with friends in Germany. In addition, our daughter and been with me all this time and she needed to get back to work at Rhein Main AFB. So I arranged to stay with friends in the Frankfurt area. I said my temporary goodbyes in Italy and took the train to Frankfurt where I would stay until we received definitive word about Jim.

The morning of 28th January dawned bright and clear and I felt real upbeat for some reason. I was scheduled to have lunch with a group of friends whom we had known from previous assignments. During the lunch, the phone rang. The call was for the wife of the couple with whom I was staying. After she answered the phone, she then said that her husband really wanted to talk to me. I figured it was with regard to Jim, so I asked should I sit down or stand up. He said that it really didn't matter – Jim had been rescued.

The remainder of the day was somewhat of a blur. Our daughter drove over from Rhein Main and we all went to the V Corps HQ in Frankfurt where a celebration had been hastily staged. I had not been able to talk to Jim, but I had talked to someone in Jim's office who said that he was fine and in good shape. Later that afternoon, we were flown on the CINC's plane to Vicenza where we found Jim in the DVQ drinking wine. What began as a beautiful day with me thinking positive thoughts, turned into a great day with our prayers answered.

Debriefing
After a cursory debriefing by the Italian authorities, my wife and I were flown to Washington, DC where we were taken to Walter Read AMC for a day of psychological and physiological

examinations. After the tests were complete, we moved to the guest quarters at Fort Myer where we stayed during my intelligence debriefing. Each morning for 5 days, we were picked up by helicopter and flown to Fort Meade, MD. The debriefing was organized by the Army MI unit at Fort Meade.[1] The Army made sure that all the intelligence agencies who had an interest in the kidnapping were involved.

Judy and I sat in easy chairs in a room with representatives of the key intelligence agencies. Each asked questions in their areas of interest, but all present could hear the question and the answer – thus everyone got the same information first hand. The debriefing room had video cameras and microphones that fed both audio and video to another room where additional members of the intelligence community could see and hear. If members in the adjacent room had a question, they would send notes to the principals in the debriefing room. I thought it was a good system and a good example of intelligence cooperation and coordination that is sometimes lacking nowadays.

Miscellaneous
After the debriefing and a short vacation in Florida, Judy and I returned to Italy where we participated in the initial trial of the kidnappers.

Spies
I knew spies were causing grave harm to USAREUR and its ability to fight a successful war, if attacked. By conducting espionage against us, the East Bloc knew our order of battle and some of our defense and counter-attack plans. This is a known fact because our security experts were sent to testify at NATO espionage trials. The following narratives represent real examples of the espionage threats we faced (actual details are not revealed to protect classified information). Any real-world similarity to names cited is coincidental. The espionage techniques are true.

How many cases occurred?

The former USAREUR counterespionage chief and case officer reported… "Only HoIS (Hostile Intelligence) would know how many approaches they made and how many they actually recruited."

LTC (Ret) Ken Krantz, previously identified as an expert, reports:

According to an unclassified publication of the National Counterintelligence Executive, there were 150 cases of espionage targeted against the US from 1947-2001. Not all of those cases resulted in convictions.

Below are examples of cases of spying against USAREUR. The intent is to give you the feel of the espionage strategies employed against US Army, Europe.

Case 4
This case file revealed how the espionage agent often befriended you and played on your ego and perhaps used …
The sudden friend: blackmail
Hostile intelligence (Communist country spies) evaluated many people until they found their target and carefully selected their mode of approach. The selection was based both on

1   Author's note: probably US Army Intelligence and Security Command – INSCOM.

placement or access to classified information and the person's vulnerabilities – hopefully both.

Sam was an American soldier working at HQs, US Army Europe and had great placement in the Communications Center with those classified messages passing through. He had some debt; plus, he loved his beer!

Hans was a German civilian who appeared to appreciate the jobs Americans were doing. "Can I buy you another beer, my friend?" the German asked the obvious American soldier in civilian clothes. The buzz cut and unstylish black spit-shined shoes gave him away as an American soldier.

They were in *Das Goldenes Fass*, a Gasthaus, which is a quaint German tavern down on the Hauptstrasse or Main Street, where cars are prohibited, in Heidelberg.

"Sure," the American said, savoring his last swallow of beer. "What's the occasion?"

"I'm just trying to be sociable with our American friends," replied Hans.

"I come here most every Friday night," Sam said cautiously. "Well, unless I have to work, that is." Sam offered his hand to Hans.

Hans gripped Sam's hand and shook it hard, a smile reaching his eyes.

Main Street was packed with both Germans and Americans out for a good time at the end of a dreary working week. In a corner of the tavern, a fire roared and licked the logs sitting in a large, stone fireplace.

Sam ordered his favorite German draft beer, a Paulaner from Munich. He contemplated ordering a Schweinehaxen but he wasn't sure he wanted the rotisserie cooked pig's knuckle tonight. He knew he wanted some warm German Kartoffelsalat, it was just like his mother's potato salad. Yeah, he'd get it all because it didn't get much better than that. Hans seemed to always show up at the same tavern each Friday as Sam. After many nights together they had formed a friendship.

"No let me get the check," Hans said. "I wouldn't hear of your paying – you and your buddies are helping to keep us free here."

So Hans started picking up their tabs and acted surprised at learning Sam was a Non-Commissioned Officer (NCO) at the Headquarter's Signal Center; but he knew this already from his prior vetting of Sam.

Sam thought, "it must be my charm that got me all this attention. I hope he realizes I'm straight. No, he hasn't tried anything. But something doesn't seem right. I wonder if there's something fishy about this – no – relax and enjoy. I guess it's all on the up-and-up."

And so, Hans, an MFS East German agent, began his attempted espionage against the United States of America.

Hans would take his time as he cautiously cultivated his source. Hans became Sam's friend, buying him many dinners and beers during their time together. Sometime later the following discussion took place at the same tavern.

"Sam, are you feeling as good as me tonight?" asked Hans, laughing.

"You know I do Hans. It's Friday. I don't have to work tonight and I love this beer."

They slapped their beer steins together in a sign of *Prosit*, spilling a little beer. By this time, Hans and Sam had their own reserved beer mugs the tavern held for them.

Hans suddenly turned serious. "As you know Sam, I sell insurance to Germans and Americans. I just never seem to make the right connections with your bosses."

"Well, maybe I can help you somehow, Hans," said the bleary-eyed Sam, feeling a bit self-important and bragging a little.

Putting his arm around Sam in a friendly but conspiring way, Hans said, "That's just what I was thinking, Sam. Look, it's company money, nothing out of my pocket, but I'll pay you one hundred dollars for a Signal Center phone book so I can get some insurance leads."

Sam had to think about that for a bit. He slowly sipped on some more beer and enjoyed its cool mellow taste. Staring at the beer thoughtfully he soon had a nagging sense he should not give the FOUO (For Official Use Only) phone book to Hans. But he thought, "FOUO isn't classified, and he has bought me all this stuff."

"Well," Sam said, rubbing his chin. "Okay. Just promise you won't tell anyone I gave it to you, okay?"

"No, no, it'll be our little secret."

Sam nodded. "All right, then. I'll bring it next Friday."

A week of dull and tedious duty passed before the next Friday arrived and the two met again at the same tavern. Sam handed the Signal Center Phone Book to Hans in a paper bag. Hans had the money out but didn't hand it over right away.

"Well," said Hans, "The company demands that I get a receipt for the one hundred dollars."

Seeing the alarm in Sam's eyes, he hastily added, "But that stays in my office and nobody else will ever see it." Sam signed the receipt and got his one hundred dollars. He felt happy about that. "Wow, one hundred dollars equals about four hundred German DM! What will I spend it on?" Sam wondered.

Afterward, Sam and Hans met a few more Friday evenings to drink beer and shoot the breeze.

Ultimately, Hans started asking for more information, but this time he wanted copies of classified messages. Hans whispered that he would pay Sam handsomely for the classified information, and, after all, who would know. Sam would be rich, and the chances of war would lessen if everyone knew what the other side was up to. Hans was especially interested in Unit Defense Plans. "Well, Sam has been 'hooked'," Hans thought.

But Sam thought about this for a few minutes, and then quickly sobered up. Sam thought, "Man, I can't do this!"

Sam whispered, "Hans, a phone book is one thing, but espionage against the United States is another. If word gets out, I'll spend the rest of my life in Leavenworth." Sam tried to hide his alarm.

Hans reminded Sam that he had a signed receipt for $100.00 for a US Army FOUO phone book.

Sam's eyebrows knitted together as the edges of his lips curved down. His stomach turned and he almost barfed.

"Hans, damit, I feel sick. I'll get back to you in a couple of days," mumbled Sam.

Hans had no trouble deducing that Sam was getting cold feet and tried to stop Sam from leaving but Sam broke his handhold and quickly left. Hans worried if Sam would tell someone about his approach. Well, it was his word against Sam's. But he wouldn't like the attention it would bring.

Sam stumbled through the shadows and fog at a fast pace along the cobblestone Main Street towards a streetcar and his bed in the headquarters' area.

Sam was in trouble, and he knew it the next morning as sunlight streamed in his blinds and he woke with a start – and a hangover. He worried something was wrong but couldn't think of it right off. Suddenly, he remembered the night before.

He rubbed his eyes and looked at the clock, it was Saturday and he was late for work. He arrived a few minutes behind schedule and performed his duties normally, if not a little slower. Then at lunch, he did the right thing, he reported to the Firehouse[2], the local field office of the 527th Military Intelligence (MI) Detachment, 66th MI Group on Campbell Barracks.

After asking to speak to an Agent, Sam said, "I'm no traitor, but I've been approached. Let me tell you what I've done."

Sam told him about the phone book and the hundred dollars that he had received from the German. The duty agent listened and made notes for the subsequent classified Agent Report he would type up. The agent got all of Sam's ID data. Sam unloaded on him.

"Look, you've made a mistake and you'll probably suffer some consequences, but you've done the right thing by coming to us at this point before things got out-of-hand," the agent reassured Sam. The duty agent sent Sam back to work telling him to say nothing to his co-workers or boss, but to report back to the Field Office when he got off. Sam left and the Duty Agent called the Operations (Ops) Officer and the Field Office Commander at home, being an otherwise quite Saturday. They both decided to come in. When they arrived the Commander went to his office and the duty agent reported the encounter to the Ops Officer.

After discussing the incident for a few minutes with the agent, the Ops officer said, "Let's go see the boss."

They had a quick meeting with the Field Office Commander and briefed him on the situation and discussed different courses of action. The Commander listened, asked some questions and then quickly issued his instructions. Then an ops immediate secret message, describing the situation and intended actions was transmitted to USAREUR (CI), Battalion and 66th MI Group Headquarters.

Because of this meeting and coordination with the 66th MI Group and USAREUR, Sam started feeding Hans's misinformation that USAREUR wanted the MfS and their Russian masters to have. Sam did the right thing.

So Sam cautiously passed Hans some "classified" messages. Hans thought it might be a set-up but the messages looked real and Sam seemed scared at first. Anyway the police hadn't shown up.

Sam lowered his head and went back to his cool Paulaner beer …

Case 5

This next case file reveals that the espionage agent often offered money to whoever would sell out their country.

A more aggressive approach – for money

Ted was having money problems. His wife, Sandra was making more and more demands on him. They were living beyond their means. He was a Warrant Officer – that rank

---

2   Author's note – Why did they call it the Firehouse? Scott O'Connell answers: "It was one... if you remember the tower (which was dismantled while I was in command) that was used to hang up the fire hoses and drain them of water. In the old days, the hoses were made of leather and if they were not hung vertically the water would cause them to warp and rot."

between Enlisted soldier and Commissioned Officer – and although it produced a good salary, he didn't make that much money. But she demanded the best travel and they were already in Europe after all – they took many trips to Paris, bought new clothes and had a Porsche. If he didn't comply with her demands, she would hold back sex. He couldn't do without that.

"Let's go to Majorca and have a beach holiday," Sandra said excitedly to Ted one day. "Everyone is doing it. Think of all the quaint seafood places where we could eat right on the beach and enjoy some nice cold white wine and watch the sun go down... and the swimming!"

Ted thought for a few moments and then said, "That would be nice. What an experience!" Ted was tempted. "Get out of this cold climate and go to the warm beach."

"And think of those warm nights with me," Sandra teased as she drew close and kissed him. One thing led to another.

Ted looked longingly at Sandra and paused. "Well, it sounds all too good but let's think on it a while. Maybe somehow I can come up with the money for the plane ride. Then there's cost of the hotel, food, and whatever other necessities."

Ted worked as an Intel Supervisor in the G-2 at one of USAREUR's Infantry Divisions. Everyone liked Ted. There was a low level FIS (Foreign Intelligence Service) agent already in his unit whose only job was to spot people with access to classified material with vulnerabilities.

This agent reported Ted to his Communist FIS case handler with rumors of Ted's probable money problems. The handler would present himself to Ted not as an East Bloc agent but rather as an agent of a friendly country who just wanted to confirm the US actions (False Flag approach).

The case handler then approached Ted with a monetary offer he couldn't refuse. Ted, with thoughts of Majorca in his mind, jumped at the offer and was soon spending an inordinate amount of time at the copying machine reproducing classified documents for the FIS.

"Sandra, I'm home," Ted said, mimicking Ricky Ricardo. "I think I've worked out the money for Majorca. Don't ask me how." He slipped off his jacket. "You'll just have to trust me."

"Not a word," Sandra said. "When do we leave?"

Unlike the first man who had a conscience and reported the approach, this man had none; he sold out his country for a beach trip and made a lot of money before he was caught and went to Leavenworth.

Sandra no longer lived the high life.

The low-level FIS observer remained in the unit...

Case 6

The upcoming case file showed spite was sometimes a cause for espionage...

Another spy from within – out of spite

Ralph didn't like his boss Clarissa. He sat nervously in front of her desk, waiting for her to speak.

"These are your extension papers," Clarissa said, holding up paperwork he had painstakingly filled out the night before.

"Yes, ma'am," Ralph answered. "I don't guess you'll have any problems signing them, right? It wouldn't be cost effective having to break in a new man, and all."

Clarissa sighed and met Ralph's eyes. "Well, I did sign them but unfortunately I checked the box that states 'do not extend'."

"What?" Ralph glared at her. "You're not going to extend my duty?"

"Ralph, I am going to give you a decent rating but you know the rules on extension say I don't have to have a reason for not extending you. The fact is Ralph, that I've only seen 'reaction' from you on the job and no 'proaction'… no new security programs. You know we've talked about this. Yes, I want some new blood in here and see what they can do, and I wish you the very best back in the States," Clarissa finished.

Ralph protested before leaving Clarissa's office but it didn't work. Her mind was set. Even though there were thirty minutes left before closing, Ralph went home broken and defeated.

Ralph was a civil service DAC (Department of the Army Civilian) GS11 or a middle management Security Manager in one of the USAREUR units. He kept our nation's secrets but now he was willing to share them for the right price. At least he would make a lot of money in his remaining six months in country.

One morning he called in sick and slept a little longer. He had many sick days accumulated. Being under the covers sure did feel good on this cold wintery day. He flipped back and forth across the mattress as he thought about his plan.

At about 10am, Ralph got dressed and put his plan into action.

He went downtown, found a payphone, and dialed the number scrawled across the scrap of paper in his hand. It was the number to the nearest Soviet embassy. An operator answered and he told her his purpose. She quickly transferred him to a KGB operative named Thor, the name that the Soviet used. The operative played sympathetic to Ralph's predicament. Worried about staying on the phone too long, the operative urged Ralph to meet him the next night at seven in the evening.

The following evening Ralph met his Soviet to-be handler in the next town at the Gasthaus *Zum Goldenen Löwen*, as Thor had directed. "Yes, I see where they are not treating you fairly after just doing your job," Thor told Ralph.

After some beer and conversation, Ralph, as a token of good faith and a sign of the level of Intel he could provide, passed some copies of TOP SECRET messages wrapped in newspaper to "Thor." Thor checked the newspapers, smiled and discreetly handed Ralph $500 in crisp $100 bills.

Ralph made a lot of money for the next four months, but at the end of the fourth month and just two months shy from rotating back to States, something happened. Harry, an assistant in his office saw signs of Ralph living high on the hog with a fancy new BMW and expensive vacations. He also noticed indicators of Ralph's late evening entry into the workplace. He became suspicious and started seeing the copier counter most mornings was higher than close-of-business the day before.

Harry notified MI that something funny might be going on.

"Look this may be all wrong and I don't want to get in trouble but I think you might have to look into my boss, Ralph Carter. He has a more expensive car then the Colonel and he and his wife are always traveling around Europe and leaving me in charge of the shop. Something's not right." The local field office thanked Harry and told him that they would take over. They further instructed Harry to cease his investigation of Ralph. Before long, a surveillance of the area by our Intel caught Ralph red-handed with copies of TS messages on his person and he was quickly arrested.

Ralph never finished his tour but he didn't have to return to the State-side job he hated either. He was sent to jail. Harry was promoted and got Ralph's job.

Case 7

This next case file shows an example of the Honey Pot espionage approach and uses the lure of sex. Gordon Barland, PhD and DOD polygraph expert tells me Soviet females were called 'sparrows' and Soviet men were known as 'ravens'. Sexual encounters were both heterosexual and homosexual.

The dark side – compromised

Sex.

Brigitte lived in Mannheim, West Germany, which is a beautiful city with its centrally located Wasserturm (water tower), near Heidelberg. Brigitte performed clerical duties at Taylor Barracks for the Americans although she was a German citizen. She was blond, petite, cute, and sexy. And she smelled so nice!

The East Germans targeted Brigitte and recruited her as a spy against the Americans because she had relatives in the East, worked at US Taylor Barracks in the West, and would attract American soldiers. A handsome *Stasi* (MfS) male agent seduced her and got her to spy on the 'Amis' (Americans). She suddenly showed interest in the local NCO Club (Non-Commissioned Officers' drinking and eating hangout), attending it frequently and dating a variety of NCOs. She was looking for a mark to exploit.

Meet Tom Delany. He was the American soldier Brigitte started dating regularly. Thomas was a high school graduate and joined the Army at a young age. He worked hard and climbed the enlisted ranks to where he was now. Thomas was a senior NCO who worked at Taylor Barracks. As a First Sergeant (1SG), Delany knew all about his unit and every soldier in it. He had a special association with the unit CO. 1SG Delany only had a SECRET clearance but he did have detailed personnel and unit readiness information. If only Thomas knew he was having an intimate relationship with an MfS operative.

Over the course of time, Delany revealed to Brigitte his importance to the unit and a few problems in the organization. Delany was not suspicious of Brigitte because this all happened over a long period. She just seemed interested in his job and offered him advice and support – like a good "wife".

Brigitte kept the MfS informed of all Delany told her. Little did Delany know, but one of the other NCOs in his unit observed Brigitte's appearances on post and reported it to the local MI field office. The local office opened a case and brought it to the attention of the German LfV (*Landesamt für Verfassungsschutz* – State Offices for the Protection of the Constitution).

The LfV conducted a three month investigation which identified her ties with the MfS and her nefarious activities against the Americans. At the time of her arrest by German authorities, MI briefed the Commander about Brigitte and Delany. The Commander told Delany to report to him and sternly told him about Brigitte' arrest and the danger he had put his unit in. He was relieved of his First Sergeant duties and transferred to another unit.

Brigitte was fired and her information forwarded to USAREUR HQ in case she later tried for employment at another US location in accordance with USAREUR Reg 604-1.

Brigitte was convicted of working for a 'Geheim dienst' (secret service) and sentenced to six months in jail.

2

Allied Military Liaison Missions Potsdam – our collectors in the East ("legal" overt spies)

Below we learn of the dangerous intelligence collection missions of our "legal spies" in East Germany.

Introduction

USMLM members were US Human Intelligence (HUMINT) collectors located in Potsdam, East Germany. Heidelberg was the Headquarters of US Army Europe in free West Germany. The Imminence of Hostilities (IOH) gauge in Heidelberg began to rise when Communist military forces began gathering too near the W. German border. Was an invasion imminent or was this just training?

Heidelberg HQs would then request USMLM in the East to probe. Then, these US collectors in the East would investigate and let Heidelberg know if war was looming or if it was just an exercise near the border.

The most prevalent way they collected information was by driving around East Germany (car "tours") and taking pictures of Soviet or East German military equipment. They were sometimes known as missionaries – on mission, but not religious. Why did the Soviets and East Germans allow American Intel personnel to be in East Germany?

The accord that permits this touring is the Huebner-Malinin Agreement. Lieutenant General C.R. Huebner, Deputy Commander in Chief, US European Command (EUCOM), and Colonel-General Malinin, Deputy Commander in Chief, Group of Soviet Forces, Germany, signed it in March 1947.

The pact allowed for a Soviet Military Liaison Mission (SMLM) in Frankfurt, West Germany as well the USMLM compound in Potsdam, East Germany. Their first unclassified mission was to provide liaison to each other's CINCs. These two units were supposed to stay away from the opposing forces' military bases. Since USAREUR Intelligence supervised USMLM, we believe their classified secondary mission of collecting military information soon became their primary mission (it has since been declassified). But when was this switch in priorities of missions made? Was it from the early days at the end of WWII or did the Intel Mission develop and evolve? Recently some USMLM veterans with extensive mission experience discussed my question and provided the following insight:

Anyone who could answer the question based on personal experience is already dead. However, the "lore" surrounding the size of the various Allied military liaison missions may provide a clue. The British and French missions were larger than the Americans, supposedly because of American counterintelligence concerns in 1947, when the missions were created: they wanted to limit the number of Soviets running around in the American zone of occupation. This counterintelligence concern, if true, suggests an early appreciation of the potential intelligence role and value of the liaison missions. What it does not address is how quickly the missions became effective intelligence collectors and producers. Since the unit histories do not extend that far back in time, they are of little help with the question. One can assume that the intelligence role of USMLM started early and small (perhaps merely spot reporting), evolved over time, and developed to a high point in the late eighties before the unit was deactivated when East and West Germany united.

Mission statements
The missions statements below are from the 1982 USMLM unit history, once classified, now declassified.

1. (U) MISSION. The primary mission of USMLM was to carry out its responsibilities for liaison between (Commander-In-Chief, US Army Europe) CINCUSAREUR on behalf of US Commander-in-Chief Europe (USCINCEUR) and CINCGSFG, (CINC, Group Of Soviet Forces Germany) and to serve as a point of contact for other US departments and agencies with CINCGSFG, in accordance with provisions of the Huebner-Malinin Accord.

2. (U) The secondary and confidential mission of USMLM was to exploit its liaison status and attendant potential for collection of intelligence information in the German Democratic Republic (GDR).

FREEDOM BRIDGE
WITH POTSDAM ON FAR SHORE.
DURING FREEZING WEATHER,
EAST GERMANS RAN AN ICEBREAKER THROUGH
EACH DAY SO PEOPLE COULD NOT WALK ACROSS
TO WEST BERLIN.
MIKE STORIE 1962

(Picture by Mike Storie)

Allied Military Liaison Mission's (AMLM) – the French and British Liaison Missions to the Soviet forces in Potsdam, East Germany

France (La Mission Militaire Francaise de Liaison) (FMLM) and **Britain** (British Commanders-in-Chief's Mission to the Soviet Forces in Germany) (BRIXMIS) also had allied missions in East Germany along with USMLM and were accredited under similar accords. In their Zones in West Germany, they had to monitor the Soviets as our SMLM monitors did. COL Thorsen, Chief of Mission in Potsdam stated in the 1975 Unit History, "In no way is there competition between (allied) Missions; we exist to complement each other."

Concerning sharing information between the three allied missions, an informed source tells me, "yes, we shared all mission tour highlight reports and most IIRs (Intelligence Information Reports)". So we know U.S. collected information went back to France and Britain and vice versa.

In their own words: true Allied – FMLM (French), BRIXMIS (British) and USMLM (U.S.) tour accounts
Frank Naylor (British – BRIXMIS)

I wasn't a tour officer but in fact was a Royal Air Force – RAF (not to be confused with Red Army Faction) tour driver for two years (1966-68). I drove an Opel Admiral and a Safari long-wheelbase Land Rover used to drive to radar and airfields that were hard to get to.

There was no typical day as most days were different and no tour was the same as the last one. All were fraught with danger – most of it en route getting in and out of the target area. Sometimes the Russians or East Germans detained us. My longest detention was about 12 hours after crashing the Land Rover into a tree on black ice; we had a few short ones where we would just drive away from local Volks Police.

I remember one incident when counting a Russian convoy. An officer on a motorbike and sidecar parked in front of our vehicle and directed a BRDM (*Boyevaya Razvedyvatelnaya Dozornaya Mashina*), literally 'Combat Reconnaissance/Patrol Vehicle' out of the convoy and parked its high-rise bow over our boot (trunk). We broke out the cigars and sat there for about an hour counting the convoy from a ringside seat as it passed by.

We got into Permanent Restricted Areas (PRAs –military areas) but never passed through a sign. It sometimes involved a long way around though rough terrain and little-used tracks or through woodland involving a lot of winching and tough driving to get to the target area. We came out the quick and easy route from behind the sign.

The whole thing was a bit of an adventure and every day was new and one was never sure what would happen next or be around the next corner; sometimes it could be exciting to discover interesting activity or hardware or on the other hand it might be someone who was preparing to shoot you. I was lucky it only happened once and it was high over the head; it was a very sensitive SAM site and we were very close. We left at high speed driving back to the mission house bar!

For social life we had our own club and lots of entertainment was organized. I lived in married quarters with my wife Joan and baby Sara and most of my time was devoted to them; it was always nice to get home safely especially after a long detention. The days were long – often 12 to 14 hours driving hundreds of miles in a Land Rover. A hot bath and sleep on the hard living room floor was my cure.

BRIXMIS RAF tour Land Rover – Frank Naylor on the
right, Don Wistow on the left. (Frank Naylor)

Excerpts from: The Prödel Incident: Serendipity and an apple.
A BRIXMIS incident near Magdeburg – 26th July 1983 (P. G. Williams)

... It was at this stage that the Tour NCO said "I can get onto the train, if you like, sir! Then we can see the BMP-2 main armament without its canvas muzzle cover. What do you think?" Without pausing for deep consideration, but certain that the opportunity could only be short-lived, the Tour Officer replied: "Go for it! I will cover your every move with the camera, but don't hang about in case the Sovs turn up".

Frank Naylor's BRIXMIS Land Rover after crashing it. (Frank Naylor)

The Tour NCO sprinted to the edge of the field, scrambled down the slight embankment and then leapt up onto the second flat-car and pulled himself up onto the top deck of a BMP-2, gazing frequently down the train towards the M-wagons and up the train at the locomotive.

New uses for an apple

If serendipity had handed the Tour crew an extraordinary opportunity to satisfy one of DI60's priority intelligence requirements, it was now that 'Murphy's Law' came to the fore[1]. Having reached the perfect spot at which to establish the calibre of the BMP-2's main armament, the Tour NCO suddenly realised that he had nothing on him that was capable of providing an accurate scale from which DI60 could make any exact measurements … and time was running out! The locomotive driver could either see or sense that his train was under attack and he had started sounding his hooter in order to get the attention of the Soviet crewmen.

The Tour NCO's instant assessment of the situation revealed that his only potential 'measurement tools' were his Dictaphone recorder and a Golden Delicious apple. They might not be ideal, but they were the only options open to him and so he reacted accordingly.

Having ripped the canvas muzzle cover off the BMP-2's main armament, he *rammed* the apple into the end of the cannon's barrel, creating an impression of the shape of the flash hider. He then balanced the Dictaphone on the cannon's recoil mechanism housing to provide a reference for the Tour Officer's photographs. Finally the Tour NCO clambered onto the top of the turret and pulled off the canvas cover from the anti-tank guided missile (ATGM) launching platform[2], as the Tour Officer continued to take pictures (in colour slide format).

By this stage it was painfully clear that the Tour had overstayed its welcome and it was time to go. The Tour NCO jumped down off the moving train and sprinted back to the safety of the Opel Senator, still carrying the BMP-2 turret's two canvas covers, his Dictaphone and the badly dented Golden Delicious apple.

Waving a cheery farewell to the by-now furious train driver who was still trying to attract the attention of the Soviet crewmen, the Tour crew now sought to put some distance between itself and the area of Prödel in order to allow heartbeats to subside and an assessment of the situation to be made.

Self-preservation becomes the Priority

It was obvious that the Soviets would be angered by this assault on one of their kit trains in broad daylight, but there was no way that the Tourers could assess just how speedy and thorough their retribution would be. Perhaps the Soviet crewmen had radio communications with the Headquarters 3rd Shock Army in nearby Magdeburg?

What seemed to be most sensible was to get rid of the films, the apple and the other booty as soon as possible, preferably by handing them to another BRIXMIS Tour crew, and then for the crew of Opel Senator No. 8 to lie low for a while well away from Magdeburg and the Zerbst Gap.

Finding another BRIXMIS patrol out on the ground in East Germany was always a challenge because Tours had no communications equipment (and this was before the era

---

1   Things will go wrong in any given situation, if you give them a chance.
2   The BMP-2 ATGM launching platform could mount either the AT-4 SPIGOT (9M111 'Fagot') or the AT-5 SPANDREL (9M113 'Konkurs').

of mobile phones), but the Tour Officer recalled that BRIXMIS was currently responsible for covering the area immediately to the west of Berlin, known as the 'Local' area.

As a result there was a fair chance of encountering the BRIXMIS Local Tour somewhere in the area around the small town of Treuenbrietzen, through which convoys frequently moved between the Jüterbog and Altengrabow 'polygons' as well as along the F2 main road from Potsdam to Lutherstadt Wittenberg.

As luck would have it the Local Tour vehicle was spotted and a quick rendezvous (RV) was successfully executed. The films, the apple and the booty were handed over and, fully aware of the sensitivity and urgency of the situation, the Local Tour agreed to return to West Berlin with its precious cargo without delay.

For its part, everyone at the RV agreed that Opel Senator No. 8 and its crew should 'go to ground' in East Germany and only go back through Potsdam to Berlin the next morning in order to seem to be behaving in an entirely normal manner. To rush straight back to safety might seem to be admitting some sort of guilt to the Soviet authorities. And so the Tour crew settled down to an evening of observing railway tracks and road junctions from a safe distance and then disappeared deep into the woods to sleep in the normal manner.

MG Williams adds the following about training for and types of personnel in BRIXMIS in an email to the author dated 24 July 2008:

The British military (Army, RN and RAF) does not have and never had (in the 1970s/1980s) any equivalent to the US FAO (Foreign Area Officer) system. Bizarrely we had and still have no cadre of trained linguists/country experts – we train people only as and when required and so have no cadre of long-term experts. The key training for BRIXMIS was the Special Duties course at the Army Intelligence Centre at Ashford (Kent); it taught tradecraft (touring tactics; recognition; photography) to full-time and part-time tourers, including exercises with notional PRAs around southern England. I think that the course was three weeks long. As you know, many USMLM tourers also attended the Ashford courses – long-serving BRX Tour Officers would go back from Berlin to help train up the next cadre (I recall instructing on the course that included MAJ Nick Nicholson in 1983). Some FMLM officers also attended Ashford courses in order to ensure that FMLM remained *au fait* (up to speed) with BRX/USMLM tradecraft developments. Officers and senior NCOs in BRIXMIS were drawn from three different streams (my own classification system, invented on the spur of this moment!):

Stream One ('The Operators'):

- Chief (Brigadier; always Army, but never from Intel Corps; normally expected to be a MG/LTG in due course; one in the 1980s made it to 4-star GEN)
- Deputy (Group Captain, always an RAF pilot; normally a career-end job)
- SO1 (Army LTC, full-time tourer; did a job like a Commanding Officer, but light on the command angle! Main POC with SERB for routine matters and liaised with Joint HQ Rheindahlen on policy issues)
- Ops Officers (MAJ-equivalent Army & RAF, both with experience of tactics and Intel work; part-time tourers; Army post was given to Staff College graduates)
- Tour Officers (Army and RAF CAPT-equivalents; drawn from the 'teeth arms'; required to have tactical sense, as well as linguistic skills – normally graduates of the Russian Interpreter course)

- RAF Chipmunk Aircrew (both CAPT equivalents; normally one pilot and one observer; operated the RAF Gatow Chipmunk within the Berlin Air Zone; part-time tourers)
- Tour NCOs (Ground: Army Warrant Officer [WO] from SAS as the 'dean' of the Tour NCOs; other Army Tour NCOs from 'teeth arms'; kit recognition experts; Air Tour NCOs: 4-6 WOs/Senior NCOs; kit recognition experts)
- Tour Drivers (one Army SSGT; 10 or so Corporals from Army and RAF; vehicle experts)

Stream Two ('The Subject Experts'):

- SO2 Liaison (Army MAJ; normally Intel Corps; acted as Chief Interpreter; full-time tourer)
- SO2 Weapons (Army MAJ; Tech Intel trained, but from any arm of service; head of the 2-man Weapons Intel team; part-time tourer)
- SO3 Liaison (two Army CAPTs; Intel Corps; headed the 'Spandau Office', interpreting at Spandau Prison and exploiting the recovered non-weapons artifacts; part-time tourers)
- WO2 Weapons (Army WO/SSGT; Intel Corps; technical Intel expert)
- WO2 Geographic (Army Royal Engineers Mapping expert; updated DDR mapping; part-time tourer)

Stream Three ('The Supporting Team'):

- Adjutant (Army LTC; no Intel responsibilities; non-tourer; chief of admin; career-end job)
- Chief Clerk (Army WO1; non-tourer)
- Mission House Warrant Officer (Army WO1, normally ex-Tour NCO; ran the Potsdam Mission House; full-time passholder)
- Quartermaster (Army WO2; non-tourer)
- Admin team (Army and civilian clerks; non-tourers)
- 'Special Section' (RAF; in-house photographic processing team; non-tourers)

BRIXMIS worked for J2 in Joint HQ (JHQ = HQ BAOR + HQ RAF Germany) in Rheindahlen and reported to the Commanders'-in-Chief Committee Germany.

We ran all aspects (except personnel management) on a joint services basis – therefore, a tour crew could and often did consist of Army and RAF tourers (and we even had a Royal Navy WO in the late 1980s – an ex-special forces veteran).

All tourers were expected to be able to recognise and report factually and with intelligent comment both on ground and on air targets.

Daniel Pasquier, FRENCH – FMLM

During the Cold War, I had to inspect, on the East German territory, the implementation of post-war agreements, signed in POTSDAM in 1947. The mission involved checking, night and day, in co-operation with the American mission (USMLM) and the British mission (BRIXMIS), the training activities of the Soviet and East German armed forces to detect any hint of massive attack against the West. Missions in East Germany required *sang-froid*, the taking of calculated risks, physical robustness, the ability to speak Russian, a good knowledge of the Soviet armed forces and their ways of thinking. Prior to deployment, I attended a five week "special duties" training course in the Defense Intelligence and Security School/Ashford/UK.

An attempt at detention

At the end of spring 1989, the Soviet command in East Germany organized an exercise with the participation of western observers, according to the Stockholm agreement, signed in 1986. This agreement was a first step towards more transparency, openness and paved the way for CSBM (confidence and security building measures). We shall understand, a bit further, that such a transparency did not yet apply to allied military missions (AMLM).

This three day exercise took place in the region of Stendal, at about 100 kilometers west from Berlin. It included three stages, the last one being an offensive river-crossing over the Elbe river by the 207th Motorized Rifle Division (207 MRD) followed by a final regrouping in the famous permanent training area of Letzlinger Heide (LH), that was also a permanent restricted area (PRA), because of the number of military garrisons.

It was early June and weather conditions were perfect. Early in the afternoon, touring between Stendal and LH, I was trying to find an observation post (OP) that would allow us to check 207 MRD infantry and armored regiments, on their way to the final regrouping zone.

Rapidly, as tour officer, I selected a small pinewood located at about two kilometers south of the village of Luderitz, along the tank trail coming from the river crossing area. We left the road, drove through the cornfield, up to the southern outskirts of the wood, to hide our Mercedes Gelander in the undergrowth.

But unhappily, we discovered that a narrow but steep-edged ditch separated the wood from the cornfield. Could our vehicle cross this natural obstacle? Of course, the tour vehicle was all-purpose but both its long chassis and its heavy weight considerably reduced its maneuverability. I would have preferred, in this current situation, a Soviet UAZ 469!

In the end, on second thoughts and after talking with my NCO and my driver, I decided to try my luck! A few seconds later, anyone driving or strolling on the neighboring road could see the rear of our car, in an unusual if not dangerous position across the ditch. In spite of several repeated attempts, the driver could do nothing to improve the situation. We really were in dire straits. But, fortunately or unfortunately, we did not have the time to bemoan the sad fate of our beloved car: in the distance, we could hear the familiar noise of a T80 Soviet battle tank. We had no time to lose.

I decided to leave the Mercedes there, only asking the driver to carefully watch out the area, particularly southward and to report, if need be by hooting, in case a military vehicle would approach our position.

Equipped with our cameras, tape recorders, binoculars, we rapidly made our way to the OP, at less than 100 meters further along the western outskirts of the wood. At about 500 meters eastward, we saw the first armored vehicles raising clouds of dust.

For any AMLM member, these few seconds were absolutely magic and unforgettable: *a growing infernal and deafening noise, dust everywhere, gas smell, tank crews shouting, to put it in a nutshell, "the sound and the fury!"* Personally, at this very moment, I experienced mixed feelings such as fear, stress but also unutterable joy and frenzy.

Beside me, my NCO, Robert, began carefully and quietly recording, which sounded like a monotonous litany: "one BMP 2 number 541, another one, another one…" Simultaneously, my NIKON F 601 camera got involved in the dance and worked perfectly: "Click, click, click…" like a regular heartbeat.

It was the last phase of the exercise: tank commanders were sitting on their turrets, with the straps of their helmet widely unfastened. "So far so good," I thought, when my driver gave several toots. Where was the driver? I have to confess that we had completely forgotten him! Robert looked behind: five hundred meters southward, right in the middle of the field, we saw a cloud of dust. He took his binoculars and immediately returned his verdict: "a Soviet BTR is coming at a high rate of speed, *SIR, IT'S FOR US!*"

Unwillingly, we stopped our job, ran to the car, concealed the equipment under a blanket and locked the doors. Shortly thereafter, the BTR 60 PU 12, a signal and command vehicle, stopped ten meters from the G wagon and the vehicle commander, a lieutenant, jumped from the turret, came running to my door, trying to open it and then furiously pounded on the windows with his fists.

At this very moment, our driver made a last and desperate attempt: both left wheels on the left side of the ditch and both right wheels on the right side, he progressively speeded up and then slowly turned right. Miraculously, our heavy Mercedes got out of the ditch and reached the field! We did it! In the meanwhile, the young Soviet officer, understanding that his prey was about to escape, had run back to his BTR to resume the chase.

It was quite unrealistic: we were driving deeper and deeper into the PRA, screening a column of Soviet T80s on our right-hand side, chased by an aggressive armored vehicle that came closer and closer to our car. To escape it, in a few seconds, I made my decision and ordered the driver to enter the column, tanks being separated by about a 100-meter interval. Gradually and cold bloodedly, the driver came closer to the trail and eventually joined the column of tanks. Tank commanders did not notice us, probably because of thick dust.

We stayed only a few minutes in this uncomfortable and dangerous position but it seemed to us much longer…Soon, we saw a crossroad ahead of us: tanks turned right, towards Letzlingen. We turned left and the driver gradually speeded up. The BTR, coming from the field, lost ground and gave up the chase when we reached an asphalted road. At that moment, we experienced a deep relief, nervously laughing and congratulating each other.

We drove a few kilometers. We made sure the Soviets did not track us and entered a thick forest and stopped. The driver switched off the engine, unlocked the doors. East German nature never seemed to us so friendly welcoming!

Such was the life of AMLM "missionaries", touring in DDR. It required, in any circumstances, cold-bloodedness, decision-making ability, boldness without exceeding limits and of course…a bit of luck!

The beginning of the end

When I came back from my summer leave, in September 1989, the political situation in the DDR had changed significantly. People openly voiced their discontent about the lack of freedom. Moreover, it was public knowledge that for several weeks, thousands of inhabitants had fled their motherland to reach the West, most of the time by train through Czechoslovakia and Hungary. There were also widespread rumors about German re-unification. Nevertheless, Erich Honecker stood firm, refusing to climb down. More than once, he repeated: "Within one thousand years, the wall will still be there!"

Throughout the country, turmoil rose steadily. Many street demonstrations took place, in Berlin of course but also in Leipzig where, every Monday, thousands of demonstrators used to take to the street and to rally downtown, near Nikolai church.

On October 9, I was touring in the south of East Germany. Fall was sunny and mild. Usually, Soviets called this period of the year "babiye lieto", which means "Indian summer".

Nevertheless, days grew shorter and dusk fell early, at about 6 pm and, consequently, available hours of daylight decreased.

For AMLM missionaries, it meant hard-working conditions, particularly as far as military equipment recognition was concerned. We also had to spend long hours, at night, watching railways lines and sidings, hoping to observe a Soviet troop train.

We had left Potsdam early in the morning, driving southward, on the highway, for a two-day operational collection trip. We checked first Halle. This town was one of the most important Soviet and East German garrisons, harboring several motorized units subordinated to the 8th Guards Combined-arms Army. Then we explored railway sidings in Falkenberg, without forgetting Bad Duben, a zone that was famous for usual heavy Soviet military traffic (drivers' training). That is why we were really disappointed not to see the least Soviet regulator and, as a consequence, the least Soviet truck in this area, usually so busy. My NCO pulled a face as long as a wet Sunday!

In mid-afternoon, having observed no activity at all (my USMLM counterpart, Dionisio, a former Marine Corps officer, would have said "we did not see diddly squat") we decided to head for the town of Leipzig. As the area seemed to be exceptionally quiet, we concluded that we had a unique opportunity to visit an antique dealer, well known to all AMLM members for selling nice and cheap Meissen china tea sets. No sooner said than done! We drove lightheartedly to Leipzig that we reached at about 5pm. But, truth to tell, we had no time to visit the antique shop!

Initially, we observed nothing particular in Leipzig's western outskirts but a few minutes later, on reaching the inner ring road, something unusual drew our attention: the VOPOS began to install roadblocks and checkpoints, maybe, we thought, to deny access to the centre of the town. We rapidly drove across the ring and headed to the antique shop. Once there, we remained flabbergasted and tight-lipped, until my NCO said: "C'est quoi ce cirque?" – a column of MFS trucks, loaded with armed personnel, was parked on the right side of the street. A few officers were waiting and talking on the pavement. The column also included two UAZ 469, towing 82mm mortars!

I decided to stop our G wagon a bit further in a neighboring street and ordered my driver to lock the doors and to wait there in the car while we were checking the situation downtown. I and my NCO made our way towards the central square. It was already night. After a few minutes, we approached Nikolai church but could not force our way further so crowded was the place. Speakers addressing the mob were inside the church but their speech could be heard outside through loudspeakers. Here and there, slogans could be read on banners, such as "Wir sind das Volk". How many people attended the meeting? Such a question, we could not answer!

I must confess that we spent this evening, unforgettable and dense moments, so extraordinary were the atmosphere. We could not prevent ourselves from thinking that a few months sooner such a demonstration would have been immediately broken up by the MfS and riot police. We met there men and women, belonging to all generations and social categories, hoping in a better future that had probably never been so close! Surprisingly, we saw neither VOPO nor MFS personnel in the area.

One hour later, after collecting enough information about this event, we walked back to our vehicle and drove to Eilenburg, a small town, 20 kilometers north east of Leipzig, to spend the night along a strategic railway line, connecting Halle to Falkenberg, the biggest railway sidings in East Germany. Seeing our vehicle leaving the central part of the town, the VOPOS seemed to be surprised and annoyed and carefully registered our plate number!

During this short trip on Road 87, tenseness increased: after a few kilometers, we observed an East German military column, driving the opposite way, to Leipzig. That night, we vainly waited for a Soviet train in Eilenburg but truth to tell, it did not matter at all: our mind was elsewhere in Leipzig. The following day, once returned in West Berlin, we were told that western media had several times reported, about the demonstration in Leipzig that gathered ...more than 50 000 people!

Several years later, investigations by journalists and historians revealed that this rally had been a turning point in German history. Honecker, refusing to yield to facts, had decided to hold on to power and to restore order at all costs, which might have resulted in a bloodbath. Fortunately, a few East German decision-makers, of which Egon Krenz, but above all Gorbatchev and the Soviet KGB in East Germany made a different decision.

Exactly one month later, on November 9th, in spite of Honecker's prophecy, the Berlin wall fell. In Potsdam, young rioters ransacked and set fire to the *Stasi* building, one of

Soviet T64 on a tank trail at Redlin Jaennersdorf, 1988. (Daniel Pasquier)

Touring in the northern part of the DDR. (Daniel Pasquier)

Soviet driver training using a BTR 70. (Daniel Pasquier)

the symbols of Honecker's dictatorship. It was the beginning of the end for "a DDR" that would soon belong to History.

Without knowing it, on touring in Leipzig on October 9th 1989, we experienced a true and key historical event.

Threats and dangers

AMLM members conducted intelligence-gathering missions all over the East German territory. Main targets were both the Soviet Western Group of forces and the National *Volks Armee* (NVA), major components of the Warsaw Pact, that is to say, our conventional enemy.

Missionaries permanently worked in a hostile environment and, actually, they had to face permanent threats and dangers. Successive dramatic deaths, if not murders, of Adjutant Mariotti (FMLM) in Lettin Halle (1984) and Major Nicholson (USMLM), one year later in Ludwigslust, proved it.

Using my personal experience, I shall try to sum up the main dangers that any AMLM members faced, once they had crossed the Glienicker Bridge, between Berlin and Potsdam. If some threats seemed obvious, others were more insidious and more difficult to grasp.

The first major danger consisted in the widespread civilian and military surveillance net that one could compare with a cobweb, whose first component was the East German security guard, standing night and day at the main gate of every AMLM villas in Potsdam. This dutiful guy zealously registered the number plate and the exact time of any AMLM vehicle entering or leaving our villas.

Then, MFS or *Stasi* agents took over. Most of the time driving but sometimes walking, these "tails" were always posted to the same working area whose towns, villages, roads, short cuts and woods had no secrets for them. They were real leeches and getting rid of them required patience, time and tricks. The AMLM teams knew some of them. For instance in the Luebben area (central East Germany), one of them, for being particularly plump, was nicknamed "the biggest of Luebben".

All these agents could gather information from local inhabitants and workers: thus, any missionary refueling his G-wagon in a small provincial station, perfectly knew that the pump attendant would immediately report about the type and the number plate of the car, the number of passengers, the time of arrival and so on. Guards on duty in watchtowers, along highways, did the same.

East German and Soviet forces embodied the next threat. East German Army (EGA) personnel, regardless of their ranks, were aggressive and nationalistic to the backbone. Their gut hatred towards the Westerners was the logical outcome of a permanent and long-drawn governmental propaganda. In three years, I must confess that I never met one EGA officer able to smile!

Consequently, checking an East German target requested from AMLM members required a detailed preparation and a detailed study of target folders. We carefully selected observation posts because it was impossible to stay more than ten to fifteen minutes at the OP. EGA soldiers and sentries were very professional and their reactions were rapid and often brutal. Therefore, the hunter often became the hunted!

On the contrary, Soviet troops sometimes behaved rather unexpectedly. Of course Soviet officers did not enjoy being observed by AMLM, particularly during field training exercises at permanent training areas. Chase, detention, attempts at vehicle ramming were frequent. In this regard, I would like to tell an anecdote.

A historic photo – During the Cold War, Soviets and French breaking bread together and posing for pictures in the East German woods! Daniel Pasquier is standing fourth from right, a Soviet Major is third from right. (Daniel Pasquier)

Daniel Pasquier standing on the left side of the photo, with a Soviet major near the former's beloved G wagon! At the time, Daniel was a young lieutenant colonel. (Daniel Pasquier)

Motorized rifle units of the 2nd Guards Tank Army deployed at the Redlin Jaenersdorf training area on July 4th, 1989. On that same day, Mikhail Gorbatchev was in Paris, at the invitation of his French counterpart, François Mitterand. I wrongly and naively concluded that the 4th of July might be a truce between representatives of France and Soviet Union. What a serious mistake! No sooner had we headed into the training area than a Soviet soldier, driving his ZIL 131 cargo truck tried to ram our vehicle at full speed and to prevent us from reaching the asphalted road. I made a second attempt a few hours later, late in the afternoon, once again unsuccessfully!

Nevertheless, I chanced to meet Soviet officers that were better educated and I succeeded several times in establishing friendly contacts with them.

For instance, in September 1990, I was checking a small training area usually occupied by the 21st MRD, near PERLEBERG. At a distance, we could see a GAZ 66, surrounded by several soldiers. Seeing our vehicle, one of them made a sign for us to come. With his binoculars, my NCO, Serge, identified an officer, having his lunch with his soldiers. As the latter repeated his invitation, we decided, on second thoughts, to slowly drive to him.

Once arrived, I opened my front window and began to talk with a major of the 239 MRR, located in Perleberg. A little while later, we got out of our car and enjoyed with our friendly and open-minded officer the famous Russian "kacha" and this brown bread, called "boukhanka".

We stayed there half an hour, talking freely with our "Soviet allies" while soldiers were filled with admiration for the Mercedes G wagon. We left after taking photos and giving out cigarettes and chewing gum.

Threats that I have just described above were permanent, quite commonplace in such a hostile environment as the DDR. And I don't want to underrate their importance and their influence, as far as reconnaissance trips are concerned. But one must not underestimate another real danger that had nothing to do with Soviet barracks or EGA ammo dumps – I mean routine.

Routine was quite unknown to new reconnaissance officers, recently posted in Potsdam AMLM. These ones were always on the alert and conscientiously implemented methods of working taught during the "Special Duties" course at the Defense Intelligence and Security School in Ashford (UK). But with the passing months, all missionaries gradually got a better knowledge of the surrounding terrain, and grew more self-confident, sometimes yielding to routine.

Routine was one of our worst enemies: choosing always the same OP or the same approach to training areas or rail sidings allowed the Soviet local command to organize ambushes against AMLM teams. Thus, in 1989, they detained us at Angersdorf rail sidings, west of Halle. Ironically, a Soviet senior officer told me: "you should ask your British colleagues to show you their OP because it is far better than yours!"

Afterwards, I did my best not to repeat such a mistake and everywhere in East Germany, I tried to find alternative OP and routes to escape, as much as possible, Soviet surveillance and attempts of detention.

John E. Pendergast (American USMLM)
This is the story of a 1959 incident at USMLM, originally I wrote it for a family history project.
Shooting incident draws complaint from USAREUR
Heidelberg, Germany (Special) – USAREUR HQ has strongly protested to Soviet authorities a recent incident in which an East German Air Force soldier fired a shot at a US Military Liaison Mission vehicle carrying three men.

The incident occurred on a main road at 5pm Oct. 13 about 8 miles north of Fuerstenwalde, East of Berlin.

The shot was fired at the passing vehicle, without warning, from about 100 yards away and pierced the exhaust pipe, USAREUR said. No one was injured.

The team continued on to Berlin without stopping. Involved were Maj. Mathew Warren, Capt. John E. Pendergast, and SSgt George Budd, Jr.

Stars and Stripes, European Edition, October 25, 1959
A Friday the 13th story
The USA, Britain and France had maintained liaison missions in Potsdam, East Germany since 1947 to handle coordination with Soviet military authorities. The missions also

Here is Captain Pendergast planning a tour. Note large-scale installation map box on left and map and tour items on the desk. (USMLM)

conducted observation activity. The Soviets had similar missions in the Western Zones of occupation. Below is one day's activity.

It was a Thursday in the middle of the Cold War, and we were planning the observation tour for the next day. The Air Force sections of the three Allied Military Liaison Missions had divided East Germany into four parts so we wouldn't be bumping into each other at the Soviet and East German airbases. Each mission (USA, French and British) would take one of the areas for a week and we left one part dormant to allow any security issues to calm down. This week the USMLM Air Team was responsible for the northeast part of East Germany.

As part of the tour planning process we looked at a number of things. First on the list were collection requirements from higher headquarters. There weren't any special requests from on high, just routine checks at airfields, electronic sites and air defense sites. We then looked at recent reports from the several missions and other agencies to see if anything significant had turned up either new info on the sites or security concerns for the area where we were headed. In going over items we determined that nobody had been to Marxwalde Air Base for a number of weeks so we put it on the list of places to check. Marxwalde AB was an East German Air Force (EGAF) facility, located between Berlin and the Polish border, which had been under major upgrade construction. We thought we would try to determine what the EGAF had in mind for this old transport base.

After listing the potential sites we hoped to look at, we dug out the maps and planned the route. We also identified Army facilities and training areas where we were going. You needed to do the latter because it was difficult to travel in East Germany without running into Soviet Army units. Some thought we should let the Mission Army Section handle all the ground stuff, but Soviet tanks were hard to avoid. Besides, I always felt that if a Soviet armor unit wanted to drive in front of my camera, I'd try and get the best shot I could of a potential USAF target. We checked the Restricted Area maps too to determine the best way to avoid unnecessary conflict with the Communist security forces. Once the general route to our targets was established, we refreshed our memories of the best observation points by scanning the large-scale map boards we kept on each installation. Lastly, we restocked our equipment bags with fresh film and the like and arranged for a car and driver with the USMLM Operations Section.

So, on Friday morning at "oh-dark-thirty" o'clock, Maj. Warren and I left the Berlin USMLM headquarters; the building had been the World War II house of the Chief of the German General Staff, General Keitel. We headed to the Potsdam Mission house to meet up with our driver. We crossed the Glienicke Bridge without picking up an East German security "tail" and met SSgt Budd at the house. We called it a house but it really had been the lakeside villa of one of the Hohenzollern nobility. Here we stocked up with coffee and sandwiches for the tour.

The East German guard at the Potsdam House entrance undoubtedly had let the *Stasi* know we were there, so there was a good chance we'd have a tail when we left. But we got lucky. No tail. This happened more often lately after we learned to "blow" the radiators of the *Stasi*'s old model Mercedes cars by alternately speeding and then slowing to a crawl on the autobahn. After three or four times the old Mercedes' radiator would boil over and we could take off alone in our 57 Chevrolet. So with no tail we headed east on the Berlin to Frankfurt/Oder autobahn to an exit near Fuerstenwalde. There we avoided the populated areas and worked our way to the Soviet radar site to get a status check of the site's equipment. If I remember correctly, the key piece of equipment was an EW/GCI radar called Big Mesh. In any case, we zipped past Mission Restriction signs, photographed the site, and headed north on a main road towards Muncheberg. Of significance, traffic was light and we passed only a couple of civilian vehicles. A right turn on Route 1 headed us towards Marxwalde AB. When we reached our destination we pulled off the highway and made our way to our observation site.

Something was happening at Marxwalde. There were all kinds of vehicle traffic on the base. As we watched we saw that the construction was complete and the base was ready for service. So we watched some more. After a couple of hours of observation, an EGAF Mig-17/Fresco flew in over our heads to land west to east. Soon the MiGs were landing every few minutes. A whole Air Regiment came in and we had pictures to prove it. We now knew what the EGAF had planned for Marxwalde AB; fighter air defense for East Berlin. Later, analysis would reveal that the MiGs had deployed from Cottbus AB in southeast East Germany. We were having good luck this Friday the 13th.

Then activity quieted down, so we opted to leave the area about 4:45 pm and head home where we could report our findings. We got back on Route 1 and went west towards Berlin. When we reached Muncheberg we turned south on the road we came in on. We hadn't gone very far when we ran across military activity east of the road. Where there was nothing that morning, there now were several communications vans, plus mobile antennae. Included was an Ilyushin IL-14 twin prop transport that had landed in the unimproved field. We had stumbled on to the outer beacon landing assistance site for Marxwalde AB. There was something else that wasn't there that morning – military security personnel. As we came down the road we saw guards at the three dirt roads leading into the site. We passed the first one before he saw us. The second one wasn't ready for us either. But the third had time to react. He came up out of the ditch about 10 feet from us as we passed. At first I didn't recognize the look on his face. I soon translated it into "I'm going to get you, you SOBs."

Killing time is USMLM Air Team member Pendergast on site in East Germany, waiting for Soviet/EGAF flying operations to start. (USMLM)

Major Warren had already told SSgt Budd to step on it and get around the bend in the road. I was in the rear and watched the guard. He kneeled on the pavement and pointed his weapon at us from about 100 yards away. With all the noise we were generating while burning rubber, I didn't hear any shots. We made the bend unharmed and then had to decide how to "get out of Dodge." Did we find some secondary roads or did we head straight for the autobahn 8 miles away, which meant running the Mission Restriction signs and possible Soviet guards at the Fuerstenwalde radar site? We decided to chance the Soviet guards on the assumption that by the time the EGAF coordinated with the Russians, we would be past them. It worked. We got on the autobahn and headed towards Potsdam. We pulled off once in a secure spot to catch our breath and confirmed that we were not followed. We weren't, so we headed home. I think we bypassed our normal stop at the Potsdam Mission house and went direct to the bridge checkpoint to West Berlin. We were interested in getting out of East Germany as quickly as possible before news of the incident spread to the *Stasi* security forces.

At the Berlin Mission House we briefed folks on our success at Marxwalde AB. The expression "fat, dumb and happy" comes to mind. Then the motor Sgt asked to talk to us about the bullet hole in the exhaust pipe. Luck on Friday the 13th had just turned bad.

A shooting incident causes all sorts of things to happen. For starters, coordination with HQ USAREUR, Berlin HQ, the US State Department, and in our case HQ USAFE was warranted. First impressions were that this would be a good incident to protest. The thinking went as follows: main road, no restricted area or signs, normally no military presence, and limited warning from the security forces. So I was directed to call the Soviet External Relations Branch (SERB) on our "hot line" and brief them on the incident and our intentions. The call required me to look up several words in Russian that I didn't normally have to use. What is "tail pipe" in Russian anyway? USAREUR later followed up with a written protest. The protest process percolated for about a month with press releases appearing in most US newspapers. The East Germans claimed they had only fired a warning shot into the air. The Soviets eventually rejected the protest. The Group

Soviet Forces Germany Chief of Staff officially asserted that the USMLM team was guilty of "undisciplined behavior." We thought the East German sentry taking a pot shot at an auto on a main road was the undisciplined one. The toughest part of the ordeal was trying to figure out how to tell my pregnant wife that I had to work late because I got the car shot up, and not cause a miscarriage. My advice: avoid shooting incidents.

The Cold War continued for another 30 years until President Reagan sorted things out. And the Military Missions planned and went about their business in a manner similar to the Marxwalde story. As for Friday the 13th being lucky or unlucky, you decide.

John E Pendergast, USMLM Air Team 1959-1961, North East, MD, Friday 13 June 2008

James R. Holbrook

Jim is the author of a new, second edition of *Potsdam Mission: Memoir of a US Army Intelligence Officer in Communist East Germany*. His website is www.potsdammission. com

The Military Liaison Missions

The Western Allies' missions grew to the point where they soon established operational centers in their respective sectors of West Berlin. USMLM's operation center was at 19/21 Foehrenweg. USAREUR took operational control of USMLM's intelligence collection and reporting activities. By the time I arrived at USMLM in 1976, all USMLM staff, with the exception of a Potsdam House Duty Officer, lived in regular military quarters in West Berlin. The Potsdam House was used primarily as a jumping-off point for trips into the interior of East Germany. It served also as a place for official meetings and social functions with

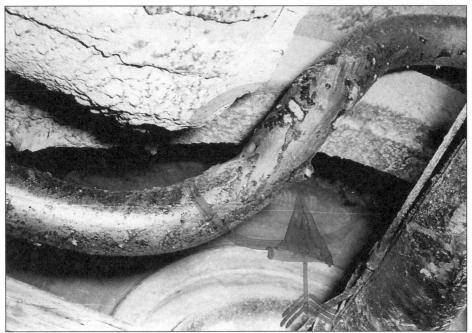

The 57 Chevrolet's exhaust pipe with bullet hole – see John Pendergast's story on the previous page. (USMLM photo)

Soviet and Allied military representatives, for casual entertainment of guests of Mission members, and for the rest and recreation (R&R) of Mission families.

In 1976, the Army section had 45 personnel, the Air Force section 16 and we had one U.S. Marine officer—a total of 62 military personnel. Four civilians rounded out the Mission roster. Since our main base of operations was in West Berlin, the Soviets could not monitor (or dictate) how many people we had assigned. The official limit of 14 applied only to USMLM members authorized to be in the Soviet Zone at any one time. The fourteen Soviet passes, authorizing travel in East Germany, were rotated among a select contingent of officers and noncommissioned officers (NCOs) who performed the actual travel and intelligence collection. Additional support personnel who remained at the Berlin headquarters provided indispensable administrative, analytic, film processing and logistic support. The situations for FMLM and BRIXMIS were analogous to ours. (At one time, BRIXMIS had nearly 200 assigned personnel, including at least one Canadian officer in their operations section.) Consequently, all the Allied Missions had a distinct advantage over their Soviet counterparts in West Germany, who were far from any Soviet military support base.

USMLM was not a secret military unit. We lived in the open and drove vehicles around Berlin, sporting very conspicuous yellow license plates with a number and Russian lettering. We operated in the open; we were overt intelligence collectors. Very few of us would ever claim that we were "spies". True, we did much of the same type of intelligence collection that agents were doing for the OSS and the British SIS in East Germany before they were

James R. Holbrook – here is a picture that shows an Opel, damaged during a chase through the woods. Obviously, we got away. My driver on the left was Sgt Jim Rice. Taken in 1977 in the E. German woods. (James R. Holbrook)

Postdam House, East Germany. The car in the foreground
shows USMLM plates. (James R. Holbrook)

The real Ops Center – back in free West Berlin. (James R. Holbrook)

shut down in 1947. True, we did sneak around and attempt to mask our specific tasks and we did "spy" on the Soviet and East German forces. But, in contrast to the work of OSS and SIS agents, the Soviets knew our identities and what we were doing. We used vehicles and wore uniforms that clearly marked us as American military. In a manner of speaking, we were overt agents and reporters all in one.

An intelligence collection mission into East Germany was called a "tour." We referred to each other as "tour officers" and "tour NCOs." Occasionally we called ourselves "missionaries" — a word sometimes used in Soviet documents to refer to members of the Allied Military Liaison Missions. A tour usually consisted of one officer and one NCO who, after a few days preparation in West Berlin, would go out into East Germany with a specific set of intelligence collection tasks. During my time at the Mission, we traveled

---

ATTENTION! PASSAGE OF MEMBERS OF FOREIGN MILITARY LIAISON MISSIONS **PROHIBITED!**

ATTENTION! PASSAGE AUX MEMBRES des MISSIONS MILITAIRES **ETRANGERES** de **LIAISON** est **INTERDIT!**

ПРОЕЗД ЧЛЕНАМ ИНОСТРАННЫХ ВОЕННЫХ МИССИЙ СВЯЗИ ЗАПРЕШЕН!

Durchfahrt für das Personal der ausländischen **Militärverbindungs- Missionen** ist **VERBOTEN!**

Military Restriction Sign. (James R. Holbrook)

Major Ed Hamilton's badly-damaged Bronco, 1979. (James R. Holbrook)

in Opel sedans or Broncos that were specially modified for our travel and intelligence collection circumstances. A tour normally took 2 to 3 days.

During USMLM's history, many detentions, shootings, rammings and assaults occurred. For the most part, however, only a few of these incidents reached the press. The most sensational news story occurred toward the end of USMLM's existence in East Germany. In 1985, a Soviet sentry shot USMLM tour officer, Major Arthur D. Nicholson, Jr. His death was a direct result of the Soviets brutal refusal to administer, or to let his driver administer, first aid.

Numerous vehicle rammings over the years injured several Allied Mission personnel. In March 1979, a large Czech-built Tatra-813 truck struck a Mission car, hurtling it off the road. The tour officer, Major Ed Hamilton, and his driver Staff Sergeant Hans Tiffany, were injured badly enough that they were incapacitated for six weeks. Soviet personnel broke into the Mission car and removed all the equipment. In March 1984, one year before they shot Major Nicholson, a large East German truck rammed a French Mission vehicle, instantly killing French Adjutant-Chef (Sergeant-Major) Mariotti. A statement made by a Soviet general to the Chief of USMLM confirmed the premeditated nature of such rammings; the next time a certain tour officer went out, "his wife [was] liable to become a widow. He might collide with a tank or a big truck."

Not all our encounters with the Soviets and East Germans, however, were violent. Probably the Soviets or East Germans detained every touring officer and NCO on a collection mission several times during their time at USMLM. We called these detentions "clobbers." I was clobbered four times.

My first clobber occurred shortly after I began touring. A zealous Soviet lieutenant thought we were in a Permanent Restricted Area, while in fact we were just refueling our car in an open area in northern Germany. When he took me into the Rostock *Kommendatura*, a Soviet version of a military police office, he found the crusty old major who had to attend to us was very unhappy about being rousted from bed. The major agreed with me that we weren't in a restricted area, berated his lieutenant and let us go.

Soviets in West Germany at US Combat Training Base Grafenwoehr. (James R. Holbrook)

The second clobber occurred in the Potsdam local area. My driver, Staff Sergeant Ralph Germaine and I were returning to Berlin after a 2-day intelligence collection mission in Leipzig. As we started across a bridge, a chain snapped up in front of us. Sergeant Germaine slammed on the Opel's brakes and we screeched into the chain barrier. From underneath the bridge a squad of armed Soviet soldiers scrambled up onto the bridge and pointed their rifles at us. A lieutenant led them. When I at first refused to give him my Soviet pass, the lieutenant turned back to his soldiers and gave some kind of signal. They all drew back the mechanisms on their AK-47 assault rifles, presumably putting a round into the firing chamber. I was concerned one of the soldiers would make a mistake and bump his trigger. In retrospect, the weapons were probably not loaded, or the rounds were blanks, as the Soviets rationed their ammunition very carefully. Moreover, given the lack of trust in their own soldiers, the Soviets probably wouldn't have let a patrol run around with live ammo. Later, at the Potsdam *Kommendatura*, the Soviets reluctantly agreed they had mistaken our car for that of a French Mission team that had been observing the uploading of Soviet tanks onto a train earlier that morning. Once again, I was released without any negative consequences.

My third clobber came because of poor planning on my part. Tours were supposed to plan their targets so there would always be a viable egress route in the event they were detected and had to flee the area. But I got us mired in heavy brush by an army installation near Prenzlau and soon found our car blocked by a Soviet warrant officer on a motorcycle. That detention turned out to be an interesting one, perhaps even a positive one for getting the true American story across to a bunch of Soviet officers. I spent several hours discussing the pay, medical treatment, promotion procedures, educational and retirement advantages, etc of the U.S. and Soviet Armies. (I used myself as an example of a former enlisted man, whom the Army had sent to civilian universities all the way through my doctorate.) When I departed, I'm sure I left a lot of food for thought for the Soviet officers who probably never heard such things about the American "imperialist" Army.

My fourth clobber could have been avoided, but I chose not to risk injury or death to a large group of soldiers who had surrounded our vehicle. My driver was anxious to break through the encirclement, but I said, "No, let's not take a chance." Our Chief of Mission, Colonel Pete Thorsen, had instilled in us the need to be careful of the civilian and military population wherever we traveled. My immediate boss, LTC Randy Greenwalt (now Brigadier General, Ret), who had served earlier at USMLM, described very well the new environment at the Mission in the 1976 USMLM Unit History:

> The intelligence collection atmosphere has decidedly improved. Previous "escape and evade" tactics which often led to exciting, but pointless, high-speed chases and concerted efforts to detain tours, have been replaced by a more subdued, stealthful style of collection and a preparedness to accept detention, rather than escalate a situation.

Perhaps in appreciation for my discretion during this incident, I wasn't even taken to the *kommendatura*, but rather, after an hour of discussion with a couple of Soviet captains, I was just released. My driver and I then continued our collection mission in the Potsdam local area.

The biggest event for me during my service at USMLM was the CINC-CINC visit. The Commander in Chief of Soviet Group of Forces, Germany, Army General Ivanovsky, paid an official visit to the Commander in Chief, USAREUR, General George Blanchard in July 1977. I was in charge of all interpreter support and was fortunate enough to both help on the planning and to be in on all the exchanges between both CINCs during a visit that opened the Soviet party's eyes to a well-trained and motivated U.S. Army in Europe.

As the only U.S. military intelligence unit actually on the ground and traveling among the hundreds of thousands of Soviet and East German military forces of the Warsaw Pact during the entire span of the Cold War, USAREUR had a unique window into the daily training and equipment status of a possible enemy.

James R. Holbrook, LTC, USA (Retired), USMLM 1976-77

Charles Stiles

There were two broad categories of personnel assigned to USMLM, administrative/support, and tour (or operations personnel). Administrative people did about what administrative people do in any military organization: typing, communications, personnel actions, maintaining the automobile fleet (very important), preparing final copies of intelligence reports for distribution, etc.

LTC Stiles, USAF, Deputy Chief USMLM, shaking hands with Soviet CINC of GSFG Yevgeni F. Ivanovsky on the occasion of the meeting of CINC, USAREUR and CINC, GSFG in East Germany, November 1974. (Charles S. Stiles)

Collecting information – on a camouflaged car with 35mm
camera and 1000mm lens. (Charles S. Stiles)

A Ford sedan. Note the plates – some of these cars had special
adaptations for their unique missions. (Charles S. Stiles)

"Tour" personnel actually conducted the collection operations into the Soviet Sector of Germany, also known as Communist East Germany. Tours lasted at least two days on the road in East Germany. A "tour" consisted of one officer, who spoke Russian, an NCO who spoke German and a Ford Interceptor sedan or Ford Bronco. A typical day for the officer, when he was not on tour, could include: time off with his family, preparing the raw intelligence into report format, getting the resulting film developed, reviewing collateral intelligence data, attending MLM staff meetings and planning the next operation with the assistance of the NCO driver. Often the tour officer had to attend social functions with the French and the British MLMs and with the Soviets; normally these were evening affairs. Every social event with the Soviets was a bit of adventure, whether formal, e.g. celebrating the meeting on the Elbe River of American and Soviet troops during WWII, or informal such as the huge outdoor picnic yearly on July 4th, which included the US hosts, Soviets, British, and French MLM members, plus members of the US Army Berlin Brigade.

A typical day for the Chief and Deputy Chief of USMLM could be to meet with the Soviet Liaison Officer and staff in Potsdam. There would be rare meetings with the Chief of Staff, Soviet Forces in East Germany, and with the Soviet Commander-in-Chief (General Ivanosky in the mid-Seventies). So, there were purely liaison activities in addition to intelligence activities.

Therefore, the composite name of the mission: The United States Military Liaison Mission to the Commander-In-Chief Soviet Forces in East Germany. The Soviets rarely would use the name "East Germany". They would say only "Germany". Likely this was a political practice and a matter of policy.

USAF driver Master Sergeant Konrad Spitzenberger is by the USMLM
Bronco. The Soviet-supplied license plate is not visible because of it
likely being covered with mud and dirt. (Charles S. Stiles)

A 4th of July celebration at Potsdam House. (Charles S. Stiles)

The Soviets killed a USMLM Tour officer, an Army Major, on March 24, 1985. This certainly shows that "danger" was an important factor where the USMLM mission was concerned. The Major and his Army driver were on a collection mission when the tragedy struck. The Major was outside his vehicle at the time and was attempting to see if a building was an in-use tank "barn". We did not see the Soviet guard who fired the shot. The soldier and the Soviet officers, who came to the scene after the shooting, would not allow the USMLM driver to approach the downed Major, nor would they call for medical assistance. The Soviets took away the body even before the arrival of the Chief USMLM. The Soviets returned the Major's body after a few days. This event went all the way to the President of the U.S. It has been said that the USMLM Major killed in 1985 likely was the "last casualty of the Cold War".

Another incident, not to be compared with the Major's death, was serious from the standpoint of the location of the "hit" and because it involved the Deputy Chief of USMLM. The location was in a Soviet restricted area and near a Soviet air base. The Deputy and driver saw Soviet vehicles approaching at quite a high speed from a forest area. They did not run for one of their planned exits because they could see armed Soviet soldiers revealing their presence all around the tour's location. The Soviets ambushed them. The captors, Soviet officers and one apparently German "technician," spent considerable time inspecting the photo equipment of the tour and confiscated all the equipment and film. Finally their escorts took them to the Soviet facility in Potsdam and released them about midnight after 12 hours. They returned the purloined photo equipment without the exposed film.

Some adventure was included in just about every trip into East Germany! Tour personnel would go into areas in East Germany where no American had been for decades: East Germany in general, and cities such as Dresden where some East Germans had

A specially-adapted car as used by USMLM members – its functions are described by David Perk on the previous page. (Paul Nikulla via David Perk)

very strong and bitter memories of the American raid in WWII that practically destroyed Dresden with fire bombing.

Short Term detentions, blocking, harassment, vehicle ramming were quite common and many had the potential for escalation in seriousness. An example of a not-so-serious "hit" but a simple case of harassment: the Soviets picked up the USMLM Deputy Chief and family (wife and three children) in Potsdam. They accused the officer of a parking violation and took the family to the Potsdam headquarters and released them after a short time. The family was doing some Christmas shopping.

Sufficient to say that membership in USMLM dating back to 1947 or so is membership in a rare and proud fraternity.

Specially-adapted Cold War cars – Cold War '007 James Bond'?

These cars were mentioned and described in the declassified USMLM unit histories. I found reference and description of these cars in the 1966, 1967, 1974 histories and others. These accounts also describe the special cars receiving the conversion to four-wheel drive in England. Below are exclusive descriptions from USMLM members.

Army Sergeant David Perk[3]

The switches in the photo above enabled the tour driver to do a number of things with the vehicle's lighting. The Master Kill switch on the left disabled all the lighting on the vehicle, including headlamps, tail and brake lights, and the dome light. This was used

3   Visit www.keepsakemedia.net/keepsakemedia/USMLM_DVD.html to view details of a DVD history of USMLM produced by David Perk, entitled *In Plain Sight*.

during stakeouts and while sleeping at night in the vehicle, and prevented the driver from accidentally giving away the vehicle location by inadvertently touching the brake pedal. Another switch disabled the right side headlamp to give the car the appearance that it was a motorcycle when traveling at night. One switch disabled the brake lights only and another made the rear lighting completely dark. One activated an extremely bright halogen light mounted on the rear bumper. Not only did this provide a very effective backup light, we could use it to disorient anyone giving chase at night as we focused it at eye level with the driver of a vehicle at close range. The last switch activated the front auxiliary driving lights.

Air Force Staff Sergeant Thomas Tiffany

We had specially modified Mercedes SUVs and sedans as well as Range Rovers and an old Ford Bronco. In addition to the external features like skid plates, electric winches, and bulletproof glass on the sedans, we also had a row of toggle switches inside the vehicles. These toggle switches did several things: turned off horn (not good for that to go off accidentally in the wrong place), turned off rear tag light, turned off brake lights, turned off all rear lights, turned off one side of vehicle's lights (made you look like a motorcycle at night) and there was one more that shut down the entire vehicle's electrical system. That was practically never used and was only to be used if your vehicle was compromised. I think they also had extra horsepower engines.

Air Force Master Sgt Mert Pennock

They assigned me to the USMLM Air Team, as a driver, from September 1974 to October 1979.

The Broncos had winches installed over the front bumper, but were operated from inside by disengaging the transmission from the drive train and engaging the transmission directly to the winch. Being the driver, I would sit behind the wheel, after, of course, hooking the cable to the nearest tree, or whatever, and engage the winch and also be prepared to hit the floorboard if the cable ever broke, which it didn't.

The Police Interceptor was a 1972 Ford Sedan that had the following features:

The Interceptor was special from the rest of the vehicles assigned to USMLM in that they set them up to engage a four-wheel drive system. When the rear wheels started to slip, the front wheel transmission drive would automatically engage and when the rear wheels were on the ground again, then the front wheels would disengage. This vehicle also had dual shock absorbers up front.

All Ford Sedans had the following in common:

- ¾ inch steel skid plate which extended from the front of the engine to behind the transmission.
- 45 gallon gas tanks. The expression on the East German attendant was something to watch as he would pump and pump before the tank was again full.
- I believe the interceptor was 450 hp. We were able to take a flat autobahn exchange at 105 mph. We arrived in Potsdam with a couple of minutes to spare and sat down to an enjoyable meal and afterwards a couple of drinks and watched a movie. We were in the AAFES (PX) movie circuit.
- Light switch panel which controlled turning off and on the following outside lights: All lights, Brake lights, turning off all lights on one side which at night looked like a motorcycle from a distance, and turning off all rear lights.

- Recaro racing seats [to make sleeping in cars more comfortable – James Holbrook].
- Rear window curtains.
- Capable of going 60 mph *in reverse.*
- We carried a hand winch, 3 foot long waffle skid plates to put under the tires if we were stuck, an axe, and each driver had a tool issue for vehicle repair, if need be, while out on the other side; we hoped that we would never have to call home for a wrecker because we might have to walk up to 20 miles to find a phone. I never had to.

Army Staff Sergeant John Schniedermeier

To start out, we had 429 Police Interceptor engines in the cars. Underneath the vehicle you had a ½-¾ inch steel plate to protect the oil pan and the engine, in case we had to go cross-country. Inside the car we had, among other things, bucket seats and curtains on the rear window, so the Tour Officer could do his job without being seen from the rear. On the front panel we had toggle switches to control the head and taillights in case we being tailed by EG Vopos or MfS vehicles. In the trunk we had a come-along wench and steel cables with snatch blocks in case we would get stuck in a field or muddy road.

Air Force Senior Master Sergeant Mel Ratz

First of all the Ford Police Cruisers were a very fast car for the Mission - sturdy as a rock and it would go up to 120 mph real quickly. But someone in the US that helped modifying learned of a company in Coventry, England that could convert our cars to four-wheel drive. The hardest thing to do was to make it look like a normal car including hub caps. We made several trips over there to learn more and to watch the progress being made. They had to modify the frame and beef it up considerably. The secret to the conversion was a small cylinder the size of a roll of toilet paper. The system allowed maximum torque to all four wheels that won't cause it to slip. This would allow us to go up a snowy hill, stop half-way up, and just sit there. Well, our buddies in the E. German *Stasi* would try the same thing and when they stopped they could no longer go forward, and would just sit there and spin their wheels. We would then slowly creep on up the hill and disappear from them. This also worked in sandy areas as well. They also installed a non-skid brake system which made it harder for them to tail us on the autobahn. The Air Force was the lead in this conversion and a little later the Army followed us. The only bad thing about the car was the upkeep. It really was a nightmare at times.

From the USMLM histories

The 1985 USMLM unit history is dedicated to Lieutenant Colonel Arthur D. "Nick" Nicholson who was shot and killed by a Soviet guard in Ludwigslust, East Germany on 24 March 1985. Nick's supreme sacrifice on behalf of this country and in defense of our national security will never be forgotten. His courage, patriotism, and selfless commitment will remain an inspiration and example to all of us at the Mission and those who follow in our footsteps.

Roland Lajoie
Colonel, GS – Chief of Mission

SERIOUS INCIDENT: A relatively grave occurrence occurred whose resolution may require action at a higher level than Chief USMLM / Chief SERB. Action taken frequently included an exchange of letters at Chief of Staff or higher level.

LUDWIGSLUST: 241520A March 1985. A Soviet sentry shot and killed Maj. Arthur D. Nicholson, Jr., a member of USMLM

CINCUSAREUR protest letter on shooting (declassified from Confidential)

General Mikhail M. Zaytsev
Commander in Chief
Group of Soviet Forces in Germany
General Zaytsev:
With this letter, I am lodging an official protest of the gravest nature.

At approximately 1545 hours, 24 March 1985, one of your soldiers deliberately shot and murdered an unarmed member of my military liaison mission, Major Arthur D. Nicholson, Jr., in the vicinity of Ludwigslust, East Germany. Following the shooting, your Soviet soldier also prohibited the administering of emergency lifesaving measures by major Nicholson's driver, Sergeant Jessie G. Schatz. This wanton act of violence is the most serious in the 38 year history of the Huebner-Malinin Agreement.

You are aware that the Huebner-Malinin Agreement provides that the members of our liaison missions are to be permitted complete freedom of travel wherever and whenever desired over the territory and roads in both zones. The only exceptions to this free travel guarantee have been the permanent and temporary restricted areas periodically established by our sides. Major Nicholson was not within one of your restricted areas; he was exercising his legitimate right of free travel. The fact that the sentry clearly recognized the mission vehicle and mission personnel and still opened fire indicates that this action had the tacit approval of Headquarters, Group of Soviet Forces, Germany (GSFG). It is also unconscionable that your soldier and his superiors did not allow Sergeant Schatz to administer first aid to Major Nicholson.

On 19 March 1985, personnel from your Soviet Military Liaison Mission-Frankfurt, were detected violating a permanent restricted area in the U.S. Army, Europe zone near Hof. When they were detained by our forces on 20 March for that violation, they were treated, as always, in a civil, safe, and professional manner. No one was harmed. Conversely, the actions by your soldier in this latest incident were completely uncalled for and show a total disregard for human life.

I strongly protest this violent action by your soldier which has resulted in the needless and unjustified death of one of my officers, who, like your liaison officers, was unarmed. I demand a full investigation and explanation of this incident, that measures be taken to insure that the personnel responsible are punished, and that measures be implemented to insure that an incident such as this will not recur.

Glenn K. Otis, General, U.S. Army
Commander in Chief

(For more information search on the internet for USMLM Unit Histories and select 1985).

Extracts from the 1988 USMLM unit history, once classified, now declassified

This was the last USMLM history.

From the Introduction
In Potsdam the door creaked twice. On 14 June, the apology for Maj. Nicholson's death was announced to an unprepared USAREUR and GSFG. The pregnant pause that followed made us wonder if anyone knew what to do after so much blind, accusatory confrontation.

The door that slammed shut in December 1979 with the invasion of Afghanistan, and then was double bolted with Nick's death in March 1985, was suddenly open again. We renewed broader contacts with the Soviets. After how many years of riding by his garrison, we had the Potsdam Artillery Division Commander as a guest for Thanksgiving dinner and for good measure had the priest from the Russian Orthodox Church of St. Alexander Nevsky in Potsdam say grace with the Berlin Catholic chaplain.

Potsdam House, after its extensive restoration looking like a sleeping princess, suddenly was kissed and awoke. Liaison was alive, and it was exciting. To have been Chief of Mission with the men and women of USMLM in a year of achievement and fundamental change was privilege, pleasure and a most kind gift of Providence.

Gregory G. Govan, COL, GS
Chief of Mission

Arms Control Development
SS-12 Withdrawal: After the signing of the INF Treaty in December 1987, the Soviet Government announced that, as an act of good faith, all SS-12 missiles would be withdrawn from the GDR ahead of schedule. Capitalizing Mission access to the GDR, USMLM organized a series of road and rail watches in an effort to provide coverage of the event independent of that provided by the Soviet and East German news medium. Results included the 25 February confirmation of 27 departing SS-12 TEL and the first ground level photography of SS-12 associated support vehicle, such as the C2 vehicle, generator vehicle, and the SS-12 associated crane.
ABOVE NOW DECLASSIFIED.

The following is a selection of tech ops reporting at the former SECRET = Warning Notice = Intelligence Sources & Methods Involved (now declassified):
- (S/WN) Examination of the exercise scenario developed by a GSFG ground army for a NATO attack.
- (S/WN) Analysis of the vehicle assignment in a ground army headquarters. Sensitive command and control vehicle groupings were isolated and all vehicles assigned to senior army command personnel were identified.
- (S/WN) Summary report on the structure, manning, training, morale and related details of army-level Spetsnaz Company.
- (S/WN) Near verbatim coverage of a meeting of a military counsel of a GSFG ground army.

PRAs – Permanently Restricted Areas / TRAs – Temporary Restricted Areas (Exercises)
While on tour and collecting military information, USMLM members were not supposed to violate PRAs OR TRAs. Did they? My source tells me:

As a matter of standing policy the three Allied liaison missions (USMLM (US), FMLM (French), BRIXMIS (British)) respected PRA and TRA (Temporary

Restricted Area), although we heard reports of SMLM (Soviets) in West Germany routinely violating PRA/TRA. Even though the three Allied missions, as a matter of standing policy, did not violate PRA/TRA, any detention near a PRA or TRA was liable to be documented by the Soviets as a PRA/TRA violation. Occasionally, USMLM tours entered the outskirts of PRAs inadvertently through either map reading errors, poorly printed maps, or just inattention. It was unit policy that such incidents be reported to the USMLM leadership immediately upon the tour's return, in case an official Soviet protest later resulted. Such protests did occur.

My source continues:

In addition, the Soviets applied a very liberal definition when it came to "restricted areas." They included in this category any area in East Germany posted by Mission Restricted Signs (MRS) (printed in English, French, Russian and German) or "Sperrgebiet" signs (printed only in German). These areas included garrisons, training areas and rail sidings outside PRAs and were routinely visited by the three missions,

CONFIDENTIAL
(U) SS-12 Command & Control Vehicle

A declassified surveillance photo of a Soviet SS-12 command
and control vehicle. (USMLM History)

A declassified surveillance photo of a Soviet T-80. (USMLM History)

because the signs protecting them had no basis in the 1947 agreements signed by the Soviets and the three Allied powers. As an example, when Maj. Nicholson was killed, I'm told that the Soviets at one point claimed he was in a PRA. This was not true; portions of the training area were posted with MRS, but the nearest PRA was across a nearby highway and clearly marked on maps. The Ludwigslust training area where he was killed was clearly outside PRA.

3

Soviet Military Liaison Missions – their collectors in the West ("legal" overt spies)

Thanks to Ron Gambolati for writing the great majority of this chapter.

After the defeat of Nazi Germany and its surrender in May 1945, the Allies settled in with the pre-agreed occupations. The occupiers designated American, British, and Soviet zones during earlier high-level allied meetings. They created the French Zone by realigning the US and British zones to accommodate an ally the West felt deserved a major role in the post-war occupation.

Early in the occupation, it became apparent that the occupiers needed some means of coordinating their actions. Coordination among the Western allies was going as smoothly as could be expected under the circumstances, but the Soviets were beginning to appear less cooperative with their wartime allies. The British led the way in the fall of 1946 with the Robertson-Malinin Agreement, an exchange of liaison teams between the military headquarters of the British and Soviet occupation forces. This action was followed in short order by the French (Noiret-Malinin) and American (Huebner-Malinin) agreements in the spring of 1947. The Soviet liaison missions were called SOXMIS (Soviet Exchange Mission) by the British, MMS (Mission Militaire Soviétique) by the French, and Soviet Military Liaison Mission (SMLM – somewhat derisively pronounced "smell 'em") by the Americans. The authorized strength of each mission was established by each individual agreement: SOXMIS was the largest with 32 Soviet officers and men, MMS with 18, and SMLM with 14. SOXMIS was quartered in Herford in the British Zone of Occupation, MMS in Baden-Baden in the French Zone, and SMLM in Frankfurt-am-Main in the US Zone. Under the agreements, the hosting headquarters provided lodging, rations and a fuel allowance to the Soviet missions. The three western missions were quartered in Potsdam, just outside Berlin, deep in the Soviet Zone of Occupation.

Soviet mission vehicles in West Germany were issued special license plates which clearly identified them.

US Zone SMLM vehicles were issued license plates numbered 1-29, British Zone SOXMIS 30-59, and French Zone MMS 60-89. While the liaison missions were granted freedom of travel within their zones of accreditation, the activity of the missions in using their freedom of movement to gather information on their hosts became readily apparent. As a result, the various headquarters introduced restrictions on mission travel. Military installations and training areas were put off limits and the missions were given a map which clearly delineated these Permanent Restricted Areas (PRA). When units went on maneuvers outside the PRA, headquarters declared a Temporary Restricted Area (TRA) and presented the appropriate Soviet mission with a map outlining the TRA and declaring

Major Michael Ian Burkham MBE, unknown RMP, myself – Corporal
Tommy Nibloe, SOXMIS Maj Banov, CinC SOXMIS Lt Col Zeitzev. All
are watching motorcycle cross country trials. (Tommy Nibloe)

the dates and times of the restriction. While the number and total length of TRA would vary
from year to year, for some strange and unknown reason, the sizes and total percentage
of PRA varied from zone to zone. For the longest time, Soviet PRA equaled over 30%
of the Soviet Zone of Occupation while only 18% of the US Zone was under permanent
restriction. In the late 1980s, the US was able to reverse this inequality and published a PRA
map with the identical percentage of restricted area as the Soviets restricted in their zone.

Soviet mission vehicles caught in a restricted area or showing "undue interest" (e.g.,
following and photographing a military convoy outside a restricted area) were subject
to detention. Unlike the treatment afforded Western missions in the Soviet Zone where
vehicles were broken into, material "confiscated," and mission members roughed up (two
mission members, one French and one American, were actually killed by East Germans
or Soviets), Soviet mission vehicles and members were simply detained until released by
order of a general officer. Official protests generally followed a detention inside a restricted
area while detentions for "undue interest" were glossed over as the price of doing business,
i.e. monitoring military activity. All US and allied military were required, as a minimum, to
report any sighting of a Soviet mission vehicle and to take appropriate action should they
commit any violation.

In the world of "open spying," the Soviet missions generally played their role well.
Soviet "touring" activities monitored US and allied training, ensured there was no military
build-up during periods of increased tension, checked for new and improved military
equipment as it moved in convoys along the German roads in non-restricted areas.

Occasionally the Soviets would penetrate a PRA or TRA if the "take" was deemed worth the risk (rather low in light of potential consequences). One example was the detention of a Soviet mission vehicle and crew well inside a PRA near a sensitive weapons site during one of the numerable Middle East crises. While the violation was serious in itself, it can be argued that Soviet verification that sensitive weapons were not being deployed during the crisis would have a good calming effect on a tense situation. Touring activity was also particularly heavy during the build-up period of the First Gulf War when US forces in Germany deployed large military units to the Middle East, and again during the period of reduction because of the Conventional Forces Agreement in the 1980s.

While there were certainly many indications that the Soviet missions participated in illegal activities, because of the restrictions on searching their vehicles, there was never any concrete proof produced other than one instance which came to light after the fall of East Germany: MMS had assisted a wanted East German spy to flee West Germany. In addition, the Soviets certainly had the assets and capacity to provide support to illegals in the Federal Republic of Germany as well as to capture signals from US and Allied military installations and vehicles.

As the Soviet missions were accredited to the respective Allied military headquarters – SOXMIS to the British Army of the Rhine (BAOR), MMS to Forces Françaises en Allemagne (French Forces in Germany – FFA), and SMLM to United States Army, Europe (USAREUR), the Germans, most reluctantly, accepted their presence in German sovereign territory after the end of Allied occupation in 1955. German reunification in 1989 and the announced dissolution of the Soviet Union made the presence of military liaison missions unacceptable to a sovereign Germany and all missions were dissolved at the end of 1990.

Gene Chomko, Col, USA (Ret), former USAREUR Contact Officer for SMLM-F and an expert on the matter adds:

Detained Soviet tour vehicle blocked by 3 US jeeps. (Douglas S. Otoupal)

Whenever a SMLM vehicle was detained, it was always done very carefully. The Soviets were not mistreated or roughed up. One had to keep in mind that our guys were doing the same job in East Germany. If we treated the Soviets harshly, our guys would get the same or worse treatment.

During a detention, the Soviets were held until I arrived to escort them back to their mission in Frankfurt. Once in Frankfurt, they would surrender their identification cards which we issued to them in the first place. The ACSI (Assistant Chief of Staff, Intelligence)[1] in Heidelberg would determine how long the Soviet tour officers would be without documentation. If we kept the Soviets off the road for three days, they would keep our guys off four days. It was tit for tat, a cat and mouse game.

I wanted a picture of the old Soviet SMLM compound in Frankfurt (as I have of the USMLM House in Potsdam) but it is gone, as reported recently by Gerry[2] from the State Department in Frankfurt:

Went out there yesterday: It's all gone, and they've got fancy little row houses there. Ran into the old local mail carrier – still on a bike – and he told me that as soon as the Sovs pulled out, right after unification, the place was turned over to the Germans, and they tore the whole thing down and started building what's there now. The power station is exactly where the guard shack, manned by Labor Service Guards, used to be.

Police didn't have any pictures of the old site, either. They destroyed their stuff when obsolete/no longer needed for reference.

---

1   Author's note: ACSI also known as DCSI.
2   Gerry Thielemann, Regional Security Office, American Consulate General Frankfurt, 2008.

4

The Military Intelligence
Field Office (counter spies)

Thanks are due to Scott O'Connell for writing this chapter. Scott is a retired counterintelligence officer (Special Agent in Charge) and currently a Senior National Security Official. In the first chapter, you heard me refer to the "local MI Office." What follows is a good description by Scott of the Military Intelligence (MI) Field Offices set up around our units in Germany and elsewhere in Europe. The male and female Special Agents who staffed these offices "fought" the spies and terrorists – head on.

Throughout the Cold War, the front line of defense against the Warsaw Pact was the constellation of field offices that Army intelligence placed across occupied Europe. Clearly, the center of gravity for counterintelligence was in the Occupied Zone of Germany under the famed Counter Intelligence Corps, and later in the Federal Republic of Germany. Throughout the Cold War counterintelligence went through myriad organizational and institutional changes but its overall mission and focus never wavered – protect US forces and its allies from the intelligence services of the Warsaw Pact, and later, from a variety of terrorist threats that proliferated throughout Europe.

The expression, 'field office' is a term of art. Counterintelligence organized tactically, strategically and operationally, conforming to the nature of the threat and the needs of the service. Divisional, Corps and Army-level counterintelligence units arrived in Germany with the 12th Army Group under General Omar Bradley with a well thought-out and crafted plan to support the invasion, but more importantly, to support the occupation that necessarily followed.

Their mission broke down into five distinct areas that military counterintelligence organizations generally follow today: secure US forces against enemy espionage, sabotage, and subversion; destroy the enemy secret intelligence services' police agencies and affiliates; assist in the dissolution of the *Nationale Sozialistische Deutsche Arbeiter Partei* (NSDAP – the Nazi Party); aid in the disposal of the German General Staff Corps (who acquiesced in, and ran the war); and insure the detention of selected scientists and technologies.

Without a doubt, the plan succeeded although not without great difficulty. The principal issue was resources. The Army Group's CI Branch, which oversaw these operations, consisted of sixty personnel. The CI detachments assigned to each Army, Corps and Division consisted of, on average, twenty men each. The Corps and Divisions typically had no more than a dozen special agents. In addition, the plan recognized that when forward troops cleared an area, CI "static" units needed to stand up. Static units became the forerunners of the strategic CI field offices of later years. These came from the tactical elements so resources stretched more and more as the CI need became greater. In all, there were less than 400 special agents assigned to the Army Group. These men had an impact on US national security and the events which unfolded throughout the Cold War not reflected in their numbers. They had tremendous success eliminating German espionage, sabotage, and subversion, identifying Nazi Party members and neutralizing or exploiting a variety of threats to US forces. Working with the Provost Marshal and tactical commands the occupied zone was quickly secured, but the challenge was to posture for the emerging threats that few in the high commanded comprehended or were willing to comprehend. Communism, as a hostile ideology and the driving force behind the new espionage, would soon replace Nazism.

The idea of 'tactical' and 'static' CI units is a concept that continued little changed throughout the Cold War and remains even today, the difference being that the 'static' units became strategic CI units. During the balance of the Cold War, these units divided themselves between US Army Europe (USAREUR), which owned the tactical units assigned to Corps and Division, and so-called 'strategic' CI units owned by the US Army Intelligence Agency (USAINTA) and later by the US Army Intelligence and Security Command (INSCOM).

By the mid-1970s there were approximately thirty five 'static' or strategic field offices in Germany and sixteen 'tactical' field offices with V Corps and VII Corps and their subordinate divisions and armored cavalry regiments. The breadth and scope of what these elements did to support the US Army in Europe varied with unit mission and, unfortunately, with the whims of the various commanders they served. After World War II, the Counterintelligence Corps in Germany had tremendous authority, if not resources. They continued to track down Nazis but began to posture themselves to combat the emerging threat from Communist, Stalinist, Russia and later, on, the Warsaw Pact. There was no German government so they functioned as the *de facto* counterespionage service for Germany, as well as the US forces. The challenges overwhelmed them and they had mixed success, largely because of the magnitude of the effort against them.

As the German Federal Republic matured, the role of US Army counterintelligence focused more on supporting the US forces and North Atlantic Treaty Organization (NATO). Their authority greatly (and appropriately) reduced, they worked with the new German counterespionage organizations and police, as those agencies now had primary authority for countering hostile intelligence within their country. However, there was more than enough work for everyone. The efforts of the Warsaw Pact, especially the emergent East German Service, *Ministerium fuer Staatssicherheit*, launched a barrage of spies against the West that overwhelmed the Western counterintelligence services and proved damaging to NATO.

In the forty-plus years the Cold War waged, the activities of the field offices varied but there were constants. The Army still embedded 'tactical' field offices in military intelligence detachments, companies, or battalions. These deployed to the field with the units and trained for war, exercising a variety of CI wartime functions, primarily screening prisoners and detainees and conducting CI raids. They also assisted with the effort to secure the units' rear area from a variety of threats. Simulating cooperation with military police and German authorities was also an important wartime mission for these units, although they could not conduct liaison on their own in peacetime. In garrison, they inspected unit security programs, gave SAEDA briefings, conducted personnel security investigations on cleared servicemen and civilian employees.

The 'strategic' field offices that worked for USAINTA and later, for INSCOM provided general support to USAREUR commanders through a number of functions. First was collection on threats to USAREUR, which they reported through a variety of media, primarily 'SPOT' reports. 'SPOT' reports involved mostly terrorism related events and were widely disseminated to all the military communities. Typically, they produced hundreds of these per month. Just like the tactical CI units, USAINTA /INSCOM field offices conducted personnel security investigations on non-tactical service members requiring security clearances. This was the bread and butter mission for most of them as the number of cleared individuals in the 'non-tactical part of USAREUR', euphemistically referred to as 'Echelons Above Corps', had large numbers of Top Secret clearances. There was always tremendous pressure on a precious few special agents to produce up to 20,000 background investigations per year. The USAINTA/INSCOM field offices had the lead for liaison with host nation counterparts. Typically, this meant the local German police and the Criminal Police (KRIPO). Selected units also coordinated activity with the other German investigative agencies on terrorism or espionage cases. Ironically, most US Army CI units had little operational interaction with their German military counterpart, the *Militaerische Abschirm Dienst* (Military Counterintelligence Service). Yes, the acronym, used by both the Germans and the Americans, was MAD! MAD excelled at local and regional threats to military forces so threat data exchanges were the primary business conducted with them. There was also some other cross-training and military skills training. However, German law during the Cold War restricted MAD actual counterespionage investigations to on-base activities. Cases involving non-military suspects (that is, most of the spies) were the jurisdiction the civilian services. Therefore, ironically, US Army counterintelligence worked more with the German civilian services than the military.

With regard to those cases, the USAINTA/INSCOM units conducted all of the counterespionage investigations and in most cases, these were done in support of the Germans who usually had primary jurisdiction. All off-post activity by the field offices was conducted by the field offices in conjunction with the Germans or with their approval. For that reason, the field offices spent a great deal of time developing working relationships and exchanging information with them. Many of the special agents had linguistics training, usually in German. Unfortunately, Americans rarely had enough competent linguists, a fact our German counterparts never hesitated to point out. Only those who had the chance to visit America and really understand its great size and relative isolation could understand why Americans did not cross the ocean with fluency in foreign tongues.

As a point of comparison, one could drive across the breadth of the former West Germany in about three and a half hours and from north to south in about eight hours. It takes five hours to fly across America in an airliner. As a further example, someone stationed in Frankfurt am Main, a major concentration of USAREUR units, could drive to any number of European countries over a weekend. From Frankfurt, one could drive to France in two hours; Luxembourg in three; Belgium or Holland in four; Denmark in six and Switzerland in three. The nearness of international borders made espionage an easier task as well. For that reason, several of the field offices, called border resident offices, operated along the no-man's land that constituted the inter-zonal border between East and West Germany. These offices coordinated closely with the German border police, the famed *Bundesgrenzschutz* (Federal Border Protection Service). Incidents that required the presence of a special agent and an interpreter occurred daily along the border where line crossers, intentional and inadvertent, appeared on a routine basis.

All field offices had German local national investigators. This unsung Corps of men and women believed in freedom, and to help maintain it, worked in the chasm between the two nations they loved. Most offices had one or two of these investigators who assisted special agents, not only in translation and liaison duties, but also in the conduct of specifically authorized investigative activity. In many cases, they mentored and trained the ever-arriving waves of new special agents as the Army did what it did best – rotate its soldiers in and out of country. The Army wrongly believed that its CI forces could be treated the same as infantrymen and succeed. Nothing could be further from the truth.

To compensate for the turmoil in the military ranks, changing jobs every three years on average, the Army created a civilian counterintelligence force. These civilian special agents, often retired or former military special agents, provided the backbone of the field office. They maintained the field office's area knowledge and had the more advanced skill sets required in a business that relied on experience and instinct more than training. Most civilian special agents were also linguists and many, the lucky ones, had German wives. They served in key positions such as Operations Officer, Senior Investigator, or Senior Case Officer. Although not required to maintain military skills and proficiency, many of them did. Because of their experience, they mentored more than their share of junior officers and enlisted men. In many ways, the CI field offices put the total in total Army force, before the greater Army invented the buzzword.

The officer or non-commissioned officer that headed up an Army counterintelligence 'field office' was called the 'Special Agent in Charge' or 'SAIC'. Depending on the size or importance of the unit, the military grade of the SAIC could range from Staff Sergeant E6 of a one or two person office to Lieutenant Colonel. Typically, though, they were Warrant Officers or Captains. Army counterintelligence requires its officers to be 'special agents' and trains them to the same technical standards as the enlisted, warrant officers and civilians. The Armor Branch is the only other place in the Army where this occurs. All Armor officers are 'Tankers' first and must learn and perform all the skills required of the men under him such as field strip his coax machine gun, do tank maintenance, calibration, vehicle recovery and the like. Just like the enlisted 'special agents', the officer 'special agent' must conduct interviews, take statements, conduct investigative leads, write various reports, plan and conduct investigations, surveillance and briefings, to name a few basic skills.

By the mid seventies, most field offices became part of larger organizations, usually Military Intelligence Companies but sometimes Detachments, both of which could be commanded by anything from Captain to Lieutenant Colonel. Fortunately, the officers at both levels of command were also special agents

The typical things that took place on a daily basis in the field office varied depending on the types of unit in the field offices' 'area of operation', or 'AO'. Since the counterintelligence field office was a military unit, there were myriad tasks that needed to be performed that had little to do with the functional mission of counterintelligence. This calls to mind the movie *Stripes*, where the group of hapless heroes disappears (go AWOL) for a while and when the Colonel finds out he asks what they were doing. The answer: training! The Colonel, needing clarification, asked what kind of training. The answer: Army training! Sir! And so it was in the field offices that fought the Cold War. Besides PT at least three days a week, military skills training such as land navigation, communications, leadership, weapons training, nuclear/chemical defense training, deployment training and readiness exercises consumed an inordinate amount of 'operational' time. In addition, noncommissioned officers had a variety of schools they might be sent to while in an assignment. All career-enhancing, but a drain on those charged with the mission.

On a typical day, in a typical field office, the men (and later, women) assigned had myriad missions and functions. Most operated independently, pursuing their cases, meeting with supported intelligence officers or security officers, scheduling or giving briefings, going on liaison visits and the like. The SAIC and his Operations Officer generally read message traffic, administrative correspondence and held meetings on a variety of subjects. The Operations Officer ran the mission for the Commander or SAIC, freeing him up to run 'interference' from a variety of places. A good Operations Officer identified his 'blue chip' special agents and assigned them the most sensitive cases. His best linguists had to do more than their share of work with the German authorities. Junior special agents generally did low level cases such as 'non-derogatory' personnel security investigations. 'Non-derogatory' cases were those that came in with no known adverse information on the subject. Normally, the more experienced investigators handled those, or assumed the lead on them if major derogatory information developed.

An example of this would be if a case came in with the subject having had a previous adverse investigation, had a criminal record, or the like. A big part of the case then focused on confirming or refuting the information or ensuring that person had not gotten into any more troubles since the last case. Financial cases posed the greatest challenge and came under great scrutiny as poor finances often trumped politics, ideology and other issues when it came to reasons for betraying your country. Finance cases could result from simple confusion in paperwork or major indebtedness and require the investigator to pore over meticulous documentation and make sense of a person's ability to stay solvent.

Cases of moral turpitude were rare but often provided an inside look into the worst behavior of people, many of them senior. Drug cases generally were open and shut – the result of the criminal or administrative investigation being grounds for a final 'suitability' report.

The most experienced investigators handled the 'complaint' cases: suspected espionage, sabotage, terrorism, subversion, or egregious security breaches where espionage could not be ruled out. These cases often became high profile, with USAREUR and USAINTA/INSCOM headquarters often in the reporting stream. Coordination with the Germans took place if activity involved occurred off-post or German citizens were involved. The vast majority of these cases did not result in a finding of espionage, but each one had to be worked as if espionage were likely.

Beginning with the early 1970s, terrorism became the greatest threat to USAREUR. A variety of terrorist groups emerged, all with different political goals and objectives but all ultimately aimed at undermining the West and the US in particular. The US military made a convenient, and, unfortunately, not so hard, target. The leftist *Rote Armee Faktion* (Red Army Faction), which sprang from the former 'Baader-Meinhof' Gang, was the most active terror group in Germany, although the Provisional IRA targeted British interests. Later, Middle East groups and even some right wing fringe groups, usually known as *Wehrsportgruppen* (Armed Sports Groups), emerged. The typical field office had but two or three espionage cases ongoing at any one time, but could have double that number of suspicious incidents that were indicative of terrorism. Many of these were threat letters, cut fences or vandalism of Army property, but they all had to be run to ground as if they were major events. The CINCUSAREUR himself was targeted by the RAF in the early 1980s and terrorist groups had successfully detonated bombs at a number of bases. Therefore, the threat was real. In response, much of counterintelligence's efforts turned to developing information about local threats to the supported commands and installations. Terrorism cases became the top priority. The field offices paid much more attention to the numerous suspicious incidents in and around USAREUR installations, which the Germans called Kasernen (Barracks). Hundreds of spot reports per month needed follow-up work, investigative activity, coordination, and liaison with the Military Police and the Germans. Anticipating the US's recent recognition that homeland security was ultimately a local matter, the German police structure included investigators who specialized in crimes against the state – *Dezernat Staatschutz* (State Protection Section). These were German criminal police, or *Kripo*, who looked for signs of right or left wing extremist activity within their jurisdiction. Terrorism fell under the banner of extremism, right or left. During the Cold War the vast amount of extremist and terrorist activity was leftist in ideology.

The cornerstone of the entire counterintelligence mission within US Army Europe was the *Subversion and Espionage Directed Against the Army*, or *SAEDA* Program. This program, promulgated under AR 381-12, required all assigned soldiers and civilians to receive a counterintelligence threat and countermeasures briefing from a special agent on an annual basis. Highly successful, the program resulted in hundreds of referrals for investigation, many of which resulted in successful cases. The only weakness in the program was the inability, due to resources, to pay adequate attention to the 'less obvious', more nuanced, cases, many of which might have indicated the presence of espionage.

Each field office maintained a frenetic briefing schedule. While the special agents fully engaged on personnel security investigations, counterespionage cases and running down suspicious activities, the Operations Officer reviewed reports from the stacks of paper they generated. Nothing operational left the office without his review and approval. In those days of the IBM-Selectric typewriter, or manual, the red pen of the Operations Officer conveyed more dread than a chemical attack! Spelling, grammar, punctuation, and syntax had to be perfect or the report was kicked back. White-out and erasure was *Streng Verboten* so a complete rewrite could ruin a young special agent's plans for an evening of *Bier, Wurst and Frauleins*.

A good 'Ops' Officer mentored and guided the special agents, some through kind and gentle prodding, others through a barrage of expletives, often in a raw mix of English with pigeon German.

The senior special agents and team chiefs, often warrant officers or senior NCOs played some role here as well – identifying sub-par work before it hit the 'Ops' Officer's desk. The 'Ops' Officer had his counterpart up higher– whether that was at detachment, company, or battalion. The food chain of review predated our current penchant for 'information sharing' but ensured quality, if not timeliness, of effort. It also allowed for dialogue and engagement over complex national security issues, not a bad thing.

So what did the SAIC do? In the smaller field offices, sometimes called Resident Offices, or 'ROs', they functioned as investigators, case officers and liaison themselves. Sometimes they doubled as the 'Ops Officer.' In the larger ones the SAIC did the higher-level coordination and liaison with supported commanders or with their own chain of command. On a given day the SAIC might visit the MP Commander, the Criminal Investigations SAIC, an installation or community commander, usually a colonel. He also might visit the commanders of some of the larger supported units such as battalions, brigades, or flag level commands. His role was part operator, part administrator, and part politician. I did mention administration, did I not? The SAIC had myriad administrative functions such as personnel, security, supply, budget and the like. If the field office were large enough he might have a Noncommissioned officer in charge (NCOIC) to assist in these functions. Again, the Army bureaucracy always took precedent over national security, except in the case of the few maverick SAICs, who felt they were there to catch spies.

To be effective, the counterintelligence special agent needed to be the opposite of the stereotypical and often pejorative term used for them, 'Spook.' Counterintelligence guys were often called 'Spooks' by the rest of the Army, by their tactical intelligence brethren, sometimes their own chain of command and, unfortunately, sometimes amongst each other. 'Spooks' are clandestine agents that must work in the shadows and keep a low profile as they prepare to lay the dagger into an adversary's back. Ouch! The successful, the professional counterintelligence special agent does his work, well much of it in the light of day. The supported commands, from the highest officer to lowest soldier, needed to know who his supporting counterintelligence 'covering agent' was, and how to contact him. To be successful, counterintelligence needs the information known by the soldiers and must be out and among them to learn what is happening and to make themselves available to those who need to report suspicious activity. The special agent uses threat briefings, SAEDA briefings, individual briefings and the entire panoply of official and casual 'contacts' to build a network of information that provides him insight into his 'AO'. That, coupled with 'external' threat information, often provided by the Germans,

A spook. (Author's collection)

enables him to understand the threat, identify suspicious activity, and report accurately. He is more a salesman than a 'Spook'.

Now that we have discussed the history, composition and general activities of life in a USAREUR field office, a few examples will complete our look into this important facet of the Cold War. The examples that follow are samples of the kinds of situations faced by the Army special agents assigned to Europe. Any connection to persons living or deceased is purely coincidence, not that counterintelligence officers believe in coincidence….

The 'walk-in'

Any person who unexpectedly arrived at the field office with information for the US government was termed a 'walk-in'. Usually, but not always, they were non- Americans and usually, but not always, they were local nationals, that is Germans. Typically, the 'duty agent' had the honor of taking the walk-ins information and performing an initial assessment as to its usefulness and veracity. Most walk-ins provided useless information but every now and then, they brought a 'nugget'. In all cases, the duty agent treated the walk-in with respect and dignity.

The special agent handling the walk-in could spend minutes, hours, or even days interviewing and questioning the walk-in. In the latter case, the field office had to arrange for food and sometimes lodging for the individual. Finally, the field office rendered a report to the Group Headquarters, which made a final determination as to their further interest in the subject matter.

The KAWOL

Arguably, one of the most frustrating types of cases was the KAWOL. The acronym stood for "Knowledgeable (person) Absent Without Official Leave". That is, a service member or civilian employee with a security clearance that did not show for work or duty formation. Usually the cases were simple and involved overuse of alcohol. Many a GI would get drunk and sleep it off somewhere. Occasionally someone would fall asleep on a German *Bundesbahn* train that transited East Germany or Czechoslovakia. That complicated things somewhat and arrangements had to be made, usually by USAREUR Headquarters, to retrieve the individual. In most cases, the "strategic" CI unit nearest to the return point interviewed the individual as soon as they crossed back into Germany and the military police officially apprehended them. Questioning could last a few hours in a routine case but go long into the night if something unusual happened. In the latter case, the *Stasi* was usually the culprit. In a very few KAWOL cases the individual might try to stay in the "East" but these were rare. Even then, they almost always returned. The austerity of life in the East was pretty stark and pretty grim, as the Berlin Wall's one-way traffic proved.

The SPOT report

As stated earlier, responding to suspicious activity was a staple of the field office. The US Army in Germany had hundreds of units and scores of installations scattered from the Alps to the North Sea. Any incident that could be an indicator of terrorist targeting was reported quickly throughout the command, enabling commands to adjust the security level as appropriate. The incident could be as simple as hole in the fence line, anti-US graffiti, a rock thrown at a military vehicle or a suspicious car abandoned near the base perimeter. However, sometimes the incident was suspicious activity around the base that might be an indicator of a coming terrorist attack. Or it could be an actual attack, usually a small pipe bomb or incendiary device. Usually these were committed low-level groups, sympathetic to but not members of, the major terrorist movements that permeated Europe from the 60s onward. Occasionally, the incident involved a more serious event, either a major bombing, or assassination attempt. The field office response was appropriate to the situation. In most cases, the duty-agent covered the event, met with the police of guard forces, rendered a SPOT report, and followed-up as necessary. SPOT reports required as a minimum, an initial and closing report, and interim reports every 30 days if not closed out sooner. The big terrorist events would require the response of several special agents who then coordinated a variety of activity: CID forensics, German off-post investigative activity, interview witnesses, and the like. In cases of an actual terrorist attack, a SAEDA case was opened and the investigation could go on for months or longer.

Toward the end of the Cold War, the political pressure to channel information up to USAREUR Headquarters and even back to the Pentagon became huge. Commanders up and down the chain were under pressure to appear that they were doing something regardless if it had any useful effect. In fact, command interference took much time away from the professionals on the ground doing their jobs. The 66th MI Group's field offices issued hundreds of SPOT reports in any given month; sometimes the numbers averaged one per assigned special agent, causing a real drain on the field offices.

The investigation

The largest and most important body of work facing any field office was the counterintelligence investigation. Whether it was a routine personnel security investigation or a *bona fide* espionage case, the investigations were run essentially the same way. The operations officer assigned the cases to the special agents based on experience, maturity and ability to write clearly. When assigned, a suspense date was given and the special agent knew the clock was ticking. Obviously as more information developed the case suspense could be extended. The special agent first developed an investigative plan. This could be quite simple or very complex. Normal background cases, as well as suitability cases, usually came with desired "leads" that needed to be conducted. Complaint type cases, especially espionage, might or might not. They all involved checking local and national records, interviewing witnesses or person with knowledge of the situation, and eventually an interview of the subject. If enough information developed, the case would then be extended in time and complexity of action. All background investigations were submitted back to the Defense Investigative Service for final compilation and transmittal to the adjudicators, usually the Army Central Clearance facility. Complaint and espionage cases would either be closed if in sufficient evidence developed or referred for court-martial or to a civilian prosecutor in the case of civilian employees.

The Cold War's end caused a reduction in US forces in Europe and a commensurate reduction in the number of field offices supporting them. The mission of the Army in Europe changed from deterrence in Western Europe to expeditionary peacekeeper. The field office changed along with it: smaller, more agile, more technical. The challenges have actually increased for the field office. The Army is an even bigger target for terrorists and spies, just a vastly different mix of them with global connections and increasingly more sophisticated ways of targeting US forces. Things have necessarily become more technical and the new generations of special agents came to the job with a different perspective knowing the adversary was different. And the field office has also become expeditionary too. Special agents, both tactical and strategic, are pulled from their day-to-day mission not just for training or field exercises, but to deploy to combat zones from the Balkans, to the Horn of Africa, to the Middle East and Southwest Asia. Despite the changes and challenges, the approach to counterintelligence promulgated by Headquarters 12th Army Group's Counterintelligence Directive dated 10 April 1945, has provided the principles by which the Cold War was fought for over 50 years, and by Army CI elements fighting the long war today.

5

Counterintelligence Division Part 1

LTC Paul Harpin, Chief, CI Support Branch

In July 1980, I arrived in Frankfurt for my first Army Counterintelligence (CI) assignment in Europe. It was my second tour in Germany; however, the first time I was an infantryman. In the interim, I had changed branches, served a year in Vietnam, two years in a CI field office in Washington, DC, two years obtaining a Master's degree in history and then four years teaching history at the United States Military Academy at West Point. In essence, I had been away from CI and the 'real Army' for six years. I had also made major. The Army assigned me to the CI Division of the Deputy Chief of Staff for Intelligence (DCSI) Staff Directorate of the United States Army, Europe (USAREUR), in Heidelberg, Germany. Upon reporting in to the Division Chief, a full colonel, and one of the largest men I've ever known, I found I was to be assigned to the Operations Security (OPSEC) Support Branch. The colonel's guidance to me was very brief: make sure he's not surprised by anything. In other words, keep him informed, no matter what.

This was also my first staff assignment at a level above battalion; 11 years before I had been the Adjutant (S-1 or personnel officer) of an infantry battalion. Consequently, I quickly learned that, with exceptions, staff "weenies", as we were affectionately called, weren't operational in any sense of the word. We were policy initiators and movers, writers, interpreters and sometimes enforcers. Above all, we moved thousands of pieces of paper from one place to another and kept numerous file cabinets full with documents, the great majority of which we hardly ever looked at.

I, of course, felt like a fish out of water. I had just come from an academic environment with all its associated freedoms and found myself in this highly secure place where virtually everything was 'need to know' and people in the next office may or may not have a legitimate, official reason to be aware of what you were doing at any given time. Also, there were badges, security guards, codes for the doors and a myriad of rules dealing with the storage, handling, transmission and even discussion of classified information. I had to learn fast. I very soon found out there were various sub-categories of OPSEC, of which SIGSEC (Signal Security) was one. I learned this within minutes after leaving the colonel's office as I was assigned as the SIGSEC Management Officer (SMO) for all of USAREUR. SIGSEC, of course, was something else I'd never heard of and I certainly had no idea what was involved. (Within a year, I was well-versed in all things OPSEC. I had to be as I became the branch chief, a position I held for two years. But I digress.)

I discovered within the first hour on the job that SIGSEC also had sub-categories, of which Communications Security (COMSEC) was the most significant. This dealt with the encryption of all classified traffic on radios, teletypes and telephones. This was before the age of computers and involved the use of so-called universal daily keycards, which had to be changed every 24 hours at the same time throughout the theater. If anyone had the wrong keycard installed, their means of transmission was not compatible with anyone else and would not operate. If anyone lost, misplaced or accidentally destroyed a future keycard, all keycards for the same day had to be replaced (there were backups). Worse, if past keycards were not properly destroyed and ended up, via people like the Walker family spy ring, in the hands of an adversary who possessed appropriate hardware and recordings of our encrypted transmissions, the information could be decrypted and compromised. If anyone lost or misplaced COMSEC material (keycards), his or her career was in severe jeopardy. While I was in this position, an incident occurred in a subordinate USAREUR unit where a junior officer placed his briefcase full of COMSEC material on the roof of his car while he unlocked the door and promptly forgot it was there and drove off. A few miles later, he realized what he'd done and quickly returned to the scene. The briefcase was gone and never recovered. Like a good soldier, he immediately reported the loss, which resulted in the required—and expensive—replacement of a series of keycards. It also led to the quick end of his career.

What a nightmare COMSEC was! Security of keycards and their proper use was a massive undertaking. At the USAREUR level, we wrote policy and oversaw the effort. We had staff control (vice real command) over the 66th Military Intelligence Group (MIG) which did the leg work and provided the technical expertise, much to my immense relief. However, much to my immense frustration, the lack of a command relationship with the 66th led to many problems, not the least of which was prioritizing their operations. They reported to two bosses – the Intelligence and Security Command (INSCOM) at Fort Meade, MD, and USAREUR – although they were a subordinate organization of INSCOM which was directly above the 66th in their chain of command. USAREUR was not in their chain of command; we could suggest, cajole, beg and negotiate, but we could not give them direct orders. A main mission of the 66th was to support USAREUR, but they were also responsible to INSCOM for the conduct of many different intelligence operations at the strategic level. This led to many conflicts over utilization and dedication of resources.

Unfortunately, due to the virtual total lack of technical expertise at the USAREUR level, especially in COMSEC, we were entirely dependent on the 66th for execution of many missions and for technical input into the various staff functions we performed. The result was often delays in getting things done and, rarely, not getting things done at all. It infrequently came down to general officer involvement at the USAREUR, INSCOM and/or Department of the Army level. No one wanted this as bad feelings were always the result, but sometimes the end justified the means.

Besides OPSEC Support, the CI Division was also organized into branches dealing with counter-espionage, Intelligence Oversight (the legal aspects of CI), and information and document security.

In addition to maintaining a close working relationship with the 66th MIG, we had a direct command relationship with and responsibility to the subordinate units of USAREUR. This usually meant interacting with counterintelligence/OPSEC personnel at both Corps (V and VII). These were the two major subordinate command units. It also usually meant dealing with the establishment and enforcement of policy. The CI division had no real command function and subordinate units regarded us as bothersome pests or staff "weenies" unless they really needed something. We were, after all, senior headquarters staffers, not troops at the grass-roots level "in the field". We didn't even wear fatigues (later called Battle Dress Uniforms) as our daily uniform like subordinate units.

Let me give you a few words about staff procedures, at which I became quite adept over the first few months. As mentioned, we lived by and for paper. Virtually everything we did involved paperwork of one sort or another. I've already mentioned the many areas where I was totally naïve – formal staff work was another. Everything had a procedural paper trail, even highly classified actions; the only difference with these was that the staffer had to observe all the rules of handling, storage and transmission of classified information. He/she also had the additional headache of making sure, as best as possible, that others in the staff chain observed the rules as well.

A relatively simple thing like informing the DCSI or another general officer about virtually anything required an Information Paper, a formal document with often voluminous tabs and attachments covered by a formulated paper which briefly laid out the gist of the document. It is my fervent belief that most generals never read any more than the cover, even though the staff normally put in numerous hours, even days, preparing the tabs and attachments. Also, if a paper mentioned another staff organ within DCSI, or, worse, outside DCSI, the staffer had to usually walk the paper through responsible officer(s) within these entities and obtain their signatures or "chops" on a dedicated page within the paper.

A challenge was a Decision Paper. We used these whenever a staffer needed a decision from a senior officer within the staff, often the CINC himself. Staffers had no command authority and for approval of most actions, especially those establishing policy or directing subordinate units to do anything, a general in the chain of command (usually the CINC or DCINC) had to approve the action. This, of course required a Decision Paper, which was an enhanced Information Paper. The Decision Paper was far more significant and thus was frequently very thick with tabs and attachments and required far more, and senior, "chops". I remember many Decision Papers that were several inches thick or consisted of multiple volumes.

Staff actions destined for the CINC or DCINC had to pass muster through the Secretary of the General Staff (SGS), which functioned as the filter for all actions submitted to these two general officers. The SGS, a colonel, was the guardian of the realm of the headquarters building where the commanders maintained their offices. Getting something through the SGS was often a very difficult task indeed. Everything had to be perfect—format, attachments in logical order, no typos, etc. The SGS had the power to stop everything in its tracks if it didn't meet his exact standards. In fact, anyone along the path of a paper could delay or stop progress. Often someone would insist on a change. In the days before we got word processors, this meant that an entire page or portion of the document had to be completely re-typed. These things could often be true battles, as close to actual combat as we would come in my time in USAREUR.

Assuming a paper cleared the SGS, often the staffer's next task was to brief a general officer at the USAREUR level, sometimes the CINC himself. If I recall correctly, I had to brief him twice, both on classified projects. This was very intimidating for a mere Major. One of these times, I had no preparatory time. I received a call from the SGS himself that the CINC wanted a briefing *NOW* on a decision paper I had written and staffed! The CINC was General Kroesen. When I was called by SGS to report to the CINC immediately, I personally informed COL Fink the CI Chief and, if memory serves, MG Parker the DCSI, before I went over there. Both told me to go immediately. Both had previously read (and MG Parker signed) the decision paper, so both were well aware of the issues. I hurried up to the headquarters building and was immediately ushered into the CINC's office. It was my first time there and not too long after terrorists had shot at him. To say I was nervous was an understatement. He turned out to be quite polite and calm and had some pertinent questions, which, surprisingly, I could answer with aplomb. He signed the Decision Paper then, handed it to me and thanked me. My head was about eight sizes larger when I left his office than when I went in. When I returned, both the CI Chief and the DCSI, of course, wanted and got a detailed debriefing from me as to what had transpired.

Approximately one-half of the Division's personnel were civilian, so the military people got to participate twice a year in another of the Division's missions: providing staff manning for command post exercises (CPX). These were designed allegedly to provide practice for wartime deployment and operation of the USAREUR staff. Unfortunately, no subordinate units participated and the entire thing was scripted. The major event of the 24 hour day was the staff briefing given each evening to the USAREUR staff principles, meaning all the generals on the staff from the four star CINC on down. Although I was only a CI staffer, I somehow became the DCSI briefer, which meant I had to brief the day's intelligence events (not just CI) to the gathered generals every evening. Everything was, by definition, artificial, so keeping all these generals awake was a challenge. And of course each staff element tried to out-do the other to make a better impression on the CINC, which in the end led to these gatherings becoming high-stress circuses. They seemed a complete waste of time, as nothing was real; we were very dependent on play hard-copy messages or spot reports, allegedly from subordinate or higher units, who weren't even involved in the exercise. We didn't use radios, hardly used telephones, as there was no one to talk to, ate in nice mess halls and slept in decent barracks. In fact, for the fall exercise, we never left Heidelberg and slept in our own beds at night or day, depending on one's shift. These things were merely distractions from our real mission to keep paper moving. They usually lasted approximately five days in the fall and a week or so in the spring. We would then rush to finish paperwork that that accumulated during the exercise. The paper came from the lower and higher units who had kept right on working on their real-world missions.

Another military-only chore was the monthly alert. These were designed to exercise our ability to gather and commence operations quickly in case of attack by Russian hordes. Alerts occurred at various times of day – usually at night – and required all military personnel assigned to the staff to gather at their office, branch or division and simply do nothing. We always just sat around until someone in authority decided we were adequately prepared to go to war on a minute's notice and let us go back home. Of course, if an alert took place during regular duty hours – a rarity – we just kept right on working and let the war pass us by.

One of the more memorable events in my time on the USAREUR staff centers on a *real* alert. It occurred on a Friday afternoon, during happy hour, in which many staff members were actively participating. An armed US helicopter had gone down for mechanical reasons in a German field far from any US facility. As this was a time of heightened tension due to terrorist activity and the powers-that-be weren't sure what had happened and were highly concerned about what could happen if terrorists got possession of the weapons on board, they called a USAREUR-wide alert. The word got to us at the happy hour and almost everyone thought it was a joke. Nevertheless, we all soon trudged over to USAREUR Headquarters only to find out the real situation and that this was serious business. This time all of USAREUR was playing for real. This time the briefings I gave involved getting real information to decision-makers. This time the staff was actually directing subordinate units in a real-world mission to secure the crash scene and protect the weapons and equipment, not to mention the personnel. The CI division even had a real-world mission to deploy CI units to the scene and immediate area to determine terrorist and/or espionage activity. It turns out all was well; it was just an accident and no one was hurt or anything compromised. The amazing (and understandable) thing to me though was the attitude of the participants. We actually staffed a wartime headquarters and made it work. People understood that lives might be in jeopardy and a real-time threat to our peaceful little world actually existed. This was no high-stress circus like the exercises; this was professionals doing their jobs. Perhaps those exercises weren't such a waste of time after all. This was the only time we ever participated in a real alert during my tenure, which includes the time the CINC got shot at by terrorists and a general officer was kidnapped in Italy by terrorists.

The day the German terrorist group, *Rote Armee Faktion* (Red Army Faction) fired an RPG rocket at the CINC was a day of brief, high panic followed by calls from, it seemed, everyone in the Department of Defense wanting information. Persons in the CI Division were directly involved in the follow-up, especially in the effort to determine who was responsible, and, of course, in contributing to the mountain of paperwork which accumulated afterwards. When the Italian terrorist group *Brigate Rosse* (Red Brigade) kidnapped Brigadier General Dozier in Italy, portions of the CI Division (not OPSEC Support) were actively involved, mainly in trying to find him. Much later, after his release, he came to USAREUR Headquarters to hold a classified briefing on all that had happened to him so we could learn from it and recommend policy to either prevent similar events in the future or to better react to them should they occur. It was a fascinating day with a fascinating and brave man.

As mentioned, the day-to-day activity of the CI staff was by far mostly mundane and robotic, with the few exceptions mentioned above. In the OPSEC Support Branch, we concentrated on COMSEC and on various "black" programs, for which we were responsible. The latter were super-secret programs which required special, extraordinary security, and for which we had staff oversight. For the most part, this meant that we had to ensure the proper security people and procedures were in place and operating effectively. This was not as hard as it sounds as these programs had backing from levels far above us; all we had to do was ask, and it was done. I wish all our COMSEC activities were that easy.

As the 1980s progressed, a new responsibility became a major task – that of computer security. We were in the infant stages of this and actually were writing, or at least suggesting, policy that became Army-wide. I was the branch chief by the time computer security became a major mission (if not the primary mission in some minds) and we devoted 100% of one officer's time to it plus I spent a majority of my time as branch chief to it. Mind you, none of us had any computer education or literacy at all. We were making things up as we went along.

During this period, the CI staff actually got its first piece of automated equipment, a Wang word processor, which was as big as a desk, but which was a Space-age miracle to us. No more IBM selectronics and carbon copies. This was great but carried with it more risk than we knew at the time. No one really knew about how to secure it or even what to secure. It was all a big puzzle and mystery. In the meantime though, we kept using it as it was an extraordinary improvement over the past. Before, if there was a major error or a portion of a document a staff officer wanted to rewrite, that meant the entire document had to be re-done. This led to much discontent and outright rebellion when some general would change "happy" to "glad" and an entire lengthy document had to be re-typed. Now, everybody got lazy, and submitted documents they knew weren't perfect, but if caught by some general or lower staffer, it could be easily changed. A new era had dawned.

In the meantime, the DA staff and us USAREUR "weenies" were wrestling with what was the risk with all this new equipment and how do we secure it? This was far above our level of expertise and seemingly far above that of the DA staff. The people who developed this new technology seemed far ahead of security folks whose entire experience had been devoted to the human threat and the danger of revealing too much over means of communication. We eventually caught up but long after I left USAREUR in 1983.

Author's Notes
1) Some functions, such as COMPUSEC and COMSEC, later moved to Security Branch.
2) Including that 1945 overhead photo of Campbell Barracks in the Preface of this book is another example of an OPSEC question. The Command Historian told me:

> That photo has been on the street in the USAREUR pamphlet 'Campbell Barracks, The Story of a Caserne' for more than 22 years, but when I checked with PAO to see if you could use it, they had to run it by the G2 and G3 anti-terrorist folks for clearance, because an aerial photograph of the facility might help the bad guys with targeting. BUT – Be of good cheer. They have decided are no objection to your use of the photo. Just credit it to 'U.S. Army.'

LTC Ken Krantz, Chief Analysis Branch
The Branch of 13 officers, enlisted, and civilian analysts focused on the two major counterintelligence threats facing USAREUR – *terrorism and espionage.* Those were the years when the indigenous terrorist attacks targeting Americans were at their highest.

The Branch worked long and many unplanned hours whenever a potential threat was credible to ensure we could get the best analysis to the operators. The analysts of the branch varied widely in age and experience, but collectively, they were unequalled in their dedication and professionalism.

The Branch was the first USAREUR staff organization to take civilians on Field Training Exercises – an experience not forgotten by them (or the military leadership).

We maintained a close working and personal relationship and many are still in touch with each other after 20 years.

Mr. John Rademacher, Chief COMSEC Section
History / Origin
It is hard to say when COMSEC started. One far-fetched rumor has it that in early times runners had their heads shaved and a message was written on their skull. In a few short weeks, when the hair would grow to a sufficient length, the messenger would cover great distances to another part of the kingdom and then have his head shaved in order for the receiving party to read the message. Of course we all know that this would take many weeks or months so this method of securing messages by our standards today would be extremely impractical and seem unperceivable.

Every government in the world uses COMSEC. It is a sub-discipline of Information Security (INFOSEC).

A short definition of COMSEC is "The protection of a nation's key and authentication systems." I guess an even simpler definition would be "keeping secrets, secret".

During WWII, COMSEC helped win the war. Our code breakers broke the Japanese code and used a captured German Enigma code machine to spy on Adolf Hitler. COMSEC was so intensely secretive that the Allies knew about the upcoming German bombing mission against the English city of Coventry ahead of time but could not say anything to anyone about it for fear of Germany finding out that we could take messages direct from Hitler and decrypt them simultaneously. One of the hardest messages to keep secret was a message the Americans intercepted telling of the Fuehrer having a bad stomach-ache. As tempting as it was, if the Germans would have received word that the Americans were laughing about Hitler's stomach problem, they would have known immediately that their Enigma Machine was compromised and most likely have cancelled the Coventry mission and changed their encryption key and authentication system.

Historical Changes

COMSEC was originally called CRYPTO. COMSEC Vaults/Rooms were known as CRYPTO Vaults/Rooms. After WWII, all CRYPTO Vaults/Rooms in USAREUR were identified by a large sign "CRYPTO Room" and every CRYPTO Room overseas had weapons and live ammunition stored inside. The weapons were the .45 caliber pistol and a couple of .30 caliber carbines. The CRYPTO clerk was always "under arms" while on duty. He wore a "side arm", the .45 caliber pistol. He also had to wear an olive-drab (OD) armband with the acronym CRYPTO in large yellow letters, as part of his uniform. When the CRYPTO clerk had to deliver messages, he was always "under arms". If he delivered messages inside of other buildings on post, he had to keep his hat or helmet on his head, as the Military Police do when under arms. The weapons were for the use of force, if necessary, to protect our nation's secrets. The armband let everyone know he was armed and not to bother him while in the performance of his duties. All CRYPTO clerks (personnel) were trained to guard our nation's secrets at all cost.

Today it is against the law to store weapons and/or ammunition inside a COMSEC Vault/Room. It is also against regulations to identify COMSEC Vaults/Rooms with any type of sign, and COMSEC personnel are not armed nor do they wear any conspicuous identification. It was not until the late 1960s that CRYPTO had expanded widely and changed to COMSEC.

Excitement

In Viet Nam, MSG Roy Benavidez was the only soldier in the history of the US Army awarded the Medal of Honor (MOH) for COMSEC heroism. He was a Special Forces SSG E-6 at the time and was off-duty when he heard that his unit was in a hot firefight and asked to get out to the fight. After arriving on the scene, he assisted his buddies the best he could. Although severely wounded, he continued the fight with all the strength he had left. He was searching the dead American soldiers on the battlefield and extracting all the COMSEC. It was then that he was wounded numerous times and the combat medics in his unit thought he was dead. They placed him in a body bag and it wasn't until the graves registration personnel were opening all the bags to find out who was in them, that Roy managed to spit up some blood and cough. The rest is written in his MOH citation which was personally awarded by then President Ronald Reagan at the White House years after the submission of his award. Normally the Secretary of each branch of service awards the MOH. However, when President Reagan heard the story of Roy, he wanted to award this brave COMSEC conscious soldier personally. His brave actions saved numerous lives and the United States millions of dollars.

Monitoring

COMSEC Monitoring is performed only on US Forces. This is done to give the commander a profile on how well his/her unit is at using the secure means available to them. It is against the law to monitor a foreign nation's telephones.

Up until the early 1990's, COMSEC monitoring was reported directly to the violator and the violator was told to refrain from saying things of a classified or sensitive nature in the "clear". However, after a few of these type violations reached the General Council, the laws were changed and only the commander could inform his/her unit that their telephones were being monitored and to please use the "secure" mode when communicating classified material up to a certain level.

Amusing Incidents

Once during a monitoring mission, a certain Major in USAREUR G2 was caught (monitored) giving a classified briefing and his STU-III was not hung up properly. When the Chief of USAREUR COMSEC confronted him about his error, the Major told the Chief that he was a Major and he could do and say anything he wanted. Well, the COMSEC monitoring person went straight to the G2, a Major General, who called the Major into his office and told him that if he was calling the PX he would "Go Secure" and did he understand that. The General dismissed the Major and asked the COMSEC person if that was good enough. This was serious then and still serious today, albeit also very funny when I think about it today.

Another time while on an "Off Site" exercise, a LTC was running around like a chicken with its head cut off barking out orders to whoever was in earshot and eventually grabbed the radio microphone and started screaming in the clear a classified movement order. The security conscious COMSEC person had unplugged the microphone from the radio during some downtime maintenance. The LTC never checked to see if the microphone was hooked up or not. The look on the LTC's face was worth a thousand words.

While conducting an annual USAREUR Command Oversight Inspection for USAREUR G2 on one of the USAREUR units, along with the USAREUR Chief of Physical Security and the USAREUR Chief of Personnel Security, I, Chief of USAREUR COMSEC, asked during the "In-Brief", if the unit had any Classified COMSEC material. Material like COMSEC Key Tape and those items associated with COMSEC Key used to encrypt and decrypt messages. Many units did not have any type of COMSEC material; they only had Classified Documents. COMSEC material was always identified with the Acronym CRYPTO in bold print at least on the top and bottom of the cover or the plastic NSA protective coating as well as the top and bottom of each page inside the document.

The unit Security Manager assured us that her unit did not have any COMSEC. Upon opening a file cabinet in the unit Security Manager's office, the USAREUR Chief of Physical Security called for me to come and look at something he found in the bottom drawer of the file cabinet. The whole bottom drawer was full of classified COMSEC. However, the unit Security Manager assured us that she did not know those items were COMSEC even though the acronym CRYPTO was clearly marked all over the items.

On another USAREUR Command Oversight Inspection of a different unit, at a different location, the same Chief of USAREUR Physical Security asked that unit's Security Manager/COMSEC Custodian, to open one of his Classified Security Containers (safes) so we could inspect the contents. The unit Security Manager immediately pulled out his wallet and proceeded to read the combination so he could open the safe. The USAREUR Chief of Physical Security turned to me and asked me if I had ever seen a GSA (Government Supply Agency)-approved wallet before. Although it was a serious violation which could have compromised everything stored inside that safe, it was comical at the time.

USAREUR G2 COMSEC

The USAREUR G2 COMSEC Section was and is part of the USAREUR G2 Security Branch, Counter Intelligence Division, which later changed to the Special Activities Division. The COMSEC Chief for USAREUR is responsible for Policy, Procedures and Oversight of all COMSEC activities throughout USAREUR. During the Annual US Army COMSEC Audit, the USAREUR COMSEC policy and COMSEC Custodian Guide was liked so well that the US Army COMSEC Audit Team asked permission to use it as the COMSEC guide for the entire world.

Summary

It is said that West Point makes young men and women officers and proper communications makes them commanders. However, Communications Security gives them the tools to make them winning commanders, officers and leaders by keeping our nation's secrets, secret.

An abridged history of the USAREUR DCSINT Computer Security Program by Dr. Julie Mehan, PhD, Chief COMPUSEC Section:

To understand how the definitely non-military "computer security lady" from USAREUR arrived in full "battle rattle" as part of the early deployment to the battle-torn country of Yugoslavia it's essential to learn a little more about the role of computer security in USAREUR in general. So, let's take a walk back in history – and look at my own and that of the full emergence of computer security in the European theater of operations.

It's October 1990 and the Berlin Wall had come down in a thundering crash just a scant year ago. I had been in Berlin since 1975 and – if there were still a Berlin Wall – might likely still be there in 2008. But after October 1989, the wall came down, East and West Berlin united, and everything changed. As the U.S. Forces closed down their presence in the newly-united city, I left my beloved Berlin to arrive in at the 1st Personnel Command headquartered in Tompkins Barracks, Schwetzingen, Germany, just in time for Operation Desert Shield and the First Gulf War. With just a few weeks to acclimate, I took over the position as the S-2 (Security Officer) as the command geared up to process the hundreds of thousands of Army soldiers passing through Germany into the Persian Gulf. Computers and their ability to process the enormous amounts of personnel and logistics data essential to the success of this deployment were critical. It was during the Persian Gulf War that the U.S. military truly realized the benefits of computers – and also the weaknesses. In fact, Desert Shield is often called the "first computer war." This was no time for computer security issues – whether intentional or unintentional – to affect the real fighters in the battle. And thus, through the computer growth years of 1990-1992, computer security experts emerged as valuable team members in the protection of the force. And I, as the security officer of the 1st Personnel Command, had the task of ensuring the continued operation of the computers responsible for personnel information – ranging from mail addresses to the processing of our battle wounded and killed. It was a grave responsibility and we all approached it as such.

Desert Shield also saw the first real information war, which began with five hackers from the Netherlands breaking into computer systems of thirty-four different American Military sites. Starting in the spring of 1990 and continuing through May 1991, these hackers were able to obtain the exact locations of the American troops, the types of weapons they had, the capabilities of Patriot missile and the movement of US warships in the Gulf region. It was an eye-opening event for the US Army Europe and me. Dependence on information and the information systems it moves around on means that networks must be secured against unauthorized manipulation and control. At the same time, these information systems must operate at or near peak efficiency. Implementing security features for any information system is similar to setting the hurdles in a track meet. *The hurdles have to be high enough to ensure reasonable obstacles, but not so high the runners can't run at all. Ensuring sufficient security for the information systems without measurably slowing essential traffic requires knowledge and understanding.*

From this point on, I became a student of information systems and the security technologies and processes essential to ensuring that these critical systems would always be available to our war-fighting forces.

In 1993, I had the opportunity to put these beliefs to the test as I joined the U.S. Army, Europe (USAREUR) Office of the Deputy Chief of Staff, Intelligence. Initially, I was the Deputy to the then Chief, Information System Security – Dick Terry. Dick quickly became my mentor, leading me into the rather arcane world of Department of Defense policy and how it supports the security of DOD information systems.

Information systems, both those in use today and those being developed for the military of the future, serve as a *force multiplier* and a cornerstone of military operations. These information technologies provide the ability for timely response to process the enormous amounts in information and turn this into knowledge for the war fighter. Policy defines the processes essential to defending these technologies. We were working on a revision of the USAREUR Regulation 380-19, Information Systems Security, focusing on changing the policy to reflect this ever-increasing reliance on information systems and their need for security.

Not long after I arrived at USAREUR HQs, Dick retired for medical reasons and I was promoted into the position of Information Systems Security Program Manager (ISSPM). Initially, I focused on completing the regulation. This focus changed radically in 1994. The USAREUR Logistics Network was experiencing significant loss of capability. It was slow, storage was decreasing at a rapid pace, and information was disappearing. Preliminary investigation showed the presence of an intruder. The worst part – the intrusion appeared to be coming from Bulgaria. By today's standards, this intruder was a rank amateur – leaving trails all over the network and almost advertising his presence. But in 1994, this was an unprecedented event in our networks and we had to react quickly.

Then and today, logistics information is largely processed over unclassified networks with a wide distribution and an enormous bandwidth requirement. Although the information is not classified, it is still critical. Among many other functions, the logistics networks support moving food, fuel, and ammunition for our soldiers. All of the addresses of the USAREUR senior leadership were located on this network. Blueprints of our installations and the critical infrastructure information could be found here. Unclassified – yes; unimportant – absolutely not!

This attack initiated what was to become a marriage between the USAREUR information systems security policy element at the DCSINT and the actual managers of the USAREUR networks located at 5th Signal Command in Worms, Germany. We did what we could at the time to contain the damage from this attack, but quickly realized that we needed help from outside to fully investigate the situation. USAREUR had no organic computer forensics capability at that time. So, we followed existing policy requirements and contacted the 902d Military Intelligence organization with our report of an attacker from Bulgaria – fully expecting them to descend upon us with all sorts of forensic assistance. Not so. This attack on an unclassified network was ignored – it just did not warrant their attention.

Much to the chagrin of our Army-focused command, we called in support from the Air Force. Within 48 hours, we had a team of forensic experts from the Office of Special Investigations (OSI) led by Howard Schmidt. Howard, who was later appointed by President Bush as the Vice Chair of the President's Critical Infrastructure Protection Board and as the Special Advisor for Cyberspace Security for the White House, continued to have a distinguished career as the Chief Security Officer for Microsoft and eBay. But at that time in 1994, he and his team were information systems security heroes arriving with their tools and technologies to execute a full forensic investigation of the extent of damage to the network. At the end of this visit, we were able to reinstate the Logistics Network with the full confidence that it was clean of any attacker. And we learned a lot about the need for our own capability for incident response, computer forensics, and network level boundary protections.

5th Signal Command and USAREUR DCSINT joined hands to address these issues. The result was the establishment of the Army's first Regional Computer Security Response Team (R-CERT) and the prototype for all R-CERTs to follow. With an initial shoestring budget and a suite of supporting information systems procured in part through "midnight requisitions,"[1] I worked on defining the needed policies and budget and LTC Leroy Lundgren, 5th Signal Command, took on the massive effort of actually putting this capability into operation. By 1995, USAREUR had a functional R-CERT.

Our R-CERT attracted attention far outside of USAREUR. LTC Lundgren and I soon found ourselves on the briefing circuit at the Pentagon. Throughout the spring and summer of 1995, we campaigned successfully to raise awareness of the RCERT – and equally successfully acquired additional funding to support its expansion. LTG Paul E. Menoher, Deputy Chief of Staff for Intelligence, Headquarters, Department of the Army, quickly became one of our greatest supporters bringing us back to the Pentagon on multiple occasions to brief senior Army leadership. General Menoher would later play a critical role in my life.

In the early fall of 1995, General Menoher provided us an introduction to the newly emerging Land Information Warfare Activity (LIWA) and the nascent Army level Computer Emergency Response Team (ACERT). This introduction would soon serve us well.

Shortly after our return from our visit to the Pentagon, I was called by the USAREUR Deputy Chief of Staff, Operations, to participate in a briefing on preparations for the proposed Bosnian troop deployment. The Operation Order (OPORD) issued for the deployment required an information warfare element – obviously something for the "computer lady." After reading all of the existing doctrine on Information Warfare (of which

1   In military jargon, "midnight requisitions" reflected an unofficial acquisition system often resorted to in order to obtain necessary items by "liberating" them from other organizations. While clearly not condoned, it frequently became a matter of necessity in light of the occasional slowness of the authorized procurement process. Note that this term is used here largely tongue-in-cheek, since none of these "midnight requisitions" involved unauthorized activity on the part of the participants.

there was little), I quickly realized that this was a task that again exceeded the organic capabilities of USAREUR DCSINT and our larger team of 5th Signal Command. General Menoher served as our conduit to the LIWA and to the resources to support this mission. I quickly met with COL Hal Stevens and LTC Tom Hudson of the LIWA to set up a task force to deploy to Bosnia. Within a few scant weeks, we had a 12-person team of notable experts in each of the original IW disciplines.

By late December, the entire team had been processed through the pre-deployment training held at Grafenwoehr. This training included everything from mine awareness to dealing with the press. We were in tents, it was cold as it can only be in Grafenwoehr, and we were all pushed through two weeks of highly intensive preparations for insertion into Bosnia. At the end of this training, we were declared ready for deployment.

The team returned to Heidelberg, gathered our equipment (computers, not weapons), got our travel manifests and set out from Rhein-Main Airport on a C-130. We landed in Kaposvar, Hungary, the staging base for transit into Bosnia. After one night in an aging barracks, our team of 12 was transported in Blackhawk helicopters across the Sava River to our destination of Tuszla, Bosnia.

This hastily prepared mission set the stage for the continued participation of information operations throughout the Bosnian engagement, as well as in all future military deployments to the Iraq War of today. Throughout 1996, this small team of 12 continued to support the effort in multiple deployments. Computer security and information operations became inextricably linked. And thus, we arrive back at the beginning of this chapter.

There is one small, additional piece of information to close this story. At the end of our deployments and 1996, General Menoher offered me the opportunity to become a part of the evolution of the LIWA. It was an offer I couldn't refuse – and so I left Germany after a total of 22 years to start a new career as the lead for developing and implementing the Army's Red/Blue Team capability within the LIWA.

6

Counterintelligence Division Part 2

There were seven different Division Chiefs while I was there. They were my bosses. They were all different people with different styles and were all patriots. They were COLs Fink, Beinhacker, Handley, Loftheim, Greife, Swift, and Sims. I learned much from them.

Mike Hennen was one of the civilian Special Assistants to the CI Boss. He was highly decorated as a "spy catcher." He was another great man who loved his country.

Along with them was the top sergeant or NCOIC of the Division. I remember especially female SFC Jean McKitrick. She helped keep us all in line! There was later also MSG Michael Pace.

You had to have a special badge with photo ID hanging around your neck to get in the Intel building past the armed MPs. The badge showed what accesses you were cleared for and therefore what matters they could discuss with you.

It was the Military Police (MPs) function to control entry into the sensitive building by only cleared personnel. They fulfilled this responsibility very faithfully, using the threat of *legally sanctioned deadly force* when required. For example, you couldn't bring in tape recorders or cameras into this intelligence facility. I remember one US full colonel who tried to bring in one of those small hand-held recorders that he made verbal notes to himself – he didn't get too far. After insisting he was going to take the recorder in, the MP told the colonel it wasn't allowed. The colonel proceeded, ignoring the MP; the locked and loaded enlisted MP stood up behind the raised glass enclosed booth, opened the window, and the colonel soon found himself staring down the barrel of a '45. He left his recorder outside.

Personnel Security
Arnie Hunter

Personnel Security looks at the person who will have access to classified information. AR 605-4, Department Of The Army Personnel Security Program Regulation (DOD 5200.2-R), then governed it. I remember some of its leaders, Gary Arrasmith, Arnie Hunter, Owen Henry and Dick Terry. They all provided knowledgeable leadership and made some hard decisions.

Is the person worthy of a security clearance?

What kind of personnel security investigation to initiate for which clearances?

These investigations would look at a person to see what arrests and other derogatory material was in their history to determine if that person should be entrusted with our nation's secrets. The Defense Investigative Service (DIS) conducted these investigations for that portion of the Subject's life in the US and the service component abroad conducted the investigation for the portion of his/her life overseas.

The least complex investigation was a NAC (national agency check or ENTNAC (entrance NAC) investigation for the clearances of confidential or secret. It checked the records of the military agencies as well as the FBI. Whatever Federal Agency you listed on your Statement of Personal History (SPH) or was developed during the course of the inquiry would be looked into.

A more thorough and exhaustive investigation was the BI (Background Investigation) for Top Secret. The name BI would evolve over the years to SBI (Special BI) and SSBI (Single Scoped BI). I call it an SBI. The SBI *really* inquired into your background with S/As doing the checking plus the above NAC records check. The examination went back to your 18th birthday or 15 years earlier (whichever was shorter) and checked on your character and background with neighbors, co-workers, supervisors, listed character references, developed character references, local agency checks (police/courts – wherever you lived for six months or more), credit agencies – again where you lived 6 months or more (here you are looking obviously for bad debt but also a person living beyond his means), ex-spouse interviews and maybe a Subject Interview to clarify the information uncovered. In the Army, the adjudicators (to judge) of the US Army Central Personnel Security Clearance Facility (CCF) would decide if you got the clearance or not – or if your current clearance should be revoked. This took the decision out of the command's prerogative for obvious reasons. Again, USAREUR security would get involved if CCF asked us to get something from the *subject*. Likewise, when some USAREUR commander was screaming that he needed a subject cleared in a hurry, we would go into CCF for a rush job. We were reinvestigated every 5 years. That was useful too. Just knowing you would be reinvestigated reminded you to stay out of trouble. Here are some other personnel security elements.

- **Limited Access Authorization**. These were "clearances" for foreign national (FN) employees. We were the adjudicators for these BIs. LAAs are discussed elsewhere in the book.
- **Laredo Leader**. This program, invented by us, checked out FNs working for us without "clearances." Program discovered a wealth of information. Discussed in a bit more detail, elsewhere in the book.
- **Travel Briefing**. Made sure travelers got the communist country briefing to warn them of the collection effort that would be made against them. Didn't allow certain folks with high clearances to travel to or over communist countries.
- **Civilian Sensitivity Positions**. We had to know about civilian US positions to get the correct investigation for a Nonsensitive Position, a Noncritical-sensitive Position and a Critical-Sensitive Position.
- **SAP**. We had a whole chapter in the reg about requirements of the many Special Access Programs.

Information Security
Bud Hiller
(December 29, 1931 – Jan 16, 2009)

AR 380-5, Department of the Army Information Security Program with USAREUR Supplement 1, governed this program. I remember its great boss, Bud Hiller, testified at trials of spies to give damage assessments (how they hurt USAREUR).

Components:

Bud Hiller

- **Original vs. derivative classification.** (Are you classifying a document related to an already classified document (derivative) or is this a brand new document that needs classification (original) – only certain positions are Original Classification Authorities.)
- **Command security inspections.** (Requires Command Security to inspect all subordinate units once or twice a year.)
- **Levels of classification.**
  (1) **TOP SECRET** – Will be applied to information in which the unauthorized disclosure could reasonably be expected to cause exceptionally grave damage to the national security.
  (2) **SECRET** – Will be applied to information in which the unauthorized disclosure could reasonably be expected to cause serious damage to the national security.
  (3) **CONFIDENTIAL** – Will be applied to information in which the unauthorized disclosure could reasonably be expected to cause damage to the national security.
- **Cover Sheets.** Appropriate classified document cover sheets will be placed on classified documents or files not in security storage.
- **Marking Documents.** Marking is the principal means of informing holders of classified and sensitive information of its classification/sensitivity level and protection required. Classification/ sensitivity markings must be conspicuous – larger print/in color.
- **Reproduction of Classified Material.** Rules established to hold down reproduction. TS document copies will be serial numbered.
- **Storage Standards.** Classified material must be stored in a container appropriate to its classification.
- **Destruction**. Describes methods of destruction of classified information such as burning, crosscut shredding to a certain size or pulping.
- **Methods of Transmission and Transportation.** Tells how the different levels of classified material may be transmitted or transported.
- **Unauthorized Disclosure and Other Security Incidents.** Tells what actions will be taken when there is an unauthorized disclosure.
- **Espionage Laws and Federal Statutes.** Puts teeth into the regulation.
- **Damage Assessments.** Tells what the damage is to our country when there is unauthorized disclosure.

Special Operations Branch
I'm not going to say much here because Special Operation to this day uses some of the same *modus operandi* to counter our enemies, but while Security Branch wrote rules and regulations to help slow the spies, SO Branch engaged with a more active methodology for catching spies from within and without.

Sharing Security Information
Security education was a priority of Security. This was a multi-faceted approach in the following arenas and was the *best* in the Army.
- **Formal Security School:** There is a chapter on the **Intel 2 Course** and that was our class taught by security experts near Nurnberg; it helped new security

managers learn the basics of their new positions. The rest would be learned OJT and through the follow-on methods noted below. We sent most security managers down to company level to that course and once a year or so we went down there to monitor it to make sure they were putting out the right information. *It was important for these new security managers to get away from the hustle and bustle of their daily jobs and just think about learning security.*

- **Visual Media**: We worked closely with Special Operation (SO) Branch to try a new, innovated educational approach. We knew Foreign Intelligence Services would try to recruit our soldiers and civilians, so we turned to Armed Forces Network to present unclassified live and recorded radio and TV spots to the USAREUR general public. We told the audience about current espionage cases after Special Operations advised on what could and could not be said. The purpose was to warn our viewers what tactics to look for in the typical spy case – so they would know if it were happening to them or in their unit. Our "talent" met about 30 minutes prior to the live broadcast or video or audio recording to discuss the segment with the host/director. The "talent" suggested comments and questions the host should ask and we agreed upon a loose mental "script."

- **Print Media**: News Bulletin for Information & Personnel Security (NIPS). It went out unclassified worldwide every month with articles from all the sections in the branch to include Information, Personnel, COMSEC, COMPUSEC and later SAP (Special Access Programs). We talk elsewhere about the NIPS in the Flag Note chapter. We received a Flag Note for its quality. It was the perfect medium to emphasize some policy that was not being followed or to introduce new guidelines for forthcoming countermeasures. Sometimes other branches would chip in an article if they wanted to pitch something they were responsible for. After the Chief Security and then the Chief CI approved the paper, it went to the two star DCSI via a Decision Paper for signature. A sample NIPS is below (they were printed on back and front pages):

NEWS BULLETIN FOR INFORMATION & PERSONNEL SECURITY
LAA CONSIDERATIONS
Are you thinking about nominating a LN employee for a Limited Access Authorization? Be sure there are no US Citizens (like local hire) that you could recruit to do the job and state that in your Commander's Statement. Also remember that LAAs are prohibited beyond SECRET.

TRAVEL SECURITY
It is your duty to ensure the personnel you are responsible for receive a foreign travel briefing if they travel to a communist country. DA's reg says the briefing will be given for any foreign travel, but we wake up in a foreign country. For now, use the briefing only for communist countries while we settle the issue with DA.

UNIT REPORTS CLASSIFICATION MARKING HAZARD
A "with-it" security shop reports all to be careful if you copy SECRET documents with the red stamp on it. The red doesn't copy well, if at all. You might have to re-mark these copies.

COMSEC
Make sure all unit members are aware not to discuss classified matters over an unsecured line. You don't know who may be listening. This caution is especially important if something unusual or urgent is occurring.

HOLD DOWN BI REQUESTS
CCF has asked us to remind you to hold down request for TS and other clearances that require a BI. Make sure the person really needs the TS before you nominate him and fill out all that paperwork. DIS and CCF need to spend their time on those actions that are truly required.

A SQUARED AWAY SECURITY SHOP
We recently inspected the Command Security Shop in Berlin (USCOB) and found "0" Major Findings. Congratulations USCOB. Call them (or us) if some security question is puzzling you.

COORDINATION WITH YOUR LOCAL MI
Security and local MI should work hand in hand. Set aside a time once a week for a sit-down in some secured area where you all can talk. Security might ask: Who is watching us when we deploy out the front gates? MI might ask: Are you reporting derog on your unit members? Even if it's a "nothing to discuss" this week, you know the forum is always there.

REPORTING DEROG TO CCF
What may appear as an isolated incident to you might not be. CCF can check its records and IRR and see if the same thing happened at other units you are unaware of. Don't take a chance. If the derog is not that serious, check the "Recommend Subject Keep Clearance" block, but report it.

MG
DCSINT, USAREUR

Security Seminars: We also budgeted for **unit inspections and security seminars**. A USAREUR unit would fill up their post theater with their S2s and G2s and security personnel. We would travel there to their unit. They surrounded the theater with MPs. Then all of our Branch section chiefs would deliver a presentation on the basics and latest in their field and eventually open it up for questions. If we didn't know the answer to a question we didn't "fake it;" we said we didn't know and we got back with them.

You *shared* classified information to those *cleared* and had a legitimate *need-to-know*.

The *Secure Telephone Unit (STU)* was very important for making classified phone calls. You also had a Secure Fax hooked up to the STU. In case some enemy broke the line to the STU, the classified conversation was protected and they would only hear a hissing sound. Sometime the STU rang with its own particular urgency, which meant the caller had selected the Immediate Precedence – (It actually sounded more urgent.)

Before email, you sent and received many *messages*. We got our electronic "mail" or message traffic through two sources. First were the messages from regular combat, combat support and administrative units that came in the front channel; messages that were delivered to us from the main post Communications Center. Second, we had our own secure Intel comms in the building or what we call "back channel messages" that came from a special circuit. You used it for sending Intel info, but it was also used in the administrative/operational support for any General Officer in the area. It's somewhat of a very specialized Army Intel Message Center. Below, the substance of the messages is a figment of my imagination and is not really classified but it is real front channel format:

Immediate

Precedence 27 Feb 95, 11AM "Classification" Special

Delivery Instructions

OO

271100 FEB 95 CLASSIFICATION IS FOR EXAMPLE ONLY (UNCLASSIFIED)

TOP SECRET

FM: 5th SIGNAL COMMAND, MANNHEIM, GE // G-2 //

TO: CINC USAREUR HEIDELBERG GE // AEAGB-CI-S //

SUBJECT: MISSING ALGORITHM SPINDLE (TS)

/ EYES ONLY / EYES ONLY / EYES ONLY / EYES ONLY / EYES ONLY /

PASS ONLY TO SECURITY BRANCH/ SETH CHERRY

1. (TS) SPINDLE # CC 07462699 DISCOVERED MISSING YESTERDAY AT 1200 HRS BY COMSEC INSPECTORS.

2. (C) REQUEST YOUR ASSISTANCE TO WORK WITH OUR COMSEC SHOP.

3. (U) PLS KEEP US ADVISED OF DATE YOU WILL BE HERE.

Current sources told me you don't see too many messages now; they now come in over the email system directly to the addressee listed on it. From there a central reader then farms out pertinent "messages" to the correct office.

We would occasionally see the Minimize Order, indicating there was a hot spot somewhere in the world with a lot of message traffic going on; we had to stop sending messages to make room in the cyber system for those messages. The only exception was if you typed MINIMIZED CONSIDERED on the message and got the approval of a boss and then it could go. Made you stop and think; does this message really have to go? Messages had precedence to them and the sender assigned them. A flash message goes to the head of the message queue and beats all other Operational Immediate (OO), Priority (PP) or Routine (RR) messages. There is only one higher precedence message, the Flash Override (I'd never seen one).

In the Headquarters, the Information Paper was the medium to get critical information to higher important personnel, such as general officers like the DCSINT or CINC. An info paper was just that, FYI only. A Decision Paper was very similar but an action officer wrote and sent it to obtain a decision on an issue or signature from a senior officer. We obtained other pertinent HQ agency concurrence signatures (called "chops") on the paper.

If the paper were going to go to the DCSINT, the CI Division Chief would sign the paper. If the paper were to leave the building and go to the Chief of Staff, DCINC or CINC in the Keyes Building, the DCSINT would sign the paper. No matter who signed the paper, the Action Officer who prepared the paper would be noted on the paper. The boss might want to talk to him. Here's an example of an Information Paper:

HEADQUARTERS
UNITED STATES ARMY EUROPE & SEVENTH ARMY
Office of the Deputy Chief of Staff, Intelligence
APO 09403

AEAGB-CI-S
8 December 1986
TO: C of S

1. FOR INFORMATION
2. PURPOSE: To provide the USAREUR Chief of Staff with what type investigation is required for a specific security clearance.
3. BACKGROUND: The C of S asked the DCSINT for this information on 7 Dec 1986.
4. DISCUSSION:
   - CONFIDENTIAL or SECRET clearances both require either an Entrance National Agency Check (ENTNAC) or National Agency Check (NAC). Upon favorable investigation, CCF always grants a SECRET clearance rather than the lower CONFIDENTIAL clearance.
   - A TOP SECRET clearance requires a Single Scope Background Investigation.
   - If there is an existing, appropriate investigation, it must be current within 5 years for TS and 10 years for SECRET or the security office must initiate a new investigation through the Defense Investigative Service (DIS).
   - Central Clearance Facility (CCF) at Ft. Meade, MD adjudicates the investigation for the Army and grants, denies or revokes the clearance.
   - Reference: AR 604-5 Personnel Security Clearance: Clearance of Personnel for Access to Classified Defense Information and Material.

Action Officer is Gary Arrasmith HM 7457
COORDINATION:
ODCSPER: CONCUR . . . . NON-CONCUR . . . .
Major General
DCSINT

And finally, when you left USAREUR …

POST CLEARANCE PAPERS
. . . . Make Furniture Shipping Arrangements with Post Transportation.
. . . . Make POV Shipping Arrangements with Post Transportation.
. . . . Deliver POV to Bremerhaven (self check)
. . . . Make Flight Arrangements with Post Transportation.
. . . . Replace catalytic converter and bring POV from German Specs to US Specs.
. . . . Clean and Clear quarters with proper authorities. (Housing or Landlord)
. . . . Pay any outstanding German bills. (self check)
. . . . Attend Retirement Briefing if applicable.
. . . . Receive clearance from local PM Office (PM & German Police Rep)
. . . . Receive last check and clearance from Finance.
. . . . Be debriefed from security & pass clearances to new unit.
. . . . Receive final Post Clearance at CPO once above completed and initialed.
USAREUR FORM

7

"US Clearances" for Germans

Consider the 1970 movie, *Patton* with George C. Scott. Do you remember him at the end of the movie riding a horse around in a large inside show paddock? He said he would hire all the Germans to help run the post-war army. That is what this chapter is about. Why employ Germans in our US Army and give them access to US classified information? The Army is less secure with Germans possessing US classified information. They owe no allegiance to the United States. Think about the following formula. You might view security on a sliding scale:

The Security vs. Operational Formula
SECURITY

COMPLETELY SECURE	COMPLETELY UNSECURE
NON-OPERATIONAL	COMPLETELY OPERATIONAL

We could have made things completely secure by leaving Europe at the end of WWII. We wouldn't be there for the Soviets to collect against us, launch terrorist attacks and recruit spies. And we could be completely secure by having rigid security rules that ignored and hindered operations.

Or we could be completely operational in Europe, overlooking security and not having any security safeguards or constraints and have a weak security posture. But the key was to slide security toward the Completely Operational end of the scale. Operations will rightfully and should, always, lead security. This way, the operators would be free to operate, with a modicum of necessary security. This from a Security Specialist!

We had thousands of foreign nationals (mostly Germans, Italians and a few English) working for us at the high point of USAREUR's existence in the 1980s. The USAREUR history Office provided us with the number of local national (non-US citizens) workers as of 31 December 1962:

- Local National (LN) Appropriated Fund (paid for by tax dollars): 78,220
  LN Non-Appropriated Fund (paid for by $ raised by the facility): 33,762
  Labor Service: (LN in quasi-military support units (non-combat) for USAREUR): 13,008
- Total USAREUR LNs = 124,990

Every big Army hires civilians to help supplement the soldiers in non-combat jobs. We brought some US Civil Servants over from the US to Germany at great expense and also hired US personnel that were already here. Foreign or Local Nationals (LN or FN) were hired to handle the rest of the workload.

What few FN positions needed LAA or classified access? The Germans that ran our trains; these higher-up train administrators needed to know in case of war classified call signals and destinations. We also needed translators. Local National Investigators worked with and much like US Special Agents and needed access to classified information.

Financial planners, Public Affair Officers, and others possessed LAAs. Thus some small per cent of the FN employees needed US type security clearances, but FN aren't eligible for US clearances. So how did this work?

We could be completely secure and not grant the FNs "clearances" or we could slide toward the operational end and grant the "clearances" with some security built into the process.

The answer is the Limited Access Authorization or LAA for the FN. An LAA is different from a US security clearance. A US clearance is broad and if you had a need to *know* and the requisite clearance (Confidential, Secret or Top Secret) you received access to the material. An LAA differed in these ways:

- **Limited to Secret**. LAAs were limited to the Secret and Confidential level only; LAAs for the higher Top Secret clearance were prohibited.
- **Limiting Commander's Statement**. An LAA required a written Commander's Statement limiting the types of documents or actual documents the FN could have access to. HQ security had to approve the Commander's Statement which also showed why it was not practical for a US citizen to do the job.
- **Higher Investigation**. An LAA required the more thorough background investigation for just the secret information. US citizens only required the less stringent NAC (National Agency Check) for a Secret clearance whereas a FN required a full blown Background Investigation (BI). If favorable, a US citizen would receive a TS clearance based on a BI.

We occasionally granted an interim LAA (the first Army Major Command to do this, I think). We *created* the procedures and they worked like this:

- The local command would nominate the FN by priority message to USAREUR security and info the local Military Intelligence (MI) Field Office using an unclassified nickname (*Certain Speed*). The Commander's Statement had already been approved for the particular unit(s).
- Upon receipt of the message, we would open a file on the individual and await interim investigative results from the local MI office. Those findings included:
- A review of the Statement of Personnel History – SPH (one's detailed history) by an Army Special Agent (S/A, noting any derogatory information.
- Interview of the FN vis-à-vis the SPH by a S/A also noting any derogatory information developed.
- Polygraph by MI.
- If all was favorable, we granted an interim LAA with the full Background Investigation to run ATF (after-the-fact).
- If these preliminary investigative activities were unfavorable, depending on the severity of the derogatory information, we could eliminate the candidate from the LAA program. Or, we could allow the Background Investigation to finish first and then review or *adjudicated* the entire investigation before considering his/her eligibility for an LAA.

8

Flag Notes And Laredo
Leader – a few successes

A Flag Note is a small letter from a General praising you for doing good work. The flag note has a replica of the general's flag at the top of the note. He has a red flag with gold borders behind his desk with the equivalent number of stars that show his rank. The recipient of the flag note cherishes it. This short chapter shows some situations when a flag note was used.

HEADQUARTERS
UNITED STATES ARMY, EUROPE, and SEVENTH ARMY
Commander in Chief
APO New York 09403

March 4, 1991

Mr. Leland C. McCaslin
Office of the Deputy Chief of Staff,
   Intelligence
U.S. Army, Europe, and Seventh Army
APO   09403

Dear Mr. McCaslin:

Thank you for your help in getting USAREUR units and supplies to Southwest Asia. Your work as Chief, Security Branch is characteristic of the magnificent contribution that many people all over Europe have made. Your's has been so good, that your staff director recommended I thank you with a personal note. I am pleased to do that for people such as yourself who did great work.

I'm proud of what you've done. People like you make the Army the top-notch organization that it is today. Thanks.

Sincerely,

Crosbie E. Saint
General, U.S. Army
Commander in Chief

The CINC USAREUR sent us this note for our use of special clearance procedures authorized under combat conditions to rapidly get troops to the Gulf for Desert Storm. Gary Arrasmith played a major role in this action and I thank him for his outstanding service to his country.

Another time we got word that a Captain had defected. After a lot of hard work the team finally clarified the issue and the DCSINT commended us.

We received the note opposite from the same DCSINT because of the joint Branch effort to put out a security education tool, the monthly News Bulletin for Information and Personnel Security (NIPS). About the middle of the month, various chiefs would present articles for the NIPS. When it was published it went down to company level within USAREUR and many other commands worldwide to include the Pentagon.

Laredo Leader
It is important to combat terrorism. This screening program described procedures to vet Local Nationals at their time of hire. We initiated the program in the 80's. After all, you wouldn't want to hire a terrorist who was member of the Red Army Faction or an

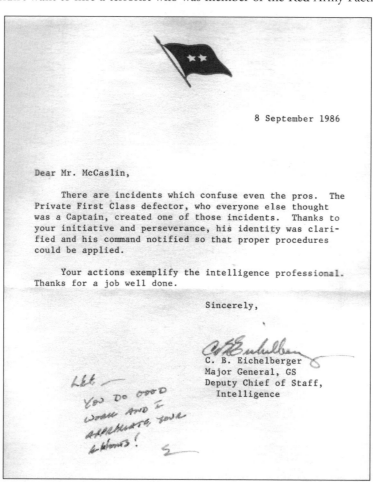

8 September 1986

Dear Mr. McCaslin,

There are incidents which confuse even the pros. The Private First Class defector, who everyone else thought was a Captain, created one of those incidents. Thanks to your initiative and perseverance, his identity was clarified and his command notified so that proper procedures could be applied.

Your actions exemplify the intelligence professional. Thanks for a job well done.

Sincerely,

C. B. Eichelberger
Major General, GS
Deputy Chief of Staff,
Intelligence

3 March 1987

Mr. Lee McCaslin
Counterintelligence Division
Office of the Deputy Chief of Staff,
  Intelligence
HQ, USAREUR & 7TH ARMY
APO 09403

Dear Mr. McCaslin:

This is to commend you on the consistently outstanding
newsletter, News Bulletin for Information and Personnel
Security (NIPS), you produce every month.

   Month after month, NIPS continues to be an informative
and highly readable publication of the highest quality.
The personal effort and pride that goes into each issue is
evident, and I assure you that it is noted and appreciated.
Thanks for a job well done. I look forward to reading future
issues.

C. B. EICHELBERGER
Major General, GS
Deputy Chief of Staff,
  Intelligence

espionage agent. They don't have "clearances," or the local national equivalent (Limited Access Authorization or LAA) but they could still do damage to you. Imagine a LN spy on base able to count the number of tanks you have! Or a terrorist able to plant a pipe bomb next to your desk!After we got the program running, we'd receive criminal information on the LN or sometimes the notation, "wanted by the German Police." By sending in the inquiry to the Germans, we knew the police knew where the individuals were.

The procedure for the firing was to prepare a classified Decision Paper with the unfavorable information received from the security check attached and recommending firing. We got chops (approvals) supporting our recommendation on the paper from Special Operations Branch, the legal men and women at JAG and Civilian Personnel before the paper went to the General for decision. Then the top Intel General (DCSINT) decided if the employee should be fired. Once the General signed the decision paper directing the LN's firing, the decision was final. We sent a classified message to the unit saying to fire the individual; the unit could not contest or appeal the decision. The fired individual usually went to Labor Court. They did not know the classified reason the individual was fired. The fired individual received compensation directed by the court based on a formula of GRADE x LENGTH OF SERVICE.

The security manager (name unrecalled) ran a similar but smaller program for the Civilian Support or Labor Service Agency and we used some of his methods for this USAREUR-wide program. Arnie Hunter is an expert and ran the program for us and is praised for his proactive assistance to the United States of America. Arnie recalls the start of the program:

If you remember, in the fall of 1981, following the car attack on the CINC USAREUR, (while I was the Security Manager at DCSOPS and before you chose me for the Personnel Security Chief Position) you came to me to obtain the list of possible "authorized names". At that time, the listing of Army names were controlled by the OPS folks, not Intel, thus DCSOPS had the listing.

As I recollect, one morning you took the listings I'd found and went back up to your office on the other side of the "H" building and made the decision to call the first ever USAREUR-wide foreign national screening program LAREDO LEADER. Then some days later, we sent a message through channels to "big Army" announcing the selection of the name, thus no other Army Command or Agency could ever use that "unclassified nickname".

Then, as my good fortune would have it, when the Chief Personnel Security position came open, you encouraged me to apply and the rest is, as they say, history. As it pertains to Laredo Leader, I did, under your supervision and guidance, work on many of the aspects of making the program a reality.

General Kroesen never knew the full impact of the program, but certainly other later senior leaders in USAREUR and most all of us for that matter, were and would remain safer because of the effort you, I and so many others made in bringing Laredo Leader to the stage.

Stan Stanton

William (Stan) Stanton came on-board to write the final Laredo Leader regulation and get staff input (and chops) from the other appropriate agencies. Especially important partners were the Deputy Chief of Staff for Personnel (Civilian Personnel Division) and Judge Advocate General (JAG). At the end of the informal coordination period Stan and Arnie got final chops from those agencies. With those signatures on the summary Decision Paper and the new Laredo Leader regulation under the Decision Paper (produced by AG Publications), the DCSINT finally approved the concept. It was ultimately approved via Decision Paper from the DCSINT to the USAREUR Chief of Staff.

Stan was in USAREUR from 1984 to 1990 and ran the program with skill and dedication. Americans can be very proud of this counterintelligence professional who helped protect the command.

And the program just keeps going:

Army Europe Regulation 604-1, 27 September 2006. See the unclassified regulation at http://www.per.hqusareur.army.mil/CPD/Reference_Library/docs/604_1.pdf

William (Stan) Stanton. (via Author)

12 May 1983

Dear Mr. McCaslin:

I'm pleased to acknowledge the exceptional staff work which
you have demonstrated in establishing the LAREDO LEADER program,
and the results which you achieved in two recent cases involving
right-radical extremists in the USAREUR local national work force.

You tackled a complex security problem head-on, and did an
outstanding job of coordinating the necessary action among the
various US and West German agencies which were involved.

This is precisely the type of persistent, dedicated and
innovative management I look for from my senior civilians.

Sincerely,

Julius Parker, Jr.
Brigadier General(P), GS
Deputy Chief of Staff,
Intelligence

9

Intel 2 Course or the in-flight icing problems!

W
e periodically reviewed the security instruction at the Security Manager's course – called Intel 2 – to see if the information taught was accurate. This chapter is about our formal course for new security managers.

7ATC in Vilseck, Grafenwoehr and Hohenfels were our large training areas which taught classroom topics as well as field training to include large force-on-force exercises.

I had to fly from Heidelberg to Vilseck to monitor the course. In Heidelberg it was a glorious morning to drive over to the Army airfield to take the flight to 7ATC. The one-way distance between airports was about 125 nautical miles, almost due east, and about 30 nautical miles east of Nurnberg.

I didn't rate a helo by myself, but I was flying with visiting Major General Albert N. Stubblebine III, Commanding General of Intelligence and Security Command (INSCOM), at Fort Meade, Md. He had come over from the States and was flying on to 7ATC on separate business. I had my desk-side briefer and took this opportunity to brief the General on a new security program (Laredo Leader) we were putting together. As an aside, I told him he looked like the actor James Coburn.

After reviewing my briefing he pulled the switch back on his helmet intercom and said "OK". The constant beating of the helicopter blades was truly deafening. If he pushed the toggle switch forward, he would be transmitting over the radio. That was truly an honor I'll not soon forget.

As we landed a Colonel picked up MG Stubblebine in a limo-type sedan and a corporal picked me up in a jeep. Oh well. We proceeded to the Intel 2 classroom where a group of new unit security managers were going to learn about their security duties for the next week.

The instructor greeted me and I said to just pretend I wasn't there and not to be nervous. Right! He did a great job and I didn't have any suggestions. It was hard for me to keep quiet and not answer the student's questions but to let the CPT do all the responding. Like Edith, I stifled myself. A couple of times the CPT did ask for my concurrence on his answer to the students. He was a fine instructor and we were lucky to have him with us. This Captain would later make full Colonel. We had some great chow at his house cooked by his wife. I caught another ride back with a Colonel and safely arrived back in Heidelberg. I drove home and did not go into work; it was after 1700 (5PM).

I'll describe one more trip to Vilseck for another review of the course that was cause for concern. You might say, like I actually did, that I almost gave my life for the Intel 2 Course.

It was a cold, wintry, snowy day. It was one of those gray overcast heavy German days and I bundled up. I met a Colonel who was going to Vilseck and the crusty old Warrant Officer (WO) who was the pilot and his co-pilot (I had previously asked the airfield to let me know when I could hitch a ride). I had a bag packed. The pilot said, "Let's go." This time we flew on a small Army fixed-wing aircraft, a Cessna 310, I think. I'll tell you this, there was much less noise than the helo!

We all climbed in and the Army pilots began their lengthy start-up procedures. Our plane finally started its run down the strip and suddenly we were airborne and flew up to our cruising altitude. It was a very bumpy flight and not one that generated much conversation. An hour or so later, after talking over the intercom, we started our descent. We passed down into the gray clouds and then broke through below them where we could see the rural snowscape coming towards us. As we neared the runway, it seemed like all hell broke loose as sirens and a Stall-Warning Horn started screaming; Emergency Panel Lights started flashing. The pilot pulled back up with more power applied and the sirens stopped as suddenly as they had begun. "Well sir," the pilot said, "too much ice; I can't land safely. Let's go back to warmer Heidelberg." On the way back I chatted with the Colonel about the incident over the intercom; we both acted like we were used to such things but in reality, at least I wasn't. I knew Happy Hour wouldn't be happy this evening, but it couldn't come too soon.

Icing

This is general aviation knowledge but is from my fellow veteran, Commanding Officer, friend and neighbor, COL Bob Huley.

An aircraft can begin to ice up on the ground, in level flight, or when climbing or descending. What you get is super-cooled liquid water particles striking the surface of the aircraft and suddenly "freezing" into ice. In a descent, you can have warmer air over top of colder air closer to the ground (an inversion layer), so you are fine flying along, but suddenly begin to ice up as you descend for landing.

When icing occurs two things generally happen. First, you can get icing on the windshield, which makes seeing where you are going/landing difficult. This is annoying, but not potentially catastrophic, unless it completely covers the windshield (of course you can always look out the side window). Windshield icing, however, is a good indicator of the more serious problem, which is icing on the wings. This disrupts airflow and lift and decreases the stall speed. This can and does result in aircraft crashing, i.e., you go to slow down to approach speed and discover that the aircraft stalls and goes into a spin, or alternatively, you go to takeoff and can never get enough lift to leave the ground and fly. This occurs in even large aircraft with fancy de-icing systems. That's why in the winter at airports when icing is occurring they spray the aircraft before departure to remove the ice. In a fixed wing, the buildup is usually on the front/leading edge, and depending on the location of the cockpit and wings, it is sometimes hard to observe. Even a small amount of icing can produce severe problems. On a helicopter, the "wings" are the rotors (including the tail rotor), and the same thing happens, sort of. In the helicopter, not only does ice reduce lift, but it can also become asymmetric because some ice is thrown off one rotor and not the other, thus creating an unbalanced rotor and severe vibrations. Icing is very bad news in either type of aircraft.

Just a little more on icing from another Army pilot:

Almost in direct opposition to logic… as you go up from the ground level, temperatures decrease 1.5-degrees per 1,000-feet. It's called the Standard Temperature Gradient.

However, strange as it may seem … when you develop ice on the wings and/or ice on the props… if you do not have "anti-icing" capabilities for either (i.e., isopropyl alcohol that shoots out on the leading edge of the propellers, and/or the leading edge of the wings)… OR … the fixed-wing aircraft does not have `de-icing boots` (i.e., the leading edge of the wing is coated with a rubberized, inflatable boot where air is pumped into, and out, of the rubberized boot, so as to inflate and deflate, and break-off the icing on the leading edge of the wing) then the only alternative you have, without "stalling" the aircraft, is to climb.

An Army fixed-wing pilot, CPT. Terrence D. Jorgensen, Sr., Transportation Corps, U.S.A.R., provided the above comments on aircraft icing.

10

The Russian Hotline

The MOLINK or Russian Hotline is real and still exists today. It's a teletype affair and not a red telephone like many believe. It's important for the two nuclear superpowers to be able to communicate and defuse a problem… before pushing the doomsday button. Thanks to my brother Jim, a Viet Nam and USAREUR veteran and now a Christian minister, for penning this exciting chapter …

I served in the Production division of DCSI, USAREUR 1976-1979. The first two years I worked in the Current Intelligence (CURIN) Branch as the Black Book Officer, published an electronic daily intelligence summary, and presented current intelligence briefings to various HQ personnel as required.

The Black Book was a compilation of highly classified intelligence briefings of the most important overnight developments for CINCUSAREUR. Early every weekday morning, I would deliver the Book to the 4-star Commander-in-Chief, GEN Blanchard in his office, standing by in case he had any questions and praying that I'd have the answers if he did. Whenever there was a weekend crisis, I'd take the Book to him in his quarters. I considered it an awesome responsibility to select, analyze, write, and present this daily brief to the CINC.

My last year in Heidelberg, I was transferred to the Order of Battle (OB) Branch, where I served as Chief of the GSFG (Group of Soviet Forces Germany) Section. We kept up with the latest developments in new Soviet equipment, tactics, and training. If too many GSFG units were out training at the same time, we'd all get a bit nervous, especially if they were out of their normal training areas and close to the East-West German border. Increased GSFG training levels would start pushing the IOH (Imminence of Hostilities) levels up, which would heighten tensions in our DCSI Watch Center and cause more collection assets to go to work to see what they were up to. One outfit that always kicked into high gear on such occasions was our USMLM (US Military Liaison Mission) based in Potsdam, a Berlin suburb. USMLM teams in specially equipped off-road sedans would head out into East Germany to detect whether GSFG was indeed training or up to no good. Our DCSI "nervousness" would make the Pentagon nervous too.

In the summer of 1979, I departed Heidelberg for Ft. Leavenworth, KS, and the Army's Command and General Staff College. No, I was not there for the "long course."[1]

My next set of orders had me reporting to serve as a Presidential Translator (PT) on the Hot Line to Moscow, arriving in Washington the summer of 1980 when Jimmie Carter was President. When I left two years later, President Reagan was in office.

I thought I would be prepared to hit the ground running, but learned upon arrival that I needed still more language training. I had majored in Russian in college. As part of my

---

1   Author's Note: Ft Leavenworth is a teaching post and home of the Command and General Staff College. It is also the home of the Federal prison. Army officers who are assigned to the post kiddingly tell others they are not there for the long course (Federal prison).

Soviet Foreign Area Officer (FAO) training, the Army had sent me for my M.A. in Soviet and Slavic Area Studies at the University of Kansas, to the Defense Language Institute (DLI) in Monterey, California for a year, and for two years of training at the U.S. Army Russian Institute (USARI) in Garmisch, Germany where all our instruction, homework, and class participation was in Russian.

Before the Army turned me loose as a Presidential Translator, I had to have 12 more weeks of intensive language training to make sure that my proficiency was sufficient to handle the highest level of diplomatic and military translation under intense time-sensitive situations. I would spend the next three months with a private Russian professor. I sat under the watchful eye of this demanding tutor six hours a day, with four more hours of homework. All of this was aimed at getting me up to speed for producing quality English language translations of Russian texts dealing with any situation, whether technical, military, political or economic, whose contents might be essential to the resolution of an international crisis. As much as I love languages, I was glad when this school was over.

By the time I reported for Hot Line duty in the National Military Command Center (NMCC) in the Pentagon, my top-level security clearances were in order. I was read on to the details of the program, and my orientation began. The Hot Line is officially known as the Direct Communications Link (DCL) with Moscow. It was born on October 20, 1963, one year after the Cuban Missile Crisis. During that crisis, with rapid escalation approaching the use of nuclear weapons, there had been no way for President Kennedy and Chairman Khrushchev to have instant communications.[2] The mission of the Hot Line is to provide the President of the United States with instantaneous communications with the leaders of the Soviet Union.

The DCL is also known simply as the MOLINK or Moscow Link. Various technological improvements have been added over the years, but, at least when I was there, it was not two "red phones," one sitting on the President's desk in the White House and another on the Chairman's desk in the Kremlin. Since the DCL had to function in crisis mode, redundancy of communications links was essential. During my tenure there were two satellite links and one underground cable link to ensure constant communications. The links terminated at our teleprinter machines. We could either type directly on the keyboard with the text showing up "immediately" on the machine in Moscow, or we could feed in perforated tapes of prepared messages.

The DCL was a joint staff operation under the control of the Joint Chiefs of Staff J-3 Operations Directorate, where all the Joint Staff's planning, policies, intelligence, manpower, communications and logistics functions are translated into action. The DCL consisted of six 2-man teams coordinated by an O-5 from one of the services. One team was on duty at all times. The team leader was an O-3 or O-4 Presidential Translator, but, as is usually the case, he would have been dead in the water without the Senior NCO Communications Specialist who ensured that the machinery was always operational.

We worked a fascinating schedule that was both good news and bad news. The good news was that we worked only 8-hour shifts and that we worked six days on and four days off. We rarely worked "overtime," and we always had a 4-day weekend. The bad news was that our 10-day cycle of "six on" and "four off" left us a bit like zombies never able to recover from jet lag. That's because our shifts continually rotated time slots. First we would work mornings 0600-1400, then come back four days later for the swing

2   See the official Memorandum of Agreement at www.state.gov/t/ac/trt/4785.htm.

shift 1400-2200, and finally work "mids" from 2200-0600. We never could quite figure out what time zone we were in.

The Hot Line was the only Army job where I had a chain-of-command with three different bosses depending on the situation. My boss for training and linguistic standards was the Hot Line Chief, who generally worked days unless he was filling in for one of the PT's who was sick or on leave. Most of the time, for routine shift operations, my boss was the flag officer in charge of the entire NMCC. He was the man on the spot to monitor and take action on developing crises around the world that could require deployment of various components of the U.S. joint commands. His burden was having to decide when to start waking up senior military and political leaders as trouble spots around the world began turning into crises. My third boss took over whenever a real, not test, message came in for the MOLINK. Whenever I got a real one, I stopped working for the flag officer and began working directly for POTUS (the President of the United States).

During routine shift hours, our main Hot Line activity was the exchange of hourly test messages with the Moscow translators to make sure that the links were fully functional. Moscow would send a test message one hour in Russian, and then we would send the next hour in English. When I was there, we were sending canned, pre-cut approved test messages designed to be politically inoffensive. In the early days of the DCL, the operators had composed their own which got a bit out of hand from time to time. Ours always talked about innocuous things like rare animals, strange plants, chili recipes, ancient inventions, or excerpts from great novels.

We always send in English, and they always send in Russian. Nuance is the reason. When it comes to Presidential crisis management, composing a message in your native language is the only way to get just the right nuance on a diplomatic communication. That's why the President and his advisors prepare all authentic outgoing messages in English. As a Russian linguist, I can pick the Chairman's nuance out of the Russian and convey its essence to the President, but I would have a much harder time putting in just the right nuance in if I had to translate the President's outgoing message from English into Russian.

Most of the time we were just exchanging test messages. One an hour was the requirement, but lazy creatures that we were, without any official agreement, DCL procedure generally worked like this. At two or three minutes before the hour, our machine would start clattering and the Russian test message would start coming in. We'd make sure it was just a test, and then at one minute after the hour we would send our test message to them. That way, we'd kill two birds with one stone and take most of the next two hours off and then the dual tests would repeat. If we really wanted to jerk the chain of the operators on the Moscow end, we would send a routine test at an odd time; say 20 minutes after the hour. Then they'd jump out of their chairs just like we would be wondering if was a real one since it was off the test "schedule."

Other than our routine test messages and sitting around studying my Russian, most of our normal shift work was as part of the NMCC team under the flag officer. Each and every shift we would run drills to launch operational and strategic forces, often generating "exercise only" Emergency Action Messages (EAMs) out of the Current Action Center (CAC) to launch control centers, nuclear submarines, recon aircraft and battlefield commanders worldwide. The NMCC would have to up the ante until the President was involved if we ever needed to execute the SIOP (Single Integrated Operational Plan). Every shift, round the clock, the NMCC team, the DCL included, would simulate an incoming nuclear attack against the United States. Various team members would be assigned role-plays as the SECDEF and the President. The exercise would usually begin with our sensors detecting incoming missiles. Often the DCL would then contribute a simulated Hot Line message claiming that the Soviets had accidentally lost control of the missiles. At that point the flag officer would begin managing the "crisis" and various simulated actions would ensue in-house and in exercise mode at outlying commands. At some point, as each exercise would escalate, the NMCC Director would say, "Put the President on the line," and the role-playing "President" would come on the line and the Director would review his nuclear options for him until he made an "execute" decision. Almost all newly-arrived NMCC personnel would go through a period of deep self-examination as to how they would be able to function if the situation were ever real. Would they take the time to call home and warn their families that missiles were incoming? What good would it do since most ICBMs could then reach key American targets such as the D.C. area in less than an hour?

Exercise in progress or not, everything would change completely if the DCL got a real message from Moscow. Whenever our machines would start clattering, especially if it were not near the hour, we would jump and hurry over to the teleprinter. If it was an "off-schedule" test, everything was fine. If it was real, our adrenaline would start pumping and our internal SOPs would kick in. First, my sergeant and I **would lock both doors** into our spaces so that we were separate from the NMCC and its Director. It was at this point that my boss changed from the Flag Officer to the President. When my doors locked, the NMCC Director understood, but at times was not happy since flag officers don't like being left out of loops, especially when they're supposed to be in charge of crisis management.

If an authentic message from Moscow began printing on my machine, my first task as I mentally translated it was to decide if it was so urgent that I needed to get the White House on the secure phone to give an immediate oral translation. If it seemed a bit less so, I was to make a written translation and send it by secure fax to the White House. The Hot Line was a teleprinter and not a phone for good reason. Think of problems with phone calls even when talking to another English speaker. You might not hear things right. Tone of voice can display emotional reactions and give false impressions. You don't have time to give any thought to your best response. A typed incoming message alleviates those problems. The written word expresses the thoughts of the sender more accurately and gives the recipient time to ponder the message. The response can still be relatively immediate if need be. At times the amount of time before a response can be a "message" in itself.

How many real Hot Line messages did I process? I can't say. The MOLINK is a private communications medium for the two heads of state. Only they can reveal when or if or how they've used it. They can mention it in press conferences, put it in their memoirs, or never mention it at all. As for me, I served at the pleasure of the President.

11

The real return of a defector from the cold

We occasionally managed real world intelligence missions. In this chapter we learn about people who leave their duty stations without permission and the true story of bringing one US defector in from the cold.

Definitions:
Deserter: A soldier who leaves his duties not on leave without the intent to return.
Knowledgeable Absent without Leave (KAWOL): A soldier who had access to classified information and is on unauthorized absence. When such a situation is detected, a report is made to the DoD Component counterintelligence organization.
Defector: A soldier who gives up allegiance for his country for another. This person is sometimes known as a traitor if he takes classified information with him.

Most defectors deserted because they were in trouble with the German or American authorities; very few defected due to ideological beliefs.

An unforgettable incident occurred as one unnamed USAREUR defector decided to come back under US control. Security at HQ USAREUR did their best to bring defectors back under US control – these defectors could and probably did give away important US information if they possessed classified data (physically or in their brains). Even their unclassified information had its value.

This particular USAREUR defector was making his way south of Germany to provide propaganda against the US, at the direction of the FIS who were handling subject. He reconsidered on his way down south; instead he surrendered to a United States Embassy south of Germany. The Embassy soon called us and told us they had our man. What did we wish for them to do?

Here were the players in this true plot.
- **The military personnel** from the southern US Embassy driving the defector north to Germany.
- **The MPs** from a unit located in southern Germany who would receive subject at the border on FRG soil.
- **US Army Pilots** who would take the prisoner from the southern border MPs and fly him home to his unit in central Germany with their own on-board MPs.

We quickly devised a plan where the Embassy personnel would drive subject north to West Germany, just over the border where the local southern based MPs would take possession of him.

"But how will we know if those MPs are legit and are the right MPs," asked one of the Embassy personnel? I puzzled over that question and improvised. I told the MPs they should take with them a page from that day's MP Desk Blotter (which listed the who, what and when of who was arrested that day) for a means of identification. I told the Embassy personnel the same thing. They were satisfied.

Next we studied the maps and along with flight operations, located a seldom used but operational civilian airstrip near that sector of the southern border that the defector would be crossing. With all these participants involved and the Embassy personnel already driving north to Germany with subject, phones were ringing off the wall and things were getting hectic. The normal business day had ended and personnel were going home.

The Keyes building at HQ USAREUR is where the top generals have offices – I call it the HQ of the HQ. We then telephoned the Keyes Building who controlled flight authorizations. We told them we had a real world intelligence mission unfolding and needed a small plane or helicopter dispatched to the subject's unit to pick up MPs and then on to that southern airstrip, receive the prisoner and return home. They agreed. They would put the plan in operation. Everyone had their instructions. I could do no more. Just sit back and monitor, and watch the clock as the wee hours of the night/morning ticked by. Had I forgotten anything?

Many hours passed; I looked at AFN TV and drank lots of black coffee, but the mission was eventually a success. The subject was turned over by the Embassy personnel to the local southern MPs at the border; they drove him to the southern airstrip where the Army Pilots and home unit MPs were waiting for him; rearrested him; and flew him handcuffed to his home unit. That was a tiring but an exciting evening and night. I think he was tried by court martial and convicted.

As the top Intel brass met the next morning in Heidelberg at the regularly scheduled Indications & Warning Briefing (I&W Brief), my boss Mr. Hennen said to the gathered group, "We have been working a problem all night. Let me brief you on it …." I was home fast asleep in bed by then …

12

The Berlin duty train

Introduction – Memories of the Berlin duty train

This chapter tells the story of the Berlin duty train that served as both a passenger and freight train that ran from West Germany through Communist East Germany to Berlin and returned; it is based on historical fact. This train helped keep what was then W. Berlin, in East Germany, alive during these wearisome times.

My mind drifts back to the "Good Ole Bad Days," as LTG James Williams, former Director of the Defense Intelligence Agency and DCSI USAREUR, called them. No discussion of the Army in Europe during the Cold War would be complete without an examination of the celebrated Berlin duty train. I think about the sinister trip by rail through the night from the West, into repressive East Germany and finally into free West Berlin, the next morning, surrounded by the Soviets and East Germany. Perhaps a cliché, but W. Berlin was truly an oasis in the middle of a figurative (Communist) desert.

That train and journey was exciting if not forbidding and legendary. Let's look at an article from the *Stars & Stripes* newspaper.

45 YEARS OF LEGEND END WITH LAST RUN

From: *The Stars and Stripes*, Sunday December 9, 1990 page 9.[1]

By: Joseph Owen, staff writer

Berlin – The end of the U.S. Berlin duty train passenger service came 45 years to the day after it began.

Freight runs had started July 27, 1945, but it was the passenger trains that assumed the mantle of legend over the years.

The trains had three purposes: to take personnel and supplies to and from Berlin, to exercise Allied transit rights on a daily basis, and to force the Soviet Union to guarantee those rights in accordance with the *ad-hoc* postwar agreements that always remained informal.

The Soviets permitted France, the United Kingdom and the United States a total of 16 trains a day to West Berlin beginning in 1945, according to military officials in the city. The number rose to 19 after the lifting of the 1948-49 Berlin blockade. The British also plan to phase out their service, but the French have made no such announcements.

The U.S. service was free to military passengers, but cost West Germany's government dearly. The Frankfurt run costs $14 million in 1989; the Berlin-to-Bremerhaven run costs $4 million. In the 12-month period ending June 30, about 70,000 people climbed aboard.

The trains have witnessed the dramatic, the comical and the bizarre. One woman gave birth on the train in 1987; another unintentionally left a baby behind in the 1970's. Porters returned it.

---

1 Author's note – used with permission from *Stars & Stripes*. © 1990, 2007 Stars and Stripes.

117

Scores of East Germans leapt onto the trains in the early years, trying to escape their country. One such incident sparked a tense U.S.-Soviet standoff at Marienborn, providing the plot for a West German docudrama.

In the West, at least one person jumped the train for another reason – to commit suicide.

For passengers, the ride was almost always suspenseful, if only because of the vaguely sinister formalities at the Soviet checkpoints. A misspelled name or an inconsistent birth date on flag orders (required since 1957) could delay passage.

And there were terrorist attacks. A bomb damaged a locomotive and some of the track in 1988. Police later arrested a Jordanian with alleged ties to a Palestinian terrorist group. Others tried to stop the train with boat anchors, tires, grappling hooks and more bombs, including some placed on the trains.

Such attacks prompted U.S. officials to guard trains carefully, keep planned routes secret and put misleading destination signs on the unmarked train cars. The Berlin train that arrived Saturday morning was marked as a Mannheim-to-Hanover run.

Army officials debated replacing the trains with busses several years ago, but never took definitive action until the inter-German border opening and German unification robbed the trains of their international political value.

The requirement for individual flag orders lapsed in June, and service dropped to six days weekly in each direction. The Soviets abandoned their checkpoints permanently one day without telling anyone.

The U.S. Berlin-Bremerhaven runs transported their last passengers on November 20, 1990. The last two trains on the Berlin-Frankfurt line arrived in their respective cities.

Further memories

I frequently rode the train through East Germany into W. Berlin. I remember the large American flags painted in color on the olive-green trains. I boarded early and in most cases, occupied a locked cabin alone because I was a regular courier of classified material.

You had to have Flag Orders that the Train Commander showed the Soviet personnel while passing into East Germany. The orders were in English, Russian and French. They had to be perfectly correct.

Drunk and disorderly on the Berlin duty train

My team was going to Berlin from Heidelberg to do an inspection of security in Berlin. You weren't supposed to bring any alcohol on the train. Well, I admit now, we shouldn't have but our team snuck on board a bottle of white wine and the three of us were imbibing of the grape (discreetly) in my cabin with the curtains to the hallway closed…. As the three of us consumed the tasty, cold German wine in my cabin before turning in, we suddenly heard a loud commotion. We quickly stashed the bottle and went out into the hallway. There was the uniformed female 2LT Train Commander with a 287th Rail MP. "And you keep him in the cabin," she commanded the soldier's cabin mate, "until you disembark in Berlin. His unit will get a report of this." Uh oh, bad days are ahead for him. I stepped up to her, glanced in the cabin, and asked, "What's up?" The soldier in the cabin was obviously drunk, disheveled and had been causing some type of problem on the train. You didn't want any problems while traveling through Soviet territory. The Train Commander replied, "Well, the soldier is stationed in Berlin. He's been in Stuttgart, West Germany attending the alcohol abuse rehabilitation course. He was celebrating passing the course!"

287th MPs at the ready, from left to right: unknown MP, SGT Dennis Edwards and SP4 Nick Cavis - train station Frankfurt. MPs are also known as 'white hats'. (Alberto Juliachs)

How important these days were to us! That train is like a city, containing hundreds of interesting stories. Share yours…. and you did. These are from the Berlin US Military's Veterans Association Bulletin Board and individual Train Commanders.

Innocent angels

It's a funny experience which shows us we all are humans, better said, the same kind of "innocent angels". Let's take a Berliner *Kindl* and say "Prost"! Greetings to ALL!

Reinhard von Bronewski – Berlin Brigade Overview (www.Berlin-Brigade.de)

Gave him a shoulder shove and away he went

As a member of the 287th MP Company, I was fortunate to be assigned to the Berlin duty train for several months in 1979. I had a great time and was able to work with some fine people. It was fun duty and the TDY pay was appreciated. I have stories about this duty I will not reveal here, however if a certain Army nurse who was on the train and reporting to Berlin during the aforementioned period happens to read this and remembers this MP and the "moment we shared" please don't hesitate to contact me. Old photos available on demand! My new photos may not be as good!

I had a great time walking alongside the stopped train with the Train Commander, a Russian officer and an enlisted Russian soldier who wore a poncho type cover to conceal what I thought was some form of nuke testing equipment. The Russian soldier would walk alongside me away from the train while the Train Commander and the Russian officer followed. My orders were to keep the soldier away from our train and that I did. Whenever he would come too close I would give him a shoulder shove and away he went. It was sort of a cat and mouse game except we always won. I guess the Army did right in picking an American soldier like me who happened to have been born in Cuba and sought refuge from the communists in the great ole' USA.

Maybe it was my youth or the fact that I can be foolish, however the feeling is the same now 27 years after the fact. I loved the idea of being surrounded by all those Warsaw Pact divisions. We had them where we could see them. Our mission may have been a suicide one, but if the balloon ever did go up we would not have had to exhaust ourselves doing recon for the enemy. We had a target rich environment!

Alberto "AJ" M. Juliachs

Train Commander stories
These were usually 2LTs or 1LTs.

Andy Smith
The Russians were mostly personable fellows, who only wanted to do a job, have a career, and retire without going to war, like us.

Interior of the duty train
Some pictures taken inside the train, November 18, 2009, at Fort Eustis, VA on the event of the train's annual inspection. Thanks to the US Army Transportation Museum.

I am Andy Smith, a retired US Army Colonel, Transportation Corps. I retired after over 31 years of combined USA, USAR, ARNG, and Coast Guard Reserve Duty. I am a Military College Graduate (North Georgia College). My last Army Job was CJ (Combined/Joint) 4, Director of Logistics, Combined Forces Command – Afghanistan.

My first job was Train Commander, US Army Duty Train, West Berlin, from June 1981 to November 1982.

Let me tell you about a typical duty day (night) for a train commander in the early 1980's. There were 2 outbound trains and 2 inbound trains that travelled to and from West Berlin 365 days a year and each had their own train crew, consisting of a Train Commander, Train Conductor, 1 or 2 Rail Military Policemen, a radio operator, and a civilian or military Russian/English interpreter. I reported to the duty site, the military-occupied Berlin rail station Lichterfelde West, also known as the Rail Transportation Office or RTO, sometime between 1830 to 1900 (6:30pm – 7:00pm). Report time was dependent upon which train, either to/from Frankfurt or Bremerhaven you had for that evening. The Frankfurt train left first each day, around 2130 (9:30pm), then the Bremerhaven train around 2200. As Commander my responsibilities included checking with all staff at the RTO for any special instructions or problems with the construct and mechanical movement of that evening's trains. I then determined whether I had any special orders for the evening from my military chain of command and conferred with the other Train Commander and Conductors. I then prepared the "schnitzel bag", the leather case with standing orders book, message keys, regulations and blank documents, for the night's trip. About 30 minutes prior to processing Flag Orders and boarding passes, I would go out and check all passengers and determine if I "might" have anyone who may create special situations for the evening (drinking, excessive numbers of juveniles, unruly passengers). I went out to the staged train and inspected for any obvious problems, damage etc. I went aboard the train and tested all water dispensers to ensure the water was potable, and the civilian crew was ready for the trip. I then would return to the RTO and begin processing identity documents, Flag orders, and boarding passes with the civilian technicians and Train Conductor. After all documents were processed and issued, I went out and presented a pre-boarding briefing to the passengers, relating standards of conduct, rules, penalties, and what to expect during the trip. I declared the train was ready for boarding, and turned this process over to the conductor with assistance from the Train MPs. Once everyone was aboard, I gave the "proceed" signal (hand wave) to the East German *Deutches Reichsbahn* train engineer to proceed.

I boarded the train, locking and placing anti-tamper rings over each door handle on the train. As the train began to move out, I checked each door lock and locking ring with an MP. I walked the entire length of the train to ensure this process. There would be small talk with passengers, and I ensured all was ok. I returned to the crew car and ensure that the interpreter was double checking all documents, preparing another "schnitzel bag" with all Flag orders and ID documents. Then I prepared 2 "test" radio messages to send out during the night. For the next two hours, the average length of the outbound leg, I read a book, walked the train, looked out the windows, conversed with passengers, etc. When everything went right it was a very boring job.

A few minutes away from arrival at Marienborn, I walked the train again. I prepared myself and the interpreter for meeting with Soviet authorities. Upon arrival, we march up to the Soviets, who would be waiting for you on the platform and exchanged military salutes and greetings (in Russian) and then shook hands (usually a test of grip strength among the male officers). The Soviet officer would invite you into a small office on the platform. In there you would present all of the travel documents to the Soviet officer, who would check every ID document and flag order for accuracy. Their attention to detail was phenomenal! The Soviet officer would then pass the documents to a soldier who would stamp each flag order to show passage had occurred. After all documents were done and returned to the bag I and the interpreter would go back outside to the platform and exchange military courtesies again, and re-board the train. In about 10-15 more minutes you passed the border and arrived at the RTO in Helmstedt. The Commander, interpreter, radio operator would leave the train and go to the RTO to await the inbound trains.

It was a reverse process for inbound after a 1.5 hour delay. Upon arrival back in Berlin, I'd write a travel report and file it with the RTO personnel. As Train Commander, you had overall responsibility for all of the personnel.

The Russians were usually a very professional group. Over time you built up nominal "friendships" with some Soviets, and learned which ones to be aloof with. They were mostly personable fellows, who only wanted to do a job, have a career, and retire without going to war, just like us.

We had alcohol confiscations from time to time. My attitude was if I couldn't see and smell it, and the passengers were not a problem, I had a blind eye. If the alcohol was conspicuous, but the passengers compliant, I would verbally reprimand them and have them dispose of any other "open" containers into the lavatories. If you were a problem then I was very tough, as I did not want my MPs and Conductor to have any problems. In 18 months I only had to put one very drunk passenger, a soldier, off the train for excessive drinking.

I didn't usually have problems with most passengers. All understood that you were the military authority on the train and that traveling was a privilege and that being barred from the train could cause many problems within their units. At one time I had to read rights to a F-15 fighter pilot (1LT) and his OIC (Major) for passing magazines out of the train to Soviet soldiers. Really an innocuous event, but the Major was belligerent and it had to be made clear to him that the crew was in absolute control and would not deal with anyone challenging our authority. After calming this major down he understood that he was in the wrong and he backed down quickly and did not create any problems for the remainder of the trip.

I did find a couple of things interesting. One night on the outbound Frankfurt train I had a couple of females 'boobie flash' a hardcore Soviet officer as I turned my back to the train. He was looking directly at the train when this occurred and when I saw his shocked expression I turned around to see these two women replacing their shirts and scurrying away. He did not get upset, understood it was a joke, and wished me a good night. It made for a humorous story later on. I did have to conduct a bus convoy for Berlin to Helmstedt and return on the night of May 27-28, 1982, when a train derailment occurred at the border and we could not conduct normal rail operations. In order to ensure that we maintained our rights of passage we hastily set up a bus convoy to take our passengers out of the city and to recover those stranded at the border. It made for a very long night.

Were these good days/bad days? Hmm, were interesting days – Not the job I joined the Army to do. I was actually glad to leave Berlin when my tour was over in June of 1984.

(Danielle Smyer Wildason)

Pictured are Volksfest Queens and BG William Moore 1979. I was the American
Queen. The German Queen was Yvonne Schijf. (Danielle Smyer Wildason)

Danielle (Smyer) Wildason

*As the Soviet officer jammed the secret note deep in my overcoat pocket, his hand
pressed on my thigh …*

My name is Danielle (Dani) Smyer Wildason. I currently work for the US Coast Guard
(Civilian) in Scottsdale, AZ, and am the Lead Contracting Officer for the Deployment of
the Rescue 21 Program via a multi-year contract with General Dynamics C4 Systems. I
attended Trinity University in San Antonio, TX, and graduated in Dec 1977. I was in the
Army ROTC program while at Trinity and requested to be an "Active Duty Reservist" upon
graduation – this request was approved, and I was commissioned a 2LT, Transportation
Corps, in December 1977 shortly after graduation. After attending the three month
Transportation Officer's Basic Course in Ft. Eustis, VA, I served in the Berlin Brigade
as a Train Commander from June 1978 – August 1981. After returning to Ft. Eustis for
Advanced Course, I was asked to stay at the school to instruct. I was then sent to several

other T-School courses and instructed various courses until I resigned my commission in Sept 1983. That ended my active duty military experience, but I later went to work for the Dept. of the Navy, Defense Commissary Agency, and the Coast Guard – I've been with the Coast Guard for 15 years. Somewhere along the way, I managed to complete two advanced degrees and a couple of marriages! While I have had some terrific jobs that I've loved, nothing has come close to the unique experience of being stationed in Berlin from June 1978 – August 1981.

As a side note, I was probably one of the very few, if not the only, Train Commander that had experienced the entire round trip on the duty train from Frankfurt to Berlin while a dependent. In 1973, while my father was stationed at Ramstein AFB and I was attending Kaiserslautern American H.S., our family made the trip to and from Berlin on the duty train. Little did I know that not only would I return, I would return as a Train Commander.

Note: What I have written here is *my* recollection – it has been almost 30 years, so I apologize if I got any of it wrong.

Train trip types: There were three trains for Berlin. There were two "troop train/duty trains" that went 365 nights a year to/from Bremerhaven and Frankfurt with a stop at Marienborn (East Germany) to process the passenger documentation (detailed below) and a stop in the W. German town of Helmstedt for the crew to change trains for the return trip. Engines were changed here as well – E. German to W. German and vice versa. The trains went on to their destinations, and the crews waited a couple of hours and took the returning trains back to Berlin. The second type of train was called a "freight train" – these went periodically to transfer equipment to/from West Germany as needed. The freight-only trip was very slow going and this was a rare time we were on the train during daylight hours. The third type was called a "command diesel" (as I recall). This was a special train much like a parlor car for VIPs – usually very high ranking military and their families – and it ran a few times a year, as necessary. I had that duty a few times to include one trip with the CINC, USAREUR and his family aboard.

The Round Trip: A typical "duty train" night started in the early evening at the Berlin Rail Transportation Office (RTO). Two crews were assigned – one en route to Frankfurt and the other to Bremerhaven. In general the Bremerhaven train was one or two cars and was considered the "easy" trip. People going to Bremerhaven were picking up their cars to drive back to Berlin the next day, so they were focused on getting sleep.

Each crew had a Train Commander (Trans Corps Officer), Train Conductor (Trans Corps E-5 or above), MPs (2 for the Frankfurt Train and 1 for the Bremerhaven – the MPs were the only ones armed), an interpreter (military or civilian) and a radio operator (military) assigned. While at the RTO, the Train Commander and Conductor checked in all passengers prior to departure. Passengers presented their "Flag Orders" along with the proper identification to ensure passage through East Germany. The slightest error could cause problems in the processing booth at Marienborn. Passengers were provided a list of "do's and don'ts" for the trip – "no photographs, no alcohol, keep curtains closed, no waving at the East Germans or Soviets, stay in compartment, etc." They were also informed that, regardless of the individual's rank/grade, for the short trip through East Germany, the Train Commander was the ranking person aboard. So, for the most part, passengers got many "don't's". They were usually somewhat apprehensive anyway, so it was generally not too difficult to control behavior, but we did have our incidents. We also had a Train Commander's SOP that covered several procedures we were required to follow if the need arose.

Prior to departure, the Train Commander and Conductor (and usually one MP) "walked" the train – we checked to see that folks were in their assigned compartments, met people and answered their questions, etc. For the most part, things were normal during these walks, but I did have a few incidents where I would pass a compartment full of male soldiers and someone would, well, smack my behind! The first time it happened, I was with SSG Russ Miller and I was so shocked I did not know what to do. I told him when we got to the end of the car and, he and the MP went back and scared the heck out of the guys in the compartment. I learned a lot from SSG Miller – he taught me how to handle just about any situation I came upon. After that, if someone did something like that, I took care of it myself! Anyway, when everything was in order, the train departed the RTO (usually on time) and our trip began.

During the trip, the radio operator was responsible for maintaining communications with Berlin. We had several checkpoints and he/she documented the time we arrived and departed. These were Potsdam, Werder, Brandenburg, Burg, Madgeburg, Marienborn, and Helmstedt. There may have been others, but I am certain about these. During the first part of the trip, the interpreters went over all the passenger documents one more time. If mistakes were found, they always made the corrections en route.

There was one car dedicated to the crew and passenger luggage (and sometimes, pets). The Train Commander had his/her own compartment, the Train Conductor and interpreter were usually together and the MPs and radio operator were together. On the trip out, most of the "down" time, was spent playing poker ("nickel-dime-quarter"). We took breaks to "walk the train", etc. as necessary, but most of the time, we were without incident – it could be pretty boring without the card games! The civilian interpreters LOVED to play (Willlie Schmoranz, Frank Pachurka, Peter Rzymkowski). We had some great times just playing cards and interacting with each other. I can say that a lot of what I learned about the Army came from the seasoned Train Conductors. Almost all of them had served in Viet Nam and the stories I heard never failed to capture my attention. SSG Russell Miller comes to mind as one of those wild guys that just seemed to have his finger in everything and was full of information and stories! I visited him and his family near Ft. Meade in the early-80s while stationed at Ft. Eustis. I think he retired in that area.

In general, I think everyone got along fairly well. We all had our "favorites" to work with and crews usually tried to switch around so we could work together. One thing I really remember is the SMOKE. Almost everyone seemed to smoke while playing poker – sometimes they smoked cigars. I think Frank Pachurka smoked a pipe sometimes. We kept the window cracked, but boy, I would never last these days. There were also some awful nights where the heat did not work on our car and the ice formed on the inside of the windows – brrrrr – we huddled up on those nights!

When we reached the checkpoint at Marienborn, only the Train Commander and the interpreter left the train. The interpreter carried the briefcase with all of the passenger documents. Initially, passengers had to keep the curtains closed the entire trip, but at some point, they were allowed to open the curtains to watch the "greetings" between the Train Commander/Interpreter and the Soviet officer in charge. This included a salute between the officers and a handshake. There were always one or two junior enlisted Soviets standing on the platform with an AK-47. It was a little daunting. For the first few weeks, the

Soviet officers refused to salute me. When questioned by the male Train Commanders, their argument was that female officers were not equal to them. I don't know what my predecessors did, but I was not the first female to be a Train Commander, so it was odd that they had this reaction. The Berlin Command filed an official protest to the Soviets (in Bonn) and soon, they were "recognizing" me as a "fellow" officer. Things changed quite a bit over the next few months with small "exchanges" of goodies. They sometimes gave me flowers and small gifts – I still have a few of the gifts – and I gave them Sears catalogs (for their wives) and candy bars.

After the "greeting" we all went into a small processing booth – just enough room for about 5 people to sit in pretty close quarters. Passengers on the train were not able to see inside the booth. We usually had a few moments of chatter (via the interpreter) and then got down to the business of the Soviet officer scrutinizing every Flag Order against the passenger documents. Once in awhile, a mistake was found and the interpreter either went back to the train to fix it or the Soviet officer let it go. When all the documents were processed on the outgoing trip, we left the booth, saluted, and shook hands again.

At some point, I started to do a very small wave to a few of the officers at Marienborn as the train pulled out – maybe I did it on a dare from Peter, I don't recall – but over time, most of them were either touching the brim of their hats in acknowledgment or waving back. It was all very subtle, but we loved it on the train.

Once aboard, it was a short trip through a "no-man's land" to Helmstedt (West Germany). Here, the Train Commander, interpreter and radio operator would leave the train and the Train Conductor and MPs would go on to the final destination of Frankfurt or Bremerhaven (at least this is how I recall it). After a couple of hours wait, we boarded one of the trains returning from Frankfurt or Bremerhaven and did it all in reverse with a crew change. By this time, it was the wee hours of the morning and most of the passengers were sound asleep.

On the return stop at Marienborn, when the documents were all processed and the Interpreter had put them all back into the briefcase, the Soviet officer usually sent out any of the enlisted Soviets – not sure what they were told, but they left – and he would pull out a bottle of vodka and a couple of glasses and exchange a few jokes. We "diplomatically" downed a good amount of vodka in the little processing booth. I'm not saying that every Soviet officer did it, but if I was with one of the civilian interpreters, the likelihood of it happening was very high. I am not sure if all of the Train Commanders had the same experience, but know I was not the only one. If there was any "gift" exchange, it would usually happen on the return trip. For some reason, they loved the Sears catalogs and candy bars. Sometimes, I would bake brownies or cookies, but they never ate them in front of me, so maybe they did not trust me and threw them away. Either way, they seemed pleased. I did receive flowers from their gardens on many occasions – sometimes they said their wives sent them to me. They also gave me other small items like perfume, boxed cigarettes (I did not smoke), and I still have the two sets of nested dolls a couple of them gave me. The paint is peeling from them, but they still have a sentimental value.

Once the return train was processed, we boarded the train and headed back to Berlin. Sometimes we played cards or went to our compartments to read or nap. In the early morning hours, we pulled into the RTO and our workday ended after our trip reports were filed. Most of the time, we all headed our separate ways, but sometimes the military crews from one or both trains went for breakfast at the mess hall.

As far as the train goes, on at least two occasions, I was allowed up front in the engine while the train was going. I can't remember the reason I was allowed, but I will guess that Peter Rzymkowski was the one who finagled it for me. That was terrific! It might have been that I was off duty or maybe on the command diesel – I can't recall.

Incidents. Incidents on the train were varied in degree. For me, the scariest were when we had a crank bomb threat (transmitted from HQ to the radio operator) as we had no choice but to conduct a search on our own. I think we had a handful while I was there. Other incidents were related to rowdy passengers – especially those that had been drinking. I remember putting off several British soldiers in Helmstedt because they had gotten into a fight on the train and we could not control them. I am not certain they even knew why we put them off, as they were so out of it. Anyone belligerent and drunk was in jeopardy of being removed from the train. Most of the time, we could get them back in their bunks and quieted down. While I never did it, I heard rumors that unruly passengers might find themselves in the cage in the back of the crew car with the luggage.

A few of the incidents I remember took place on the trip out. I remember that President Carter came to Berlin the summer of 1978. That night, I had a full train with several cars and a group of people pelted the cars with rocks at one of the overpasses. It was still daylight and most of the passengers were awake. The train sustained minor damage as a result, but purely cosmetic.

On certain occasions, they flew the E. German flag on the front of the train. I recall May 1 as one of those instances. We always protested and at some point, I think it stopped.

By the end of the summer of 1978, we had resolved the issue with the Soviet officers not greeting me. Around that time, a new officer appeared named LT Grabor. With him, it was all business – or so I thought. Once in awhile, he would give me roses from his garden. In late October 1978, he gave me a carefully folded handwritten note (which I *still* have) saying that he wanted to meet me in E. Berlin (yes, we reported it…oh, my). He jammed it in deep into the pocket of my overcoat as we were leaving the processing booth and before we stepped out on the train platform. I don't know how I maintained my "calm" as I thought he just…well….jammed his hand down my pocket – those old overcoats had deep pockets, so the truth is, his hand was pressed on my thigh for an instant. When I turned around to glance at him, he was dead serious. By that time, we were all out on the platform together, saluting each other and shaking hands as if nothing had happened. I was with Peter Rzymkowski that night and as soon as I got on the train (yes, I was shaking and furious), I told him what happened, as I knew we needed to file a protest, but it would be LT Grabor's word against mine. When I put my hand in my pocket to demonstrate, I found the note – folded up very small. Here is the actual note from the Russian military officer:

My Dear Miss Smyer
We haven't met for a long time and I miss you very much. I wanted to speak to you, but not circumstances hear (sic). Maybe we can meet in East Berlin? I can appear there in the next time. Please tell me your opinion in a small letter, but nobody must know anything about it. Let it be our secret.

Yours sincerely,

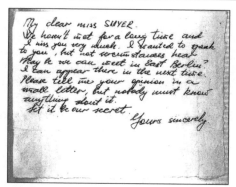

The note from the Russian officer. (Danielle Smyer Wildason)

I was speechless! I couldn't recall doing anything to encourage him. Anyway, Peter and I talked about what to do and decided to play it cool, so we did nothing on the return trip to indicate we had seen the note. As far as LT Grabor was concerned, maybe I had not found it yet. At any rate, upon my return to the RTO, we wrote it up and, after talking to my boss, we contacted the proper people (MI Agents of the 766th MID, I believe). At first, they considered whether to let me go ahead with giving him a note back and setting up a meeting, but I was dead set against it and that quickly became a non-starter. They really wanted to know why he would take such a chance and were fairly sure he was doing it because he was told to. We then had a few more sessions where they asked me even more questions – I suppose they wanted to see if there was something the Soviets could benefit from – guess there wasn't. I don't know why they let me keep the note – I remember telling them I wanted to keep it, so all they did was make a copy of it. The next time (and subsequent times) I saw LT Grabor, I acted as if nothing had ever happened and he did likewise. After a few months, LT Grabor was transferred and that was that.

All of 1980 was interesting and things were a little "off" much of the year. The Soviets had invaded Afghanistan and by the summer, the US boycotted the Summer Olympics in Moscow. We had an unusual amount of delays – especially on the freight trains. Things were a more strained, but still workable.

Upon leaving the RTO, every Train Commander received a model train that included the engine and a duty train car – painstakingly painted with the transportation wheel and everything. On the top of the train car, they painted the names of every Train Commander (and supervisor) you had worked with while on the trains. Mine is still intact with a tiny bit of paint rubbing off. Members of the Service Company also received a very nice "Lifetime Member of the Service Corps" hanging. Mine ended up getting folded by the movers way back when, but I have it hanging now – fold mark and all.

I prepared this at the request of Lee McCaslin in February 2008, as I recollect it after almost 30 years. I made every attempt to portray it as I recall it. THANKS. Danielle Smyer Wildason.

Thanks for your contribution Danielle.

More Train stories…

Fernando Bruno
I proceeded to inform Berlin Command by radio (in code) of the situation…

I graduated in 1958 from the University of PR. I received a Regular Army commission in the Military Police Corps as a second lieutenant. I attended the Basic Infantry Officers Course and Airborne School in Fort Benning, Georgia. I was assigned to the 51st Armored Infantry Battalion, Combat Command A, in Butzbach, West Germany. After my two years tour of duty in a combat branch I was re-assigned to my basic branch in the Military Police and transferred to Berlin, Germany as Executive Officer of the 570th Military Police Company (Railway Guards).

A typical duty day started a 7:30 AM until 5:30 or 6:00 PM. The company's mission was to escort the passenger trains which departed Berlin every evening going to Frankfurt. The passenger trains were commanded by a Transportation Corps officer. My MPs provided the security up to Helmstedt, which is the first stop after crossing the border into West Germany, and that evening, provided the security for the train coming from Frankfurt back to Berlin. I acted as Train Commander of the freight trains. This duty was performed once a month, the train left Berlin at 6:00 or 7:00 PM and arrived at Helmstedt, West German border town, around 7:00 AM next morning. The reason for this very long trip was due to having the lowest priority in the East German railway system; even the locomotive was East German. Upon departing Berlin, the train made stops and placed on the station sidings for as long as two hours at the cities of Potsdam, Brandenberg, Magdeberg. The train had to be cleared at the Soviet checkpoint of Marienborn. At this station I dismounted from the train with my interpreter (a sergeant that spoke both German and Russian), met the Soviet officer in charge at the *Bahnstaig*[2], went to his office, and cleared the train with the train manifest. That same evening we met the freight train at Helmstead coming from Frankfurt and went through the same procedure in reverse order back to Berlin.

I had a very nerve racking experience after the Berlin Wall went up in August 13, 1961. I was freight train commander bringing all the heavy equipment of an infantry regiment that was being transferred to Berlin from West Germany as reinforcements to the Berlin Command, and when I arrived at the Soviet checkpoint of Marienborn, the Soviet officer in charge, Captain Perevoznik, informed me that the train was being detained. I proceeded to inform Berlin Command by radio (in code) of the situation. My MPs dismounted from the guard cars and proceeded to provide security for the train for 24 hours a day. Finally, at the end of the third day, Captain Perevoznik came to my guard car and informed me that the train had been cleared for departure, at which time the train proceeded back to Berlin. I was awarded the Army Commendation Medal for my performance in that situation.

Miles Gilmore
Working with the Russians was fascinating.

I'm Miles Gilmore. I arrived in Berlin as a new 2nd Lieutenant, and left as a promotable 1st Lieutenant. I was stationed there March 1987 – March 1990. I served as Train Commander, Senior Train Commander, then Plans/Operations Officer, Transportation Division, Berlin Brigade. I graduated University of Virginia, BA, 1986. I grew up in Atlanta, Georgia.

---

2   Author's note – train platform.

As I recall the reporting time was 1830hrs the night of duty for the Frankfurt train, just after that for the Bremerhaven train. The Frankfurt train always had many more passengers; on a busy night it could be 300 or 400 passengers. We opened the booking office at 1900 hrs (7pm) and began processing the passengers. The passenger had to see the booking agent (a German local hire), the train conductor, and the train commander. All the passengers had to call a couple of days prior to make their booking.

There were usually at least one or two issues, usually administrative, where we had to retype the flag orders when they had some sort of typographical error. Usually the interpreter handled these things. Meanwhile, the train commander had to sign out a radio, a communications codebook called a CEOI, and some extra batteries for the radio. The final duty there was for the train commander to give a safety briefing to all the passengers, telling them not to take pictures, not to drink, to keep inside the train at all times, etc. Some of the train commanders jazzed this up and tried to make it entertaining; all of us could give it in our sleep after a few months.

The Frankfurt train left first, and stopped in Potsdam. None of us debarked the train there, but the Soviets had the opportunity to inspect the train, and we hooked up to an East German locomotive there. These were aging diesel locomotives, whereas the West German ones were all electric. I remember the smell of the air changed noticeably in East Germany, especially in the winter, as most homes were heated with a highly polluting brown coal; it smelled sulfurous.

At that point we all settled into a rhythm; the MPs and train conductors sometimes played cards, sometimes we chatted with the interpreter, occasionally we would bring along food and snacks. The final stop in the East was Marienborn, a tiny hamlet in East Germany. There the train commander and interpreter debarked the train and went into a small "shack" or office to greet the Soviet officer, who was also accompanied by a military policeman of the Soviet Army.

The first stop in the West was Helmstedt, a smallish city. There the train commander and interpreter debarked the train and waited for the inbound train from either Frankfurt or Bremerhaven. We did the same thing in reverse on the way back. We were usually back in Berlin by dawn.

I have some very vivid memories of all the train conductors, other commanders, interpreters, and translators. Some of them became very good friends. The interpreters were generally civilians; a few were Americans who had either married German women and settled there permanently or preferred living in Europe.

Working with the Russians was fascinating. They were a varied bunch, with some that were arrogant and self-important, others that were jokers. Some of them recognized the boring futility of their work. More than a few of them loved to drink. On special occasions they would ask if they could make a toast. Not a good habit to get in to, but I remember working on a New Year's Eve and obliging. If I had known how they drink I might have thought twice, though! When they say a "shot" they mean a tumbler at least half full with room-temperature vodka, which they could easily swallow in one gulp. And I found out that drinks come in sets of two or three; they would suggest another as soon as the first was finished. I think I took that one, as they seemed insistent, but that was more than enough!

We also had a toast when the wall came down, in November 1989. They recognized the historical significance of the occasion, the death knell of the Warsaw Pact.

Alcohol confiscations happened occasionally, but not often. More frequently some passengers would have drinks before getting on the train. Unbelievably I think smoking was also permitted on parts of the train, which would be unthinkable today.

Occasionally there were DV (distinguished visitor) cars, or even a special train. I think the most famous that came in was Senator Sam Nunn. I found Senator Nunn to be very friendly and down-to-earth; I even had a brief conversation with him about my alma mater, U.Va.

The most persistent problem I had was with passengers taking pictures on the train. I personally dealt with this lightly, though I suspect other train commanders took it more seriously. However, if a passenger took pictures in Marienborn and the Soviet officer noticed, this became more serious, and sometimes they insisted upon action. In such cases I usually nodded gravely and agreed, yes, this is a serious offense and cannot be tolerated. I then reboarded the train and conducted as quick an investigation as I could. It was easy to pinpoint where the flash came from. I then told the passenger that he/she had two choices: either submit the camera to me, or give me a roll of film that I could take out to the Soviet so he could see me expose the film. Often I'm quite sure the passenger gave me an unused roll, which I then took out to the Soviet and pulled the film out of the canister in front of him. In every case he saw this as sufficient punishment.

Though again a violation of regulations, many train commanders traded with the Russians to get memorabilia. The Russians loved getting cheap electronics – digital watches, radios, stopwatches. In return I still have a Soviet officer's cap, coins, rank, ribbons, etc. One of my colleagues traded a VCR for a full uniform. Also, many of the less doctrinaire of them wanted pictures of themselves together with us. I think most of them asked for this, but I only did it a couple of times with ones that seemed more trustworthy.

We also occasionally had special freight trains, with no passengers, just the crew of MPs, a conductor and an interpreter. From what I heard those used to get wild, as they were less supervised; they used to have beer and grill out on the caboose. However, mostly they were just somewhat boring, as our freight trains had the lowest priority on East German tracks, and it often meant sitting idle for hours.

These were definitely the good days. All the lieutenants were very young and for most of us it was our first overseas experience. Though the job could be routine, it had a very special significance, as the history of the Berlin Airlift proved. They were probably the most exciting days of my working life; we all believed in what we were doing, the camaraderie in the unit was unsurpassed; we lived in a great city that was unique in all of history. Though there certainly was some anti-American sentiment in Western Europe at the time, I think that the United States was perhaps a more innocent and idealistic country at that time, and was more universally loved around the world. The "bad guys", the Soviets, were easily identifiable; unlike today, where we're never sure who they are, when the might strike next, what country they're in, or what their motivations are.

And then there was the movie …

Stop Train 349 – real movie

This is an old black and white film about an American Army train going from Berlin into West Germany. On board is an East German stowaway. The Russians get wind of it and stop the train. The Russians and the Americans face off!

Howard Leatherwood – Special Agent
Another story from a dear friend, retired Special Agent Howard Leatherwood.

Mistaken Identity
We were stationed in Bremerhaven for two tours, totaling ca. 12 years, and the duty train trip to Berlin was a ticket to delightful short vacations. The memory that stands out was when we decided to take just such a mini-vacation. We decided to take our three older children with us, but to leave our youngest, Stephen, with our German maid for the weekend. Our maid lived in a nearby village and I had driven her home from work on one or two occasions. When the day of departure for Berlin arrived, I took Steve with me in the car to the village where our maid lived. I stopped near what I thought was our maid's house, went up to the door with Steve in my arms, and knocked. A man, who I presumed to be our maid's husband, came to the door and I explained that his wife had agreed to take care of our baby boy while we went to Berlin for the weekend. He said that would be fine, but just after he replied a lady (not our maid) walked into the room and asked her husband why I happened to stop at their house. He quickly explained that they were going to take care of the baby boy over the weekend. I explained that our maid lived nearby and apparently I'd come to the wrong house. Nonetheless, they reaffirmed that they would be happy to take care of him. I thanked them, but said that arrangements had already been made and our maid would be expecting us. (When I later related this story to our maid, she laughed and commented that the couple were nice people and would have taken good care of Steve.)

Tom Watts
Here's a story from the man who ran the train.

Colonel Tom Watts (Retired) was born in Jackson, Mississippi in 1948 and spent over twenty-seven years in the United States Army with numerous assignments in Germany, Belgium, Southeast Asia and the United States from 1971 – 1999. He was assigned in positions of Company and Battalion Commander at Fort Polk, Louisiana, Germany and Seattle, Washington. Colonel Watts was assigned to West Berlin, Germany as the Transportation Officer in the American Military Sector and Logistics Officer/G-4 for the Allied Staff Berlin. He was assigned to Pentagon in the Secretary of Defense's Office in 1992 and 1993. Colonel Watts was the Military Logistic Advisor to the United States Ambassador to NATO. His final assignment was as an instructor at the United States Army War College at Carlisle Barracks, Pennsylvania. He is married to Judy Griffith Watts who worked in the Office of Military Intelligence for Headquarters, USAREUR in Heidelberg, Germany (author's co-worker) and the American Military Sector West Berlin, Germany. Colonel Watts is a secondary school teacher of American History in the Madison County, Mississippi.

After the 1988 Bombings
There was a bombing in 1988 in West Germany of the tracks north of Kassel. The bomber or bombers had laid a series of explosive devices on the inside of the tracks at about 10 to 15 feet apart. They placed the explosives along a portion of the tracks that take a bend with a deep ravine to one side. Lucky for us, not all of the explosives (about 6 or 7) detonated and the dummies placed the explosives on the right side tracks away from the

ravine. We had about one hundred to one fifty passengers, crew and support on the train. The engineer was slightly injured from pieces of glass from the thick window of his cab. It shattered but did not break through. The bomb damaged the locomotive and some of the track. The train safely stopped and radioed ahead to the next station. There was a large university in the nearby city, and the police thought the radical students from that school could have done it. However, the Police later arrested a Jordanian with alleged ties to a Palestinian terrorist group. We had several other incidents trying to stop the train with boat anchors, burning tires, grappling hooks with the Bremerhaven inbound duty train. We painted out the American flag and fabricated a series of placards with the American flag. It would be placed on the passenger cars at Marienborn and taken off when they arrived at the Berlin station, Berlin-Lichterfelde West, to show the flag through East Germany.

Story from Colonel Tom Watts, former United States Army Transportation Branch Officer, Berlin.

Robert W. Rynerson
Irish Smile
By Robert W. Rynerson,
formerly SP5, Berlin Brigade
Thu 21-Nov-91

As the Cold War just fades away, the scholars who spent a generation trying to figure out how and why it began are turning their attention to the question of how and why it ended. They will not find the answer in documents. There is no paper trail into the hearts of the people who long stood watch on both sides of the barbed wire. Each of us who were there, however, can tell you the moment when the end began – the moment when someone let their humanity slip through. The world was watching the heavens, when I saw the Cold War begin to melt. On that day, July 20th, 1969, Americans landed on the moon. If we wanted to talk about something here on Earth, there was always the war in Vietnam. For a little group of us, however, that night was supposed to be business as usual. We were in the crew compartment of the U.S. Army's Military Train from Berlin. It was 8:30 in the evening, and Dm80610, as it was known to the German and American railway men, was rumbling over the switches out of our little station, picking its way toward the one remaining main line open to the West. After a stop at the West Berlin Wannsee station, we would roll over 100 miles through East Germany. The East Bloc called it the German Democratic Republic; we called it the "Soviet Zone of Germany" and we would report to the Soviet Army checkpoint officers, who would review and stamp the paperwork of every passenger. Out of an old German leather attaché case came the stack of military I.D. cards, passports, and multi-colored, quadrilingual documents in the languages of the four Occupying Powers. In a few minutes we would be out of the American Sector of Berlin, time enough to put someone off the train if all was not in order. Mr. Pachurcka, a civilian interpreter for the U.S. Army who had spent too many years on the knife-edge of border conflicts, gave each photo a sharp glance. "An Irish passport?" he growled. As the GI on-the-job trainee interpreter, I had been laying out the accumulated identity material, and had opened the unfamiliar booklet to the picture of a lovely Irish woman in her early 30's. All work stopped. Anything out of the ordinary could trigger suspicion by the Soviet checkpoint officer.

Quickly, I explained to the narrow-eyed Francois Pachurka and to our Train Commander what I had learned a few days earlier in the Berlin Rail Transportation Office: this passenger was traveling with her mother and young brother on papers issued by her employer, the British Embassy in Bonn. They were on holiday, a vacation that a secretary could afford, on military standby travel. Wheels turned in Francois Pachurka's head. He paused and then advanced a hypothesis. "She is actually with British Intelligence. The Irish hate the British, but she had a son out of wedlock, and had to find a job that would take her away from home forever. This woman," he fished out another Irish passport, "is truly her mother. But this boy," and he held up a third passport, "is actually her son, not her brother." The Train Commander and I stared at each other for a long moment, while the train wheels clicked over the bumpy *Reichsbahn* track panels underneath us. Now that they had been pigeon-holed, our Irish guests were welcome to be on Dm80610, as it passed into the Soviet Zone. In northern twilight, many passengers stayed awake on any trip.

That night, Mary and her mother and her "son" were listening to the moon landing on portable radios. The signal traveled for thousands of miles, and then hit the East German jamming program, a powerful station which operated on the fringe of the Armed Forces Radio Berlin frequency, so that the space message faded painfully in and out. I joined them for awhile during the lull between work projects, keeping Mr. Pachurka's cynical observation buried in my heart.

At the Marienborn border checkpoint it was a special night. We took the Soviets' salutes with undisguised grins on our faces. Their officers allowed themselves to be sportsmanlike, congratulating us on our space success, joking about when we would be working at a checkpoint on the moon. On the edges of this scene, the Russian and Asiatic enlisted men remained stone-faced and cautiously alert, as on almost every night. For twenty years they and their fathers had watched silently, while their officers smoked American cigarettes, okayed our train movements with American ballpoint pens, and (usually) waved us on our way.

Back on the train, I found the Irish family looking out at the spotlit border station. German railway workers busily serviced our train. Border police walked along it with their German Shepherds and the wheeled mirror, checking the undercarriage for refugee riders. A Russian soldier stood watching this scene from the platform, his face locked inscrutably.

Mary, the Irish employee of the British, had dutifully read the six pages of rules on travel to and within Berlin. She repeated some of them back to me.

"But there's no rule that says we can't smile, is there?" she said, adopting a leprechaun voice. At 11:59 p.m. of July 20th, 1969, the Cold War began to melt, as Mary turned on a wider and wider Irish smile.

The soldier tried to maintain his composure, but he could not. His lips began to quiver, a silly grin crossed his face, and then finally he beamed a smile of sheer enjoyment. He lost his military bearing, and was only saved from complete collapse by our conductor's signal. The train started, and he faded from view.

I walked back along the long corridors of the sleepers to the crew car on the end of the train. I always enjoyed those moments, as our sleeping passengers crossed the deadly border behind the closed doors of their compartments. Intense spotlights probed the corridor windows for a moment, and then I felt the surge of acceleration as we hit the smooth track of the *Bundesbahn* and West Germany.

That night, Mary's smile seemed like an amusing incident. But as memories of other details fade, it has stuck in my mind. How far in space and time did that smile travel? Pachurka, the cynic, would not have extended his improbable hypothesis to imagine a Russian soldier taking that warm glow home. Still, Mary's smile was a step in the right direction. And if Pachurka was right, it was from a woman whose own life was being lived in exile from her small country.

13

Berlin Armor: just a step away from a Cold War to a 'Hot War'!

… either run over it or blow it out of the way!

T his true story was written by SP5 Conrad (Connie) Schornhorst, Tank Co., 6th Infantry Reg. and Co. F (Patton) 40th Armor, 1958-1960. Source: Reinhard von Bronewski. www.berlin-brigade.de

According to some newspaper clippings I have, it was on the evening of Nov. 15, 1958 and it seems to me that it was just before the sun went down, at least it all started about that time.

I was in Berlin's Turner Barracks and in my skivvies, on my way to take a shower when I stopped by a friend's room to talk. While talking, the CQ (Charge of Quarters), a Sgt in our Platoon stuck his head in the room and yelled "1st PLT on ALERT!"

It was 6pm or so and we never have alerts at that time of the day; they are always around 4:30-5am in the morning, so we thought he was joking and didn't pay much attention to him. We continued to talk when I heard some noise outside the door and went to see what was going on. Guys were running in and out of rooms.

I told my friend: "It is an alert." So much for my shower. I ran back to my room and put on some clothes but it wasn't much of a uniform - fatigue pants, t-shirt, field jacket, Class A shoes plus my crash helmet and ran for my tank. Our driver (I was the gunner) was right behind me. I don't know where the loader was, he was a bit slow. Frank was saying: "Conrad, this is a practice alert isn't it?" I said to him, "When have we ever had a practice alert at this time of day"? When we got to the tank, Frank, our driver, and I pulled the tarp off and for once didn't bother about folding it. Frank started the engine to let her warm up. In those days, 1958-1960, our small arms, .30 cal and .50 cal machine guns, .45 cal grease guns and our personal weapons, the .45 cal pistols, were all kept in the arms room. I never could understand that 110 miles behind the Iron Curtain they claimed that we only had 15 minutes at most to get out of our Company area before the 'Russkis' started shelling it and our weapons were locked up in the arms room! There were guys from other platoons helping us get the weapons in our tanks. I've got no idea who handed me the heavy .50 cal machine gun but it never ever wanted to go in the brackets that held it in the tank, but this night I gave it one shove and in it went the first try; I couldn't believe it. We screwed the barrel in and it was a GO. Then someone handed me the .30 cal Browning and I put in its brackets and it was a GO too. Our crew ran to the arms room and got our grease guns and .45 pistols and got in our tanks. We were sitting in our tanks when over the radio we heard our Platoon Sgt, SFC Gene Sergeant (known to us as Sgt Sgt), say to move the tanks over to the front gate. The CO's tank was at the head of the line, I heard a click in my ear phones and Frank asked me: "Conrad, this is a practice alert isn't it?" To which I said: "Frank, when have we ever moved our tanks to the front gate on a practice alert?"

So we moved to the front gate on Huettenweg and were sitting there when Sgt Sgt said over the radio: "Open a can of …50 cal ammo and load the .50; also, open a can of .30 cal ammo and load the .30 co-ax and open a can of .45 cal ammo (it was vacuum sealed) and load all the grease gun mags and pistol mags that you have or can find." I heard another click in my ear phones and Frank said, "Conrad, this is a practice alert isn't it?" to which I replied: "Frank, when have we ever loaded all these weapons and ammo mags on a practice alert?"

I'm here to tell you that things were a little tense and I was loading every mag I could get my hands on. I just sat there and kept on loading mags. I had pistol and grease gun mags sticking in every pocket I had. If someone would have shot me I would have blown up like a bomb! Then while sitting there, over the radio, Sgt Sgt said for everyone except the driver to come out and gather around so he could tell us what was going on. We gathered just in front of the barracks and I was facing the Huettenweg (road). Now he told us the reason; he said that the 'Russkis' had stopped a US convoy and would not let them come ahead to Berlin or go back to the Western Zone and we were told to go to get them out and we were only waiting for the MP escort.

He asked if everyone had this and that's when we all said we did; then he asked if we all had our gas masks. One guy said he didn't and Sgt Sgt said he didn't have time to go get his own so ask one of the guys that was hanging out the window (must have been about 15 guys watching) to throw him one. Just like someone had given them a command, they all left the window and then as if on command they all appeared and threw gas masks at the guy. He had to dodge them all but he picked up one and waved at the guys. While Sgt Sgt was talking to us I had noticed a VW pull up across the street and a guy got out and stood there watching us. Then we could hear the MP's coming, the old BEE BEEP BEE BEEP siren sounded our way, and that's when suddenly the guy jumped back in his VW and drove away. I'm sure that he was some kind of 'Russki' agent monitoring us.

Sgt Sgt told us to get back in our tanks (one tank driver was yelling: "I'm too short to go to war", he only had a week to go before he went back to the States) and told us over the radio to make sure that we had thrown all the empty ammo cases outside, that we didn't want anything jamming the turret when we turned it. He also said that when we went under the overpass that has the sign saying that we were leaving the American Sector (entering the GDR / Russian zone) to load a main tank gun 90 MM HE round, and from then on, if something got in our way, to **either run over it or blow it out of the way!!**

Oh boy, what emotions. My thoughts ran crazy. My head felt like a roller coaster. RED ALERT. Was this my end, the end of all my comrades? Was this the first step to hell, the small step from the so-called Cold War to a Hot War? What happens to my family, to my girlfriend, to my...? Shit, what for a damn bull shit!

We sat there for just a few minutes waiting on the MPs, speaking not a word when suddenly over our radio came the order: "Take your elephants back to the barn, they just turned the convoy lose".

Phew!

I'm sure the strange guy in the VW must have had a radio of some kind and told the 'Russkis' that we were on the way to kick their butts. I've been told that the guys in the convoy heard our tank engines start up and that it was a comforting feeling to them knowing that we were ready to come to get them.

After parking the tanks we all were headed towards the barracks when our CO told us to gather around and he told us that if anyone asked to tell them that this was just another practice alert. Frank and I found that a little funny. Our CO asked if anyone had any questions and one guy asked: "Sir, if this was a practice alert, why were you in your tank instead of your jeep?" The CO replied, "If there's going to be any bullets flying around, I'm going to be in that tank, not in my jeep." He then looked around and said that he didn't see the same uniform on any two guys but at least we were ready to go in record time. Needless to say we all were breathing a little easier when they (the 'Russkis') turned the convoy lose; things were sure a little tense for a while. I had a little trouble going to sleep that night, thinking of what might have been. We did not leave the Company area! Just another short story of some of the great times we had in the great city of Berlin.

14

Revisit Potsdam –
Lt Col Nicholson's death

T his is a formerly classified case history. It's been declassified now by the USAREUR History Office. If you want their full story, see the web page http://www.history. hqusareur.army.mil/pubs.htm

The last casualty of the Cold War: Lt Col Arthur D. Nicholson and the US Military Liaison Mission

Excerpts below are from the *Intelligencer, Journal of US Intelligence Studies*, Vol 13, No. 1, Spring/Summer 2002 by Roland Lajoie. Both the author and AFIO copyright the work.

Ludwigslust, East Germany, March 24 1985. Junior Sergeant Aleksandr Ryabtsev surveyed the situation through the sights of his AK 47 automatic weapon. The young Soviet soldier assigned to Group of Soviet Forces Germany had pulled guard duty on this sunny early spring day and had only expected to be bored. That was not to be, for there by the tank sheds in the middle of his post, a sub-caliber firing range used by his tank regiment, was that strange vehicle again. But now one individual was standing through the sun-roof keeping watch while the other was outside and appeared to be poking around the sheds where some of the unit's tanks were kept. Both the vehicle's plate and the patch on the intruders' camouflage uniforms bore the distinctive US flag patch of the "Missiya" about which he had been repeatedly warned. In fact Ryabtsev had briefly seen this same vehicle earlier in the day and had telephoned his sighting to the duty officer only to be yelled at to follow the instructions of a guard on his post if the intruders returned. Now they had returned and Ryabtsev, crouched 50 yards from the vehicle, was nervously considering his next move. At that moment the individual by the sheds suddenly turned as if to return to the vehicle. With his weapon already trained on the more prominent target on the vehicle and with the duty officer's warning ringing in his ears the sentry jerked the trigger. That round barely missed the individual on the vehicle who quickly dropped down into the safety of the cab. Ryabtsev then turned his weapon on the second man, now running toward the vehicle, and fired twice more bringing him down just short of the cover he was seeking. The person on the ground raised himself briefly on one elbo, said, "Jessie I've been shot" and collapsed mortally wounded.

The American officer bleeding on the ground was Maj Arthur D. Nicholson US Army. His last words were spoken to his driver Army Staff Sergeant Jessie Schatz. Both were assigned to the United States Military Liaison Mission (USMLM) located in Potsdam, East Germany or the German Democratic Republic (GDR) as it was officially known in 1985. All three personnel involved in the shooting had one other thing in common: they were all assigned or accredited to the Group of Soviet Forces in Germany (GSFG).

Who was Nicholson and what was this US Army officer doing on a Soviet training area in the middle of communist East Germany? "Nick" Nicholson was a Russian linguist and Soviet military specialist trained in the US Army's well-regarded Foreign Area Officer (FAO) program established after WWII to prepare a cadre of officers knowledgeable in Soviet military matters. He had eagerly sought an assignment to Potsdam thinking what better place to learn about the Soviet military than where Moscow's premier offensive force, GSFG, lived and trained. Accredited to GSFG Headquarters was a group of Americans known as the United States Military Liaison Mission (USMLM). USMLM had an unusual chain of command. As a tenant in Berlin the Mission was obviously sensitive to the prerogatives of the US Commandant Berlin who provided funding for the unit from the plentiful larder of the occupation budget. But he had no say in what USMLM did or how it did it. USMLM was also mindful of the various US diplomatic missions in East and West Germany and the several regional US military commands but none of these (often to their chagrin) had any input let alone influence over USMLM activities. USMLM had only one boss, the Commander-in-Chief US Army Europe (CINCUSAREUR), who was located several hours away in Heidelberg, West Germany.

USMLM's liaison responsibility provided the status, protection (such as it was), and access to the GDR that made possible the Mission's second and far more important mission: collecting military intelligence on Soviet Forces and the East German Army (NVA).

Within five years the Berlin Wall came down, Germany was reunited and Soviet forces began their exodus to a homeland that itself was undergoing historical changes. Collecting intelligence until the very end, USMLM monitored the withdrawal of GSFG out of Germany and across the Polish border. One of the last photos the Mission ever took was of a Soviet troop train with a large sign on the side of a railcar with the words "WE WILL BE BACK". In retrospect this seems less chilling than pathetic bluster. Russia would soon find itself in no position to defend its borders let alone threaten neighbors. But during the four decades following WWII that it hunkered in Germany it did threaten, credibly and convincingly – but more transparently thanks to fourteen Americans.

Below is a small part of the USAREUR History Office's declassified account of MAJ Nicholson's murder. Keep in mind this was just recently declassified. As previously stated, you can read the entire report by going to that web site listed at the beginning of the chapter and scrolling down to 'The Nicholson Incident – A Case Study Of US-Soviet Relations'.

Declassified now – new interviews

Comments from Col. Ron Gambolati, USAR (ret.), in response to author's questions (a member of the report)
Thursday, October 11, 2007 9:58 PM
Q. Describe your role in the affair (remember, all now declassified). Tell us what you know. Describe your feelings.
A. Let me know if you want the unpopular truth or the official version. OK, you have indicated you want the truth as I saw it. First, you must realize the report, I believe, was a whitewash. State Dept milked it for all it was worth and then SECDEF declared victory and dropped the issue … There was no way the US would admit to being wrong.

The truth will not be popular because we created a myth in order to further our ends. We only partially quoted the CG MEDCOM but I remember his remarks as clearly as if he said them today: Nicholson died in seconds. If he had been shot on the front steps of Mass General, no one would have been able to save him.

Yet we made it sound as if Nicholson had suffered for hours while denied medical attention. Also, no one wanted to hear "Soviet base, Soviet rules." We wanted to apply US/Western standards when it was their game. I will say this: LTC Larry Kelly, USMC, is one of the finest officers ever to wear an American military uniform. I respect him beyond words.

In regards to your other question: I firmly believe (and reported such to our British and French allies) that SMLM-F was tangentially involved in verification of conventional forces reduction in USAREUR.

Comments from Major General (Ret.) Roland Lajoie, commander at the time of USMLM (then COL) in response to author's questions
Friday, October 12, 2007 5:14 PM

Q. Here were my questions to the General:
1. If any, what successes do you see coming out of all this?
2. What, if anything, would you do differently?
3. Why do you think the Soviets didn't let us administer first aid?
4. Do you think it would have helped? From what I read in the 2004 declassified report, the wound was almost surely fatal.
5. Did LTC Nicholson receive appropriate recognition?
6. Do you consider him a hero?
7. How can I get in contact with the widow to interview (or her contact me)?
8. Do you care to comment on COL Gambolati's comments?

A. The most complete responses to your questions are contained in Annex F to the 1985 USMLM History. Larry Kelley wrote it under my supervision and with a lot of my personal input. We were the first two Americans on the scene that night. Our report was certainly not a whitewash. The basic facts are not in dispute. Nick and his driver were on a routine USMLM tour i.e. recon mission on the grounds of a sub-caliber training range which was located behind Mission Restricted Signs (universally ignored by all 3 Missions) but not in a Temporary or Permanent Restricted Area. Nick was dismounted and poking around and taking pictures of the tank sheds and the bulletin board which contained miscellaneous technical information. Schatz was sitting on the roof of the vehicle keeping watch. Suddenly a sentry whom they had not seen opened fire without warning. The first shot barely missed Schatz and one of the next 2 shots hit Nick in the center of the body severing the renal artery. He bled to death in a very short time.

I also remember the comment quoted to you by Ron. I agree with his recollection with a slight change. I thought the doctor said that if Nick had suffered that gunshot wound outside of Mass General he might have been saved, but not likely. That wound in the middle of a field in East Germany was fatal. The initial reaction of the sentry forcing Schatz back in the vehicle seemed to be the panicky reaction of a scared kid not a deliberate decision to deny first aid. The thrust of our criticism of the Soviets was not that they deliberately let him bleed to death but that for about an hour never even checked on him.

Nick was given a hero's funeral and considerable recognition. A small ceremony has been held at his grave site at Arlington every single year since his death. Numerous Army facilities in the US and Europe are named after him, including a monument in Ludwigslust near the shooting site.

SECDEF Weinberger may have considered this the murder of an unarmed soldier in broad daylight in Germany but we in the Mission understood that although unprovoked and unnecessary it was the unfortunate consequence of doing inherently dangerous intelligence collection against the Soviet Union's premier offensive force in Europe. We operated very effectively in a grey zone that exploited our anachronistic status. This, however, was an inherently dangerous grey zone that we preferred not be clarified. This led to considerable tension between us and USAREUR HQ, which in the aftermath of the shooting wanted to save us from ourselves. Ron, I am sure can add a lot on this subject.

I think you should respect Nicholson's widow's privacy, re. her interview.

Good luck on your project, Roland Lajoie.

Comments from Mr. Bruce Siemon, USAREUR historian, then and now – in response to author's questions

Wednesday, October 24, 2007 2:49 AM

Q. After looking at these two observations, would you care to comment?

A. I can't (and shouldn't) comment, since I was not directly involved in things. Anything I might contribute is only hearsay, my passing on of things I heard from those who were directly involved (or worse yet, from third parties who were telling me what THEY heard from direct participants). I was later involved with the research and writing of the historical monograph on the subject, but even there my role was secondary. Bill Stacy did the hard work and wrote the manuscript.

So, I don't feel qualified to comment on the incident, other than to say that I trust the accounts of Gen Lajoie and COL Kelley, and that I believe Bill Stacy did a thorough and honest job of researching. If Bill says something and has a footnote, I am certain the document will substantiate what Bill wrote.

Best regards Bruce

But Bruce later did comment:

Wednesday, October 24, 2007 7:43 AM

I attended the dedication of the Nicholson memorial at Ludwigslust in March 2005. I met and talked with Gen Lajoie and COL Kelley and Dr. Helmut Trotnow of the Allied Museum Berlin (the man to the left of the podium, from the viewer's perspective, in the photo of Gen Lajoie speaking), and a number of other people – some US (including USMLM veterans and representatives from the U.S. Embassy), some German civilian and military members of official delegations, and also some "East" Germans (i.e., people from the Ludwigslust area who were involved with the memorial project). After the formal events by the side of the road, we all went to a reception in town – finger food and wine at the cost of the city administration. I met a number of very pleasant German civilians, including one woman who with tears in her eyes explained that but for people like Nicholson and all the rest of the Americans she would be in prison, not attending a memorial ceremony for an American hero. She represented a group called Victims of Socialism and had laid a wreath at the memorial during the ceremonies. I had expected good representation from the U.S. side, and from German officials, but the local German citizens turned out in much larger numbers than I had anticipated. This was not one of those displays that were common under the Communist regime. The local people were there voluntarily because they cared and wanted to show their appreciation and respect for "Nick" Nicholson. It was a very moving experience.

New photos and comments by R. W. Rynerson

The author concludes there are some gray areas but no real deception. I will tell you at the time, I remember the impression that the Soviets let him bleed to death. You, the reader, are the final judge.

There is a lot going on in this photo. The woman at left is a local community booster who is involved with Ludwigslust's sister city (Muscatine, Iowa). The man watching me is possibly part of the hostility and monitoring that I ran into while speaking with some local people. General Lajoie is deep in reflective thought at right (raincoat). (R.W. Rynerson)

The dedication of the Nicholson memorial – General Lajoie speaks. (R.W. Rynerson)

15

Border patrol

Nickname: The Black Horse Regiment *Motto*: *Allons* (Let's Go)

Introduction
First Squadron occupied OP Alpha

One day in 1985, our team was invited to present a security seminar at the 11th ACR on USAREUR's eastern border in Fulda, Germany. The picture below commemorates our visit to this important unit. I'm in an observation post (OP) in West Germany that looks over the border fence, cleared "no-man's-land" and then into East Germany. Across the border in the distance you can see one of their OPs. The term Fulda Gap was a much used military term because the lay of the land was less harsh and flatter than elsewhere and would have been a key avenue for Soviet armor to advance west, had the balloon gone up.

Wikipedia tells us:

> The 11th ACR's principal adversary was the Soviet 8th Guards Army. The US armored cavalry (heavy, mechanized reconnaissance units equipped with tanks and armored personnel carriers) were expected to delay a Warsaw Pact advance long enough for U.S. divisions stationed near Frankfurt to assemble and move to the Fulda Gap.

The author in an observation post on the border. An East German outpost is visible in the background. (Author's collection)

Both opponents were lavishly equipped and generally received a high priority on new equipment.

Soviet armor and weapons the 11th ACR might have faced if an attack came from the East

Frank R. Shirer Army Chief, Historical Resources Branch, provides historical detail on the M-60 ammunition rounds. Its 105-mm main gun used rounds such as:

- APFSDS – Armor Piercing, Fin stabilized, Discarding Sabot.
- APERS-T – Flechette or "beehive" round (anti-personnel).
- HEP – High Explosive Plastic, a shaped charge. Also known as HESH – High Explosive Squash Head.
- WP – White Phosphorus aka smoke aka "willie pete".
- HEAT – High Explosive Anti-Tank.

જ

The 11th ACR was a critical unit in the linchpin of the USAREUR defense plan. At times I suppose incredibly boring, but just being there as a literal attack blocker, served its purpose.

"The Frontier Of Freedom" – the Fulda Gap, 1972 – 1994

On 17 May 1972 the 14th Armored Cavalry Regiment furled its colors and was reflagged as the 11th Armored Cavalry Regiment. The Regiment once again unfurled its colors in Germany. This time it was at the famous Fulda Gap. The Regiment assumed a new, two-fold mission; defending the Fulda Gap against a possible Warsaw Pact attack while also conducting day-to-day surveillance of 385 kilometers of the Iron Curtain dividing East and West Germany. The Regiment relieved the inactivated 14th Armored Cavalry Regiment and joined V Corps – "The Victory Corps."

The Regimental mission in the General Defense Plan (GDP) was to strongly reinforce the United States Army Europe (USAREUR) as the covering force for V Corps. The importance of the Fulda Gap is that it offers to any attacker from the east the shortest and most direct route across the middle of West Germany. A successful thrust through the Fulda Gap, aimed at seizing the Rhine River crossings at Mainz and Koblenz, would sever West German and NATO forces defending it.

As so often in the Regiment's history, it had to disperse its squadrons. Located at Downs Barracks in the city of Fulda were the Regimental Headquarters and First Squadron, known as "Ironhorse." Second Squadron, known as "Eaglehorse," was stationed at Daley Barracks in the spa city of Bad Kissingen. Third Squadron, known as "Workhorse," established its new home at McPheeters Barracks, Bad Hersfeld. Fourth Squadron, or "Thunderhorse," was in Fulda, at Sickels Army Airfield, where aviation elements were stationed. Fourth Squadron grew to become one of the largest aviation units in the Army with 74 helicopters. A comprehensive effort to upgrade/modernize the Regiment's various installations was begun by Crosbie Saint, (47th Colonel of the Regiment). The "Quality of Life" program made living conditions more suitable for the Regiment.

Modernization brought with it organizational change on a comparable scale. The Regiment grew in size, became more diverse in its capabilities and increased its self-sufficiency. The Regiment now numbered over 4,600 soldiers, a four-fold increase over the original 1901 troop count. In 1985 the newly-formed Combat Support Squadron, known as "Packhorse," was activated in Fulda. Maintenance Troop was the largest in the Regiment with 366 troopers. Of special note was the 58th Combat Engineer Company, known as the "Red Devils," who won the Itschner Award, symbolic of the best Combat Engineer unit in the U.S. Army. In 1991 the 511th Military Intelligence Company, known as "Trojan Horse," was selected as the best company-sized intelligence unit in the Army.

Border operations were serious business. Each cavalry troop of the Regiment could expect border duty four times a year – each tour lasting 21-30 days. Duty day began with a 0600 border briefing, a review of SOP's and an update on the latest sightings or incidents. Part of the mission was to demonstrate to potential adversaries that the Blackhorse, representing all NATO forces, was well-disciplined and ready to fight. The trooper's gear had to be clean, boots highly polished, uniforms pressed, weapons spotless, and radios operational. After inspection, the troopers were divided into reaction forces, observation posts (OP's), and patrol duty (PD's). Usually two armored vehicles with 10 men would respond virtually without notice to any contingency along the border. The crews had 10 minutes to be moving out of the camp gate – fully equipped, weapons mounted, ammunition on board. Patrolling was a 24 hours a day, 7 days a week function.

Observation Posts (OP's) served as base camps as well as vantage points for observation. First Squadron occupied OP Alpha near Hunfeld-Schlitz-Lauterbach. Second Squadron was at Camp Lee northeast of Bad Kissingen near Bad Neustadt. Troops were dispatched to OP Tennessee. Third Squadron manned two OPs; Romeo, overlooking the Eisenach-Bad Hersfeld autobahn, at Herleshausen, which was a legal crossing point.

The Wall Came Down, 9 November 1989

The Warsaw Pact and the legitimacy of the Eastern Europe's Communist military regimes was disintegrating. The stage was clearly set for a dramatic transformation of the European *status quo* that had existed since the Cold War began.

One historic day changed the mission of the Regiment in Fulda irrevocably. On 1 March 1990 the Regiment ceased border operations altogether and closed its OPs. Less than eleven months after the border opened for the two Germanys to re-unite, the Blackhorse lost its claim of being a "Border Regiment."

The Regiment's legacy was a justifiable pride at having played an important role in one of the greatest victories of military history, a victory all the more remarkable for having been won without firing a shot.

The above is used by permission of the U.S. Army PAO, from the 11th ACR homepage.

Incoming … True Stories from the 11th ACR

Patrick McDonald
I suppose we should have been more worried about the ammo, and less worried about the flowers.
From 1984 to 1986 I was a soldier assigned to Alpha Troop, 1st Squadron of the 11th Armored Cavalry Regiment. At that time the mission of the 11th ACR was to guard the border between East and West Germany at a place called the Fulda Gap. According to all the military experts, if the Soviet Union was ever to attack the West, most likely they would spearhead through "The Gap."

Now, one regiment against the entire Warsaw Pact was very poor odds, and so most of us lowly troopers considered ourselves dead meat should the flag ever go up. But we were young, and with youth comes that feeling of immortality which caused us to shrug off the danger and concentrate on more important things, like trying to pull a little fun out of the boredom involved.

20+ years later I was running a website to help writers find literary agents, when an aspiring writer by the name of Lee McCaslin contacted me with some questions. We struck up a conversation, and he told me a little about his book and sent me a photo. To my surprise I recognized the photo immediately, or at least the setting. It was a picture of Lee standing atop the guard tower at OP Alpha. This was the Observation Post used by the 11th ACR which overlooked East Germany.

When Lee asked me to write up a little blurb about my experiences on the border, he asked me to include some stories about my "adventures." Well, I hate to disappoint anyone, but there wasn't much adventure going on. We traded shifts standing in the tower watching some East German who was watching us watch him. When we were not doing that, we were cleaning the compound so when the inevitable dignitary came to visit, it would be presentable. This cleaning took the majority of our time.

I remember one spring when the compound became overgrown with wildflowers. It was colorful and cheerful and, I thought, gave the place a nice homey look. But the Squadron Sergeant-Major didn't feel that way, and so he had about five of us spend the entire day walking around the area pulling up flowers. I suppose they just weren't military enough for him.

On one of our more boring days, when for some reason I don't recall, we were left without any officers or high-ranking NCOs to keep an eye on us, we decided to have a little fun. Whenever a dignitary visited, the East Germans would notice the extra activity and break out a high-powered camera to take pictures of whoever it was visiting, so we decided to put on a show for them. One of our guys stuck globs of aluminum foil to his hat and uniform epaulet, so from a distance he would appear to be a general or something. We then held a little ceremony as if we were welcoming him to the OP, and made a very big fuss of over-saluting him. Still in character, he went up to the tower for a look around, as all the dignitaries did, and we watched the cameras come out and start taking his picture. I like to think that somewhere in KGB Headquarters these pictures still exist, and that they spent a lot of time trying to figure out just who this guy was.

I can think of only one situation that may be considered "adventurous." One day an East German car was seen driving along the border between the fences. There were two fences on the border, both within East Germany and about 30 feet apart, with the land between fences often patrolled by East German soldiers or dogs. But in this case a civilian car was driving between the fences. We had received a radio call from a sister observation post that the car had passed through their area and was headed our way. Me and another soldier were sent up into the tower with an M-60 machine gun and told that if the car or passengers attempted to flee to the West, we were to cover their escape, opening fire if necessary. Now that I think about it, that may have been against U.S. policy, but those were our orders. It didn't matter anyway. All ammunition was in sealed containers only to be opened in the event of an emergency. When we were given the go-ahead to break the seal on the ammo canister, we were horrified to find that the links which held the rounds together were so old that they had rusted away. Of course, this made firing the weapon impossible and we could do nothing but watch as the car continued to drive past us. As far as I know, it never attempted to escape and the East Germans never did anything to stop it.

After this we were told to enter the ammunition locker and clean things up. We discovered the entire stock of ammo to be in the same poor state. Yup, the links fell apart in our hands because they were so rusted. I suppose we should have been more worried about the ammo, and less worried about the flowers.

Patrick McDonald, Specialist-4, 1st Platoon, Alpha Troop, 1st Squadron, 11th Armored Cavalry Regiment. (November 1984 – October 1986)

Curt Poppe
Crazy bunch of dudes
I am a retired SFC, was a PLT SGT with 501St MI Bn out of Katterbach, FRG 1980-1983, in support of 1ST A.D., prior to the Wall coming down of course. We covered the Fulda Gap and had some run-ins with the 11 ACR. They were a crazy bunch of dudes.

Our area of deployment included Cheb/Eger on the border. Had some of my teams deployed one time on the border for training exercise and they were overrun by 11 ACR. These guys treated my guys as enemy, raided the camp, tried to enter the Intel area [preceding term changed by author] and my guys locked it up, staying inside the hut. They threw down on rest of the platoon and searched them, etc. WENT NUTS! One of my guys in the hut (a no-balls kind of guy) gave in to their threats and let them in, comprising info!

Ended up my guy that gave it up lost his clearance (ditto) and the 11 ACR guys got nothing, including the LT in charge!

Definitely a lack of NCO leadership. Any self-respecting, knowledgeable NCO would have kept his LT in check!

Curt Poppe, SFC, RET

Dick Hinderliter
It is a smell a person will never forget.
Although not during the Fulda Gap era, SFC Hinderliter tells us this exciting story about what he faced in Viet Nam.

I was attached to the 11th ACR, Black Horse Div, in Viet Nam in 1967, at Xuan Loc and Long Gao. Being Signal, they told us when the perimeter was under attacked, we were to just stay in our bunkers and let the tanks, APC's, etc. take care of the problems. Our perimeter was hit many times but was never penetrated.

On the outer perimeter, they had cleared fields with claymores and land mines (Personnel), then came the barbed wire fences stacked roll on top of roll for about 10 feet.

The next protection line was tanks with flame throwers and fiftys, APC with sixtys and big search lights. They had armor about every fifty feet completely around our camp.

We also had many Huey gunships on the air strip. Of course, nightly we would get incoming mortars trying to knock out the gunships and occasionally they would rush the barb wire with the first wave throwing them on the wire so their next wave could run up over their backs and get over the wire. That did not work very good for them though because all the flame throwers would light up and the machine guns would get the ones that didn't fry on the wire. It is a smell a person will never forget.

Dick Hinderliter, SFC, US Army 1954-1977.

Dick Hinderliter died since he wrote and sent me this story. We celebrate and are thankful for his life (03/09/29 – 01/21/08).

16

SETAF – Rapid Reaction Force – Paratroopers

Below is from the SETAF Homepage.

Introduction

Q. What is the SETAF Mission?

A. On order, USA SETAF (Airborne) forms, deploys, and employs Joint Forces as a Combined, Joint, or Army Task Force to achieve full spectrum dominance across the range of military operations where directed.

Above, define **Combined** as multinational and **Joint** as multi-US Service.

SETAF is USAREUR's Southern European Task Force located in Vicenza, Italy, not far from the beautiful island of Venice. With its 173rd Airborne Brigade and other fighting units, SETAF is the only rapid deployment force in USAREUR.

A real G-2 there tells us:

The *Alpini* had a contingent at Caserme Ederle to guard the base and our housing area, Villagio. The *Alpini* are the elite Italian mountain infantry. The *Folgore*[1] often came to our ceremonies ... a very colorful unit. Their band would always perform as a tribute to the US ... they have flowing feathered hats and run in a continuous serial column as they play.

SETAF is intended to remain after the current draw down of major Army forces in Europe. SETAF is the strategic reaction force for the European command...and handled many of the Embassy evacuations and humanitarian relief operations in Africa.

Will this change with the forthcoming AFRICOM? When I asked the new J2 of AFRICOM, Terry Ford, if he thought SETAF would play a lesser role in Africa he said, "Don't know, but suspect SETAF will continue to play a big role in Africa once AFRICOM is fully stood up. We still will need trainers, humanitarian assistance support, etc."

Commander's staff in SETAF and elsewhere

Commanders have staffs to assist them. Depending on the configuration and size of the unit, the staffs will either be an S, G, or J staff (with the same staff designation numbers, such as S1, G1 or J1). These letters and numbers are explained below.

First, let's discuss the letters.

- An "**S**" staff is in a smaller unit, such as a brigade or a battalion, commanded by a Colonel or lesser rank.
- A "**G**" staff is in a larger unit, such as a division or a corps, commanded by a General Officer.
- A "**J**" staff is in a larger unit with different service components (Army, Navy, AF, Marines) in the staff. The new command in Africa is going to be a joint command

---

1   Author's Note: The *Folgore* Parachute Brigade is the largest unit of paratroopers of the Italian Army.

with a J Staff (J1, J2, J3 and J4). This type unit is known as a Purple Suit unit, figuratively blending the colors of the separate components uniforms.

- In a small unit, such as a company, the staff to assist the commander may consist of only one person, the Executive Officer (XO). Larger units have more staff personnel which are divided into at least 4 sections, with these numbers.
- Personnel, the first staff section, deals with everything to do with the people in the units. They handle the unit's personnel paperwork such as issuing orders for assignments, travel, salaries, and awards. In a civilian company, they would be known as Human Resources. A small unit's personnel staff would be called the S1.
- Intelligence, the second staff section, is responsible for collecting and analyzing information on the enemy situation confronting the commander. They advise him as to what the enemy's capabilities and intentions are. A small unit's intelligence staff would be called the S2.
- Operations, the third staff area, writes all the detail plans for accomplishing the Commander's mission. This section plans, executes and evaluates military operations. It is usually the largest staff section and considered the most important. A small unit's operations staff would be called the S3.
- Logistics, the fourth staff section, is concerned with supplies and services for the unit, such as ammunition, material, maintenance, food, water, gas, and transportation. A small unit's logistics staff would be called the S4.
- Other staff elements of larger units may be represented by the number G5 (Civil –Military Operations), G6 (Command, control, communications and computer operations) and the G7 (Information operations officer). These numbered staffs 1-7 are called the Coordinating Staff Group.
- The Commander may also have a Personal Staff Group consisting of the Command Sergeant Major, Aides, Inspector General, Staff Judge Advocate, Chaplain and Public Affairs Officer.
- Finally, there may be a Special Staff Group consisting of many functional area experts such as the Surgeon, Resource Management, Staff Weather Office, Civilian Personnel Office, Safety Office, Veterinarian, Protocol, History, Aviation and others.

Back to SETAF …

Separate ground, sea, and air warfare is gone forever. If ever again we should be involved in war, we will fight it in all elements, with all services, as one single concentrated effort. (Dwight D. Eisenhower)

SETAF has many airborne qualified units to reach objectives quickly and carry out its mission, no matter what it might be. Some of the subordinate units are the:

- 173rd Airborne Brigade Combat Team.
- 1st Battalion (Airborne), 503D Infantry "First Rock."
- 2nd Battalion (Airborne), 503D Infantry "The Rock."
- 4th Battalion, 319th Airborne Field Artillery Regiment "King of the Herd."
- 1st Squadron, 91st US Cavalry "The Airborne Cav."
- 173rd Special Troops Battalion
- 173rd Support Battalion (Airborne) "To Our Upmost."

Stories from airborne paratroopers – and their first jumps!

Frank R. Brown III

I'm not sure I would feel comfortable jumping tandem like they do nowadays. I think I would insist on going it alone. That is … airborne all the way!

I climbed out on the strut of the Cessna. It was October 4, 1964. The Cessna was about 2500 feet above the ground, flying at about 90 miles per hour. I waited for the signal to GO. I released my hold, arched my back, and stuck out my arms spread eagle as the Army taught me. I fell away from the aircraft and started to roll. I resisted that motion. I anchored the parachute to the plane by a "static line". It opened automatically.

I had reentered West Virginia University Graduate School in February. I say reentered because you will see what I mean later. To be honest I was not doing too well. I found it hard to settle down. I joined the Morgantown Sky Divers. They held a mini course on how to land with several of us. I executed the Parachute Landing Fall or PLF easily. They complimented me on learning so quickly. If they only knew! Next, after they outfitted us with boots, which I already had, they gave me a jump suit, hard hat, and goggles.

With the parachute opened I looked up to see the panels removed. Ordinarily if I saw a hole larger than a helmet, I would have considered activating my reserve chute. I reached up along the risers and found the toggles. I was not used to having them. With a moment of experimentation, I rotated to face the "T" on the ground that was the landing spot.

I was drafted out of West Virginia University Graduate School in 1962 after the Berlin Wall went up. Basic Training was at Fort Dix, NJ. There were many college graduates in my basic training company. Somewhere the staff presented a program on the Airborne. They emphasized that it was the first step to getting in the Special Forces.

I have experience as a Boy Scout hiker and camper and felt I was able to take care of myself outdoors so I signed up. I thought nothing would come of it because I already had an assigned MOS, Military Occupational Specialty (MOS), as a crewman on an Honest John Artillery Rocket. I attended Advance Training on the Honest John at Fort Sill Oklahoma. There I was a squad leader because I had had ROTC some years before at MIT. Six of us were sent to Fort Benning, GA to the US Army Airborne School.

Rotating to face the "T" was the wrong idea. This put the cut-out panels at my back and jetted me along over the ground. I was way off course. I was descending… directly toward a nearby farmhouse. I thought I would collide with the sidewall and slide down the house.

Once at Ft. Benning I was put to gardening. We had to wait for the cycle to come around. Then we began Ground week. It began with a physical testing. I was in good shape. I had saber fenced in college and now had been through army basic training. We faced our fears and ended up having a lot of fun jumping out of the 32 foot tower and riding the pulley to the mound at the other end. I sure did my share of push-ups. Tower week followed. I got one jump from the 250 tower. I do not know whether it was because I did it so badly they would not let me try it again or I just happened to do it right. Jump week came next. The Staff and Cadre did not really harass us during that week. Monday morning after the usual PT with run, we went out to the hanger and they issued parachutes.

I had flown in airplanes many times before, but we had one student who had never been up in an airplane before. So, for him it was a big thrill. The airplane was a C-119. The seat was uncomfortable. We flew around a bit so the Air Force Reserve Pilot could get in his airtime and to gage the winds over the drop zone. I napped. Most future parachutists were slightly apprehensive, but very well trained. I accomplished my first jump without incident. As a college graduate in engineering, I trusted what I knew about physics and air resistance, i.e. how a parachute works. After four more jumps, including two on one day we received our wings as certified paratroopers. Then the Army sent me to the 82nd Airborne Division at Fort Bragg, NC. There after spending a night or two in the Replacement Company they assigned me to Battery B 377th Artillery. It had just converted from an Honest John to a "Little John" rocket battery. The Little John was a smaller and air-transportable rocket. It could deliver an atomic warhead. Remember the Cold War was on.

I was in the Battery when the movie the Longest Day came out. I remember the scene where the paratrooper comes down in the garden and scares the old lady.

I slide-slipped the house. Next up or down in this case was an apple orchard. I passed right through the treetops lifting my feet and made a perfect PLF in the garden. Just like in the movies. My sky diving log reads TFTM, Too Far To Measure. Usually sky divers land very close to the "T". I wrapped up my parachute and walked back to the Drop Zone mightily embarrassed.

Most people, who are old enough, know right where they were when they got the news of the shooting of President Kennedy in Dallas. I was delivering a message to the second platoon. When I heard it, I thought they were kidding and said, "Good, I hope we get a holiday."

Within a month of arriving at the 120-man battery I knew everyone's name. Now 50 years later I can only recall a few. For instance I do remember we had a soldier named "Black" but he wasn't, one soldier named "White" (he wasn't), one named "Blue" (and he certainly wasn't) and one named "Brown" (and I'm not). I have never run across anyone from the same Battery. I had a POV, privately owned vehicle, after a while. My car was a rear wheeled air-cooled engine Corvair. I took several paratroopers, at different times, into caving country in West Virginia. We would explore caves on the weekends. Two of the soldiers, Ed and Walt, ended up marrying local West Virginian girls.

In the 82nd I made 16 jumps total. Later after discharge and returning to Morgantown and WVU, I made five more jumps. On the fifth jump, I cracked a leg bone. A green stick split they called it. I made one more jump in NJ. But somehow the adventure had worn off.

I have often thought I would like to try jumping again. But I got married to a nice Lithuanian girl chemist and raised four boys to be engineers. I'm not sure I would feel comfortable jumping tandem like they do now a days. I think I would insist on going it alone. That is going AIRBORNE – All the Way!!

Frank Tapparo

I had a bit of a scare on the fifth, mass, jump when I landed on the chute of someone jumping before me. I remember taking those giant steps to get off the chute before mine collapsed...

I'm Frank Tapparo, LTC, USAR (Ret), who spent eleven years on active duty with service, that included almost four years in Germany and about a year and a half in Vietnam. Following active duty, I was on the staff of the Secretary of Defense in the Pentagon for twenty-three years and a member of the Senior Executive Service for twenty of those years.

Why I wanted to be Airborne (and Ranger)? I think vanity was the strongest reason. Although I came on active duty assigned to the Infantry, my basic branch was Chemical

Corps and I felt that I needed all the "merit badges" I could get to show that I was as good as any "full-time" Infantry officer. I was a Regular officer ("short" service number, "lifer") in the Chemical Corps as the result of my being a Distinguished Military Graduate from MIT, where all senior cadets were assigned to a technical service. Being a chemical engineering student, I was "automatically" in the Chemical Corps section of the ROTC. While all Regular officers had to go to either Airborne or Ranger school, I chose to go to both of them. I arrived at Ft. Benning in September 1960 and left in April 1961 proudly wearing both Airborne wings and a Ranger tab.

I finished the basic infantry officer's course in December 1960, too late to begin an Airborne class before the Christmas holiday break. Nevertheless, I, along with a number of others from my infantry class, were assigned to the Airborne School and given bunks in a barracks near Lawson Army Airfield. Incidentally, at that time we spent some of our idle time watching trials of the CV-2, Caribou, the Army designation for the aircraft later transferred to the Air Force and renamed the C-7. Those weeks between completing officer basic and the Christmas holidays were spent doing E-1-type duties. I recall having to police the billet area; a platoon or so of second lieutenants being led by a master sergeant, master jumper saying as we picked up butts and other trash, "All I want to see are asses and elbows!" After police duty we were given packs of stickers and sent to empty buildings in the Airborne Department area where we affixed "turn out the lights" stickers to every light switch. On 24 December I was relieved of my duties and headed to New Hampshire, where I was married on 31 December and returned to Ft. Benning and Airborne School with my bride.

I have saved my Airborne School "classbook," so I can tell you that I was in Airborne Class 19 that graduated 3 February 1961. There were 159 students in our class, 146 of us newly minted lieutenants, as well as a colonel and two captains. Also in the class were nine privates from the Utah National Guard and a reserve sergeant from Florida. We were there four weeks, with the first week devoted to PT and air transportability and aerial delivery techniques using mock-ups of a C-123 and a C-130. An interesting feature of the class was that we did not have class on Wednesday afternoons. I recall that breather was to allow us to get our uniforms in order, as enlisted men (EM) were required to have only three sets of fatigues and the free afternoon allowed EMs to have their laundry done and, thus, a fresh uniform for the remaining two days of the week. Whether that explanation was true or not, I do not know. I know I had sufficient fatigues to be able to "break starch" every day. I also remember having my boots shined by the bootblack in the student officers' mess across the street from Benning's jump towers. Along with a bunch of other guys, each morning I would put my dirty boots in a closet by the bootblack's work area and retrieve my newly shined boots. I think that service cost us 25 cents a day. I also recall that one day class was cancelled because of a severe ice storm the night before; also that we were given an extra long lunch hour on 20 January to watch John Kennedy being inaugurated.

After that first week of PT and air mobility techniques we began the "real" jump class. My experiences were no different from thousands of others—"first week, trolley troopers; second week, tower troopers; third week, paratroopers." A few things about the training stand out vividly today, especially the morning inspections with toes on the cables lining the ground. There were the behind-the-buckle inspections to make sure no Brasso lingered there. (The buckle that I shined so well for Airborne school—inside and out—I used throughout my Army career, several times buffing it on a rouge wheel in a post craft shop after scratching it.) And then there were the "drop down and give me ten" for the slightest infraction. Yes, I remember the "suspended agony," the swing landing trainer, and the 34-foot tower. Although my classbook says that about ten percent of a class typically washed-out for fear of jumping from the 34-foot tower, I do not remember the first tower jump being that scary. The real thrill came from the free-fall jumping from the 250-foot tower. Those jumps gave you the freedom to act individually with just a bit of instruction from the NCO on the ground. I loved it.

You ask about the emotion of the first jump. We jumped from C-123's and what I recall was the opportunity to be on one's own and not being yelled at by an NCO. The thrill was jumping from the noisy airplane into the silence of the air and the all-too-quick descent. I had no fear on the first jump; that came on the second, when I began to think of all that could go wrong. My apprehension did not keep me from jumping on command, nor did it cause me to throw-up in the plane, as happened to one of my stick mates. After landing, he was hustled back to Lawson where he had to clean up the mess he had made in the plane.

I had a bit of a scare on the fifth, mass, jump when I landed on the chute of someone jumping before me. I remember taking those giant steps to get off the chute before mine collapsed, which I succeeded in doing. After that fifth jump we were allowed to stay in the jump area with our wives who had come to the jump area and who all knew which plane carried their husbands and his position in a stick (the line of paratroopers in a plane ready to jump – or stick). We joked that the wives would say, "My husband is coming down faster than your husband!" After the last stick had jumped—and one of the guys on the last plane had dealt successfully with a "cigarette roll" and used his reserve chute—we assembled on the jump zone and received our coveted wings.

For me, it was then a quick kiss to my wife and onto the bus, as we were late for the PT test that would get us into Ranger school. But that's another story.

Hakon Hansen
Accidents were never amusing! I knew some fellow soldiers that had been tragically killed while jumping. They will not be forgotten …
I'm … Sgt Hakon Hansen.
Why?
I wanted to be "AIRBORNE" because of the *esprit de corps* that went with being in the 82nd Airborne Division that I always heard about and wanted as a soldier. As an Airborne soldier, you were never ever considered just your average soldier, but one of the best and bravest that would meet any challenge brought forth, and you could always count on the man to your right and left of you!!! "Airborne."
Training.
Training was easy for me physically and mentally but neverending for three weeks. The slow pace of the runs was daunting and painful on the shins, but I made it through without injury to myself. Whoa …
First Jump (emotion?)
In my first jump, I was very scared, unsure and exhilarated of what it was going to be like jumping out of a perfectly good airplane! When the "jump master" started giving the hand commands to stand up! And hook up! This was it, no turning back now. I would think to myself, then the silent commands of 'One minute', then '30 seconds', and all the time looking at that red light knowing that the light was going to turn green at any second. Then

you hear the words, 'GO' and soldiers on both sides of the plane start to shuffle to the exit door of the plane like little penguins loaded with all the gear that weighed approximately 100 to 130 lbs, that made you waddle like a penguin, depending on your mission. Then as I got to the door and gave my static line to the jump master, and looked him straight into his eyes and turned into the air to drop 30 feet and to suddenly feel the shock of the static line pulling the chute out of your pack tray on your back was something that I had never felt before. This was followed by the opening of the chute looking up and knowing that everything was going to be alright. Then I watched the plane gently fly out away, the silence of slowly falling to "God's" earth was truly breathtaking and unforgettable to this day. I felt like a proud Eagle!

Night jump
My first night jump was very intimidating for me. Think about it, you're jumping into an unknown drop zone where other soldiers and their equipment had already landed. And guess what? You were jumping very close to where they were or right on top of them.

Danger
When you're "Airborne," there is always the element of danger that present.

Injury
Oh yeah!!! Cracked my tail bone a few times, slight concussion, and of course the back injury.

HALO
No HALO[2] for me I wanted to try it, but you had to be on a Ranger team to get the school.

Amusing incident
Accidents were never amusing! I knew some fellow soldiers that had been tragically killed while jumping. They will not be forgotten....

William Brazil
This was the old airborne training command. Nothing was easy.
3 Feb 2008 – I'm William Brazil. I joined the army to go directly into the Airborne. This was Sept. 10, 1955. I had just turned 17 and my education was formally at an eighth grade level; that in reality wasn't even equal to a fifth grade rank.

When I first got into the army I went directly to Fort Dix, N J for training. This lasted nine weeks. I then went home for two weeks leave. Then I reported in to Fort Bragg, NC, 82nd Airborne Division, for artillery training. In those four weeks, we were drilled relentlessly and physically pushed. We were given constant classes on the stripping and use of infantry weapons such as the .30 and .I 50 caliber machine guns. No howitzers. No artillery at all. It seemed the airborne always wanted to see if you would quit. Many guys did. Numerous guys went AWOL. This was the old Airborne Training Command. Nothing was easy.

After I finished artillery basic, I was supposed to go straight into jump school. That was not to be. I wore glasses. They stopped me from going to jump school and assigned me into A Co., 317th Airborne Field Artillery, 82nd Airborne Div. The captain was a guy that rose from the ranks in WWII, and he asked me right on out did I want to stay in the Airborne. I said, "Damn right I want to stay. That's why I joined." He then said, "Well, in a few months we'll get you past this glasses problem." Two months later, and a lot of harassment as a leg (non-airborne), I was sent up to take the eye test again. This time the medic said, "I'll be back in a little while to give you the test." I was right next to the eye

---

2   H.A.L.O. = High Altitude Low Opening.

chart. I was in that room for ten minutes and memorized the lines. The medic came back in and naturally I passed with excellent results. But now there was a new hitch.

Since I didn't come directly into jump school from airborne basic, I was now required to go through pre-jump school. What you did during the four hours was all physical exercise, calisthenics, running and a half hour in the guerilla pits. The guerilla pits were a place with the perimeter lined with logs, sand and sawdust and other material about ankle-deep filling the pit. Half the class stripped to their t-shirts, the other half stripped naked from the waist up. The object was for one side to throw the other side out of the log perimeter. Anything went. No rank permitted. Officers and Enlisted Men were equal. The side that won got a break. The side that lost was drilled without any break. It was common to see a half a dozen guys knocked out on the ground. I got through that training and went into jump school.

Jump school to me was a picnic. At Bragg we only had 34 foot towers. They were nothing.

My first actual jump was early on a sunny morning. When I went out the door I had every intention of saying as trained: "Hup one Thousand" slowly through "Hup four Thousand" but I stopped suddenly. I felt as if I was floating through mist that was actually a cloud flowing past me and engulfing me. I got out the first part "Hup One thousand" and then the thought flew through my mind because of this cloudlike mist, "God, what the hell am I doing here?" Suddenly my chute opened; I looked all around in amazement at how beautiful everything seemed.

The rest of jump school was anticlimactic after the first jump.

My first night jump was a little unusual. I remember bouncing off someone else's chute. My fear was being entangled in the air with other chutes. That's one of the only things that made me nervous. Also, wind made me nervous.

One time while our company was assigned to West Point to train cadets in the summer of 1956, we were going to make a jump onto the cadet training field from planes that were just glorified oversized Piper Cubs. We were supposed to have four men because of the shortness of the jump field. One side of the field is around two or three hundred feet down, almost a sheer drop to the Hudson River. Well, that morning we got up to jump. We got on the trucks. Here we were in a heavy rainstorm with thunder. I kept saying to myself, "They're out of they're minds. We jump in this, and we're all dead." I couldn't believe they were going to make us jump, but that's the way it looked. Finally, thank God!!! The jump was called off. We unloaded from the trucks and went back into the barracks.

I eventually ended up in the 11th Airborne Division, Hvy Mortar Co., 502nd Airborne Infantry. It was a great outfit. I got sick while I was on the pistol team in Dec. 1957 and was I was sent home in 1958. The Colonel at the hospital asked me what I wanted to do, I said, "Well my time is just about up. I can just go home, and if I have continuing problems, the VA will take care of it." Was I ever wrong. I started on a journey, physical disability and difficulty, that looking back on it, I don't know how I survived. I honestly can say that.

I've achieved my BS in Accounting, *magna cum laude*. I say this because the paratroops got me to see the need of education.

I had some rough times but I always look back on the Airborne with great pride and a sense of nostalgia for many great, wonderful young guys I became very close to.

Casama Ederle, Vicenza, Italy, 9 December 2008 – SETAF cased its old colors, ending the airborne chapter of its history, and uncased its new colors, signifying assumption of a new mission – serving as the Army component in support of U.S. Africa Command.

17

It was a grand affair – the
annual MI Ball

A ll work and no play … First the G-2 or DCSINT selected a Division Chief to put on the Ball (Colonel Handley, Chief of the Counterintelligence Division in my case) and then he selected a Chairman for that year's MI Ball. The colonel monitored the planning, but the main effort was accomplished by the Chairman.

I knew it was time go to work when I received the thick folder on the event from the past Division that hosted the event. I scanned the substantial folder. That's when I realized the magnitude of the project and felt rather panicky and depressed. This was going to be harder work than my regular job. So many details! To start the project, after coordinating with the boss, I "invited" certain members of CI Division to be committee members. Planning started about a nine months out from the event and I held meetings with all the committee members about once a week. The different committees were flowers and decorations, reservations, entertainment, advertisement, invitations, budget, accommodations for General Officers and seating. It was a very complicated party to throw considering its size and VIPs attending!

MI Ball at the Heidelberg Officers and Civilians Club ('The CINC's Own') (Author's collection)

160

At about 6 months out I met every day with the committee chiefs and the MI Ball became my full time job. In the image below you can see some of the US and foreign organizations participating and the meal choices. The food was good! It was expensive then; I wonder what it would cost today? I had the Prime Rib!

Finally the day of the banquet arrived. It opened up at 5:30pm but I and my crew were there at 4:00PM to make sure everything was in order. Not only did I have to check out the work of the committees but also the work of the Officers' Club, where we held the ball. To say the least, I was nervous. If this went wrong, it could be a career stopper! General officers of many intelligence organizations were coming as my General's guests and everything had to be just right. We placed the wine and goodies in their visiting quarters. I saw my career passing before my eyes! The DCSINT General was depending on COL Handley. My boss was depending on me. I certainly had to depend on the committee members. Delegate, delegate! Surely the invasion of Normandy could not have been this difficult!

Branch Insignia: On a gold color metal dagger, point up, 1¼ inches overall in height, a gold-color metal heraldic sun composed of four straight and four wavy alternating rays surmounted by a gold heraldic rose, the petals dark blue enamel.

The insignia was originally approved in 1962 for the Army Intelligence and Security Branch and redesignated to the Military Intelligence Branch on 1 July 1967. The sun, composed of four straight and four wavy alternating rays, is the symbol of Helios who, as God of the Sun, could see and hear everything. The four straight rays of the sun symbol also allude to the four points of the compass and the worldwide mission of the Military Intelligence Branch. The placement of the sun symbol beneath the rose (an ancient symbol

MENU:

MEAL A: PRIME RIB, BAKED POTATO, BABY CARROTS, GARDEN SALAD, AND DESSERT $35.00

MEAL B: CHICKEN BREAST ARIANA, RICE PILAF, BABY CARROTS GARDEN SALAD, AND DESSERT $30.00

MEAL C: PASTA PRIMAVERA, BABY CARROTS, GARDEN SALAD, AND DESSERT $30.00

SEATING PREFERENCE: (CIRCLE ONE)

EUCOM	LANDCENT	MIG EUROPE
650TH MI GRP (SHAPE)	BAOR	5TH SIG CMD
USAREUR (HQ)	CAN ARMED FORCES	21ST TAACOM
DCSINT — cI Air	66TH MI BDE	32ND TAACOM
V CORPS (HQ)	18TH MI BN	1ST AD (HQ)
205TH MI BDE	204TH MI BN	501ST MI BN
1ST MI BN	527TH MI BN	3RD ID (HQ)
165TH MI BN	JAC	103RD MI BN
302ND MI BN	STAFF WEATHER OFFICE	11TH ACR
OTHER: (SPECIFY)		511TH MI CO

of secrecy) refers to the operations and activities being conducted under circumstances forbidding disclosure. The partially concealed unsheathed dagger alludes to the aggressive and protective requirements and the element of physical danger inherent in the mission. The color gold signifies successful accomplishment and the dark blue signifies vigilance and loyalty.

I knew when the bomb-sniffing dogs arrived to check-out the club and White Hats arrived to walk perimeter security, it was getting near the start of the occasion. The guest started arriving in their formal uniforms, tuxedos and long flowing gowns for most of the females (of course some in uniform). Music started playing. The cocktail hour commenced. COL Handley called the hall to order. The MPs posted the colors. We had the invocation. So far, so good. We charged our wine glasses for the toasts. There were enough toasts to start to feel good:

1. TO THE PRESIDENT
2. TO THE REPUBLIC
3. TO THE ARMY
4. TO THE CORPS
5. TO THE ALLIES
6. TO OUR SPOUSES AND GUESTS

There was the welcome, the dinner (that's when I relaxed because it was all in the Club's hands now), guest speaker, retirement of the colors, and then dancing.

All was OK. That year of planning had paid off. Colonel Handley came up to me and congratulated me on a job well done. That meant a lot. But he added that I made one mistake during the set-up for the ball: we accidentally mixed the table setting country flags of The Netherlands and France. Ouch! Well now, they do sort of look alike!

18

Three significant CI women
who broke the glass ceiling

Glass ceiling – an intangible barrier within the hierarchy of a company that prevents women or minorities from obtaining upper-level positions.[1]

I was lucky enough to be associated with three women who all broke that glass ceiling.

Elizabeth Ryan
In the mid 1980s at USAREUR, I hired a secretary as an entry-level GS-5 and through the years she rose through the ranks with great tenacity to run USAREUR's LAA Program. She is now in Washington, DC as a GG-14 and Command Security Manager, Joint Force HQ-National Capitol Region, Military District of Washington. WOW! She broke the glass ceiling. She tells me I'll always be her boss.

We held a USAREUR G2 reunion in March 2007 in the DC area.Liz helped me set up the reunion with a friend, Linda Sell and about 100 people attended, including several General Officers. Only military units can feel the emotional ties at such an affair.

Words from Liz in February 2008:

I think that you would be proud of what I have achieved during my career that YOU started me in; I am so involved in areas I never thought I would be – it's rather neat and all because in 1989 you selected me, believed in me, sent me off to be educated in the security arena. I owe much to you.

Maria Dimarco
Before USAREUR, I was at the US Army Central Personnel Security Clearance Facility or Central Clearance Facility (CCF). This Army unit grants, denies or revokes security clearances for Army people. We were adjudicators (to act as a judge), reviewing their most recent investigation. In my position, I only reviewed derog cases that the subordinate adjudicators had recommended denial or revocation of clearance.

One hot day a Mrs. Dimarco made an appointment to interview for a base line adjudicator's position, GS-7. I wondered why she had a coat on and didn't take it off. Oh well. The interview went well and I hired her. A little while later I learned she was pregnant and had to take some time off. Good move with the coat! Of course one couldn't make a non-hire decision based on a reasonable medical condition. I'm glad I made that choice. What is amazing about Maria is that she is an immigrant from Italy along with her dignified husband Rosario. She was naturalized a US citizen (a requirement for a clearance) and she made it to the highest standard rating of Civil Service as a GS-15 (beat

1   Definition used by permission from the Merriam-Webster Online Dictionary 2009, © Merriam-Webster Inc. (www.Meriam-Webster.com).

(Author's collection)

United States Army
Central Personnel Security Clearance Facility

Certificate of Appreciation
is awarded to

LELAND C. McCASLIN

For your outstanding support to the United States Army Central Personnel Security Clearance Facility, Fort George G. Meade, Maryland, while serving as Security Manager and Special Security Officer for Headquarters, United States Army Europe. Your oversight of the personnel security program for individuals assigned to USAREUR and your responsiveness to our requests for information have greatly enhanced the Army's personnel security clearance program. Additionally, your expertise in the Limited Access Authorization program for foreign nations has also been of an immense value to this command. Your commitment in providing timely support underscores your professionalism and profound sense of personnel pride and reflects great credit upon you and the Department of the Army.

5 April 1995

USA Central Clearance Facility
Fort George G. Meade, MD 20755-5250

DENNIS A. BASSETT
Colonel, MI, Commanding

me!) and Chief Adjudicator for CCF! Talk about breaking that 'Glass Ceiling'! Several years later I worked closely with her at CFF (Maryland) and me in USAREUR (Germany). We worked together for me to get her the information she needed to finish a case and for her to expedite a rush clearance for me (USAREUR). I'm sure Maria was the originator of the certificate on the previous page which reflects our work together over a long distance:

She recently honored me by inviting my wife and I up to Baltimore for me to speak at her retirement, since I had hired her into government. Where does the time go?

Brigadier General Julia Kraus

At USAREUR, when my office (Command Security) and local DCSINT security were combined, Julia, as the head of DCSI security came to work for CMD SEC as a GS-9. I knew she was a reserve officer because she was doing some CGSC (Combined General Staff College) homework by correspondence. She has risen through the civilian ranks. She now has also made it big time in the military and does active duty stints at Department of the Army as a General Officer. Talk about breaking that glass ceiling! I am honored to have worked with her. Julia was treated with great respect and special handling due to her Senior Officer statue at Maria's retirement. She also spoke.

On a personal note, since we didn't receive AFN US TV in my Heidelberg apartment (weren't in the AFN beam) she always had a source of American TV VCRs (remember them?) from home and was very kind to lend them to me.

19

Travel in Europe

S ure, we understood the importance of our work, but we all took leaves and visited beautiful places in Europe. As long as you had your passport or ID cards (active military), travel in this small continent compared to the United States was very possible. Most civil servants had official passports that were maroon in color, contrasted with the blue tourist passports.

(Author's collection)

Heidelberg, Germany

Enjoy Heidelberg! I wanted to capture the feel and spirit of Heidelberg. If you've lived here, and can afford it, you'll be back. As usual, we took this place for granted while we lived here. Don't!! Get out and away from your jobs and appreciate this town and its beautiful and historic surroundings. Take a "tramp" (walk) around Heidelberg like Mark Twain! Or, take a river cruise on the Neckar River with a friend and a bottle of chilled white wine. If I had one place to recommend, it would be to the Hauptstrasse (Main Street) of Heidelberg. Located in the city center, it is an old cobble-stoned street where no cars are allowed. But, the street has many European- styled bars, cafes, and restaurants along the way, as well as numerous trendy shops.In the 1900s many Italian families immigrated to Germany and opened Italian restaurants operated by the entire family. There are several fine Italian restaurants in Heidelberg, for example, the *Piccolo Mondo* Italian Restaurant comes to mind.

Another great one is the *Ai Portici!* You can take public transportation there. You know one clever point about mass transportation in Germany is that no matter what type of transportation you're on (or switch to), the original ticket is good all the way, as long as you're going in the same general direction. You must buy a new ticket for the return trip.

Or take a cruise on the Neckar River that runs through Heidelberg:

The German cruise-boat people presented it like this: "– River Cruise: Stadthalle, Heidelberg > Neckargemünd > and back. Departure: 1000 hrs. Stadhalle. Departure: 12:45h p.m. back from Neckargemünd to Stadthalle. Time: 1½ hour one-way. Price: for passengers from Stadthalle (Congress-Center) and back: Euro 13.70pp. Prices included

Christmas shopping on the Hauptstrassse, Heidelberg. (Author's collection)

Heidelberg castle. (Author's collection)

(Author's collection)

CINC's mansion in Schlierbach. (Author's collection)

7 % Tax.... PAYMENT AT THE DAY ON THE BOAT ONLY CASH: WE ACCEPT NO CREDIT-CARDS."

"Einsteigen bitte," said the Captain, in German. My wife (Charlotte) and I started walking up the gangplank. We gave them our DM. We boarded and took some outdoor seats on the open top deck on the Heidelberger and settled down. I walked down to the inside bar and bought a big bottle of Riesling white wine for us and was given two little green German wine glasses and returned with it all to my upstairs, outside seat. I filled our glasses to the brim and felt very tranquil. We sat back with our wine, wind coming at our faces, with a good breeze that one feels on the water, and enjoyed the experience of being on the boat and the scenery about us. It was so relaxing to look at the old architecture and the green hills rising. The air smelled so clean. And it was a sunny blue-sky day!

We sailed by the little town of Schlierbach, a suburb of Heidelberg, where the ★★★★ CINC USAREUR lived in a mansion. We also lived in Schlierbach but in an apartment. There was just one way down to the river road to head into Heidelberg and onto Campbell Barracks. I remember being tangled up in the CINC's chase and lead cars entourage one morning coming in to work. Well, they thought I was a terrorist and I thought the chase car was full of terrorists – after the CINC. I reported them to the local field office of the 66th MI Group and they informed me that the CINC's protectors had reported me too. It was just a mix-up that was soon forgotten. But I felt embarrassed.

We kept going ever so slowly until we rounded a bend and one hour later landed in Neckargemünd. We stepped off the boat and had a quick lunch. We ordered a couple of biers and some Nurnberger sausages and kraut. This was outside under some big oaks, near the river in the *Biergarten* covered with white stones on the ground. Very pretty! By the way, if you like kraut in the States, you'll love it over here!

A view of Neckargemünd old town. (Neckargemünd tourist information)

Later we reboarded and showed our tickets and climbed up the stairs to the upper level and took our original seats. The boat made a long meandering turn-around in the river and started back. We again watched the scenery of this beautiful and historic region and retraced our steps to Heidelberg. We docked downtown at the Old Bridge near city center, as they call it. We strolled a little in the old part of Heidelberg on the ancient cobbled stoned streets visiting a couple of *Gasthauses* to include 'Sepples' and 'the Red Ox' and then headed home by taxi, thoroughly relaxed.

Eat or stay on the Hauptstrasse in Heidelberg at the *Zum Ritter Hotel*.

My wife and I stayed there one time on vacation on the top floor. Stay there and the entire floor is yours and with each side window you look up and down the Hauptstrasse. All the staff is most helpful and I highly recommend.

Venice, Italy

Take time to roam through the back lanes of Venice as well as Piazza San Marco; these paths and canals are just as unique. These alleyways retain the romance and the feeling of Venice. There was the famous Bridge of Sighs where prisoners were escorted from the courtroom to the prison in Venice. The bridge got its name centuries ago and is believed so named because doomed prisoners last saw their beautiful Venice through the bridge's windows.

You will be impressed with the splendor of Venice with its dazzling colors and of course the blues of the sky and water all about you.

And spend some time on the Grand Canal and eat at one of the fine restaurants along the canal and feast on their seafood (it is an island after all).

I cannot describe how great eating a seven course French dinner with remarkable wines over the waters of the canal is!

French Alps from Italy by train. (Author's collection)

Colmar, France – the 'Venice of France'

Hostellerie Le Maréchal. (Author's collection)

Colmar is just over the German border, in France. It's in the Alsace region of France that has switched hands between the Germans and French over centuries.

Colmar is special among its French neighbors. The building style reminds you of the Germany. The cooking is that of a German and French mix and the dwellers speak French with a German tongue.

Hotel Le Maréchal is a unique hotel which is rustic but elegant, great timbers in the walls, German-style, flowers hanging over the windows, and located in the charming old district of "Little Venice." The rooms are bestowed with historic pieces from yesteryear and 20 or 30 rooms overlook the canals. The hotel was constructed in the 1500s.

It's not a square box hotel with straight hallways like in the US. You go up a few steps in the hallways, maybe turn right … well you get the idea!

Or go on a Spargle hunt
Kir Royale
Ingredients:
- 1 part Crème de Cassis (Black Berry Liqueur)
- 5 parts Champagne

Mixing instructions:

Pour Crème de Cassis in glass and gently pour champagne on top.
- VARIATION: Kir – Same but with white wine instead of Champagne.

Champagne is a sparkling wine produced by inducing the in-bottle secondary fermentation of wine to effect carbonation. It is named after the Champagne region of France. While the term "champagne" has often been used by makers of sparkling wine in other parts of the world, many claim it should properly be used to refer only to the wines made in the Champagne region of France. This principle is enshrined in the European Union by Protected Designation of Origin (PDO) status.

Spargle (asparagus) is produced white in the German farmer's field by continuously mounding dirt over the Spargle during its growth period. No sun; no green producing photosynthesis of the chlorophyll.

And finally in this travel section, go on a 'Volksmarch'

A Volksmarch is a time-honored healthy tradition among the Germans and Americans living there. You usually walk a 10k hike at your own speed through a town and adjoining fields on a pre-determined route. There are food and beverage stations along the way. You are marching (walking) against yourself and not others. At the end, if you make it, you receive a medal to add to your collection. Let's go on a VM that really occurred recently. The flyer below is a copy of the real thing. The Group Captain of the March, Connie Wise, edited my story from Germany and made suggestions to bring it to near-reality. Anyway, the following reenactment describes a true Volksmarch:

Heidelberg International Wandering Club Bus Trip
Strasbourg Christmas market & Erstein 10km evening Volks March!
8 December 2007
€20 per person includes bus transportation and start card (stamp only)
Last date for sign up and payment is 26 November 2007

Join the Heidelberg International Wandering Club on 8 December 2007 for a trip to the Strasbourg Christmas market and a 10km evening Volksmarch in Erstein. We will depart PHV and upon arrival in Strasbourg spend several hours at the Christmas market where you can "shop til you drop" or just enjoy the festive atmosphere. After the market we will make our way to Erstein and enjoy the easy "Marche de la St. Nicolas" walk through the lighted city, woods and fields (recommend you bring a flashlight for when the lights get a bit dim). Bus departs PHV Park & Ride at 09:00 on 8 December 2007 Returns to PHV Park & Ride about 21:00.

Charlotte and I reached the PHV housing area and the bus in plenty of time to make the 0900 boarding. Naturally, there was sparkling wine served on the bus. Charlotte and I cut up with the other passengers which made the 1½ hour drive to Strasbourg go by quickly! We off-loaded near the Christmas Market and both of us enjoyed wandering around the bazaar, buying Christmas ornaments and eating nuts and drinking hot *Gluhwein* (mulled wine). It's made by heating up any inexpensive red wine, jazzed up with cinnamon, cloves, sugar and garnished with a lime or orange. It's really tasty and warm against the frosty air. After about four hours of walking through the old city it was time to get back on the bus and travel to the start of the Volksmarch. We traveled the short distance to Erstein and left our Christmas purchases in our seats.

Charlotte and I got to the "start gate" in Erstein and then took off at a slow pace walking through town. Although it was a Christmas Volksmarch, the weather was unseasonably warm. We both had flashlights for the evening walk but didn't need them yet. "Charlotte, are you warm enough?" I asked. She smiled and looked in my eyes and said "I'm warmed by all this walking." We followed the pre-determined route through town which was easy enough and were surprised to find the 'extra' muddy patches were carpeted! It was neat to see all the Christmas lights and decorations in town and especially the colored lights along the wooded trails.

A path soon took us out in the fields around the town. There were some gentle hills to negotiate. A lot of farm animals. We skirted a lake along the trail. We walked for miles in the pretty scenery as night descended and we soon arrived at a lighted food and beverage station where we enjoyed the free broth. Remember we were not walking for time but completion.

Wondering how much further we had to go for some *Gluhwein*, Charlotte asked, "you ready to start walking again?"

I smiled and replied, "lead on."

At that point we started walking again but the path led us in to some serious wooded sections. It soon became evident that this was a forest. It got thicker, darker – and quieter. We paused and just looked up at the dense pines around us. The scent of the trees was thick with resin. In those woods, it was time for the flashlights. We navigated the eerie trail; my imagination ran away from me – I thought, would we meet Bilbo Baggins or the Elven king of Mirkwood?

Soon, after several hundred meters, the trail was lighted in various colors which was beautiful. A few kilometers later in the forest we were at another checkpoint, with cheerful Christmas lights apparent. "At last, *Gluhwein*," Charlotte said. Although it wasn't really cold enough for *Gluhwein*, we enjoyed a cup of the sweet liquid before moving on. There were two 'houses' in the woods where local children put on skits depicting Father Christmas at one and the Nativity at the other. We paused and watched both enactments. We finally took off again and the lane eventually took us out of the forest and through some fields and after some time back into town.

We finally arrived at the finish hall. We got our IVV Books stamped and enjoyed the party in the hall with over a thousand other Volksmarchers! We also received our much-coveted Volksmarch Medals.

We soon boarded the bus and headed back to Heidelberg. We slept most of the way back. It was getting colder as we headed northeast towards Heidelberg. After we got off the bus at PHV, we drove back home to a snowy Schlierbach (a suburb of Heidelberg).

Afterword

From the G2

U se of the term "Iron Curtain" in the context of Soviet-dominated Eastern Europe was not popularized until Churchill used it in his "Sinews of Peace" address March 5, 1946, at Westminster College in Fulton, Missouri:

> From Stettin in the Baltic to Trieste in the Adriatic an "iron curtain" has descended across the Continent. Behind that line lie all the capitals of the ancient states of Central and Eastern Europe – Warsaw, Berlin, Prague, Vienna, Budapest, Belgrade, Bucharest and Sofia; all these famous cities and the populations around them lie in what I must call the Soviet sphere, and all are subject, in one form or another, not only to Soviet influence but to a very high and in some cases increasing measure of control from Moscow.

> *Wikipedia*

I was very fortunate to get such a personable, insightful and knowledgeable officer to write the close-out to this book. We learn from him that what we did was important. The officer, in the highest ranking intelligence position in Army Europe in the mid '90s, the retired USAREUR G2, Colonel Jack Hammond, provides a truly interesting and historical summary of USAREUR intelligence in the Cold War.

What we did in USAREUR was important. If you look at the potential for war between the United States and NATO, and the Soviet Union and the Warsaw Pact, up through the end of the eighth decade of the Twentieth Century, you begin to realize how serious this threat actually was. We lived and worked in that period defending the United States and its Allies – making sure that the Soviet strategic perception was that we were a credible threat to their success if they chose to attack Western Europe.

This was serious business – our tanks and armored personnel carriers (APC's) were up-loaded with war ammunition; we carried full sets of updated maps in every vehicle for our defensive plans and counter-attack options; when we were alerted (exercised at least every month) we rushed to the *kaserne* not knowing if we would return home; and we trusted the NEO (non-combatant evacuation operations) plan to take care of our families so we could do our jobs. REFORGER (Return of Forces to Germany) would deliver four additional combat divisions to Germany within ten days to fall in on division-sets of equipment in POMCUS (Prepositioning of Material Configured in Unit Sets) storage areas.

Today, this seems hard to imagine. If you asked a German born in 1990 if he or she could comprehend this threat, they probably would express disbelief that we stood toe–to–toe with the Soviets at a place called the Intra-German Border (IGB), a place that today has almost been "erased" by the Germans as a bad memory. However, the facts were that we faced a determined opponent who was every bit as serious as we were, and our objective was to make them believe we were a threat to them.

The threat

From my own personal experience after the Berlin Wall came down, I know that "they" did believe we (NATO and U.S. forces) were a serious hurdle to any incursion into the West that they may have contemplated. In German-sponsored visits to the former East Germany military *kasernes* and command posts, and discussions with former East German *Volksarmee* personnel (non-commissioned officers, officers at the grade of Lieutenant Colonel and Colonel; from senior NCO to political officer up to regimental commander; all in the temporary employ of the former West German Army), it was clear to me that they feared us and our capabilities, but that they were also quite aware that their Soviet masters did not exactly trust them. The *Volksarmee* probably "mirrors" the Soviet relationship with the armed forces of its other allies.

The *Volksarmee* was assessed to be the "best of the best" in the Warsaw pact, even in comparison with the Soviets, but they labored under Soviet control and mistrust. Soviet officers had essentially "co-command" of the *Volksarmee* Divisions, occupying seats in their commands posts with the only direct line to higher headquarters being to the Soviet Headquarters (Group of Soviet Forces in Germany (GSFG)) at Zossen-Wünsdorf, south of Berlin. The *Volksarmee* military maps, classified *GEHEIM* (Secret), had no more than 40 kilometers of the western portion of East Germany on them, but stretched west all the way to the ports on the English Channel and well into France. *Volksarmee* regimental commanders knew no more about their operational plans than the local dispersal area for their units off their *kasernes* to protect against NATO air attack. Control of and distrust of their allies by the Soviets was endemic to their relationship as master and servant.

One *Volksarmee* regimental commander related to me that he could never be more than thirty minutes away from his *kaserne* to include nights and weekends. In his entire tour in command (which ended with the German reunification) he had never had a leave. His primary focus was the readiness of his forces and their ability to escape the *kaserne* before a NATO air attack. He did not understand that we and our Allies, although we were constantly trained and prepared, actually had leaves and weekends off; that our soldiers could essentially go anywhere when off-duty as long as they could return for the next duty day. He told me that at that time, when he was in command, he believed that our intent was aggressive and that the Warsaw Pact and East Germany were in danger of being attacked by NATO and the United States at any moment. He was aware of our readiness exercises where we rapidly evacuated *kasernes* and deployed to local training areas or to exercises. It was obvious that he had been fed mostly propaganda about our intentions, and not much real intelligence about our defensive posture.

And it is clear that the posture of the Warsaw Pact and the Soviets was not truly defensive in nature. They did not plan a "defense" of the land area they occupied in Eastern Europe; they planned how they would attack Western Europe. In 1991, on a visit to the former operational exercise center (*Ausbildungs Zentrum*) of the former East German Ministry of Defense, I was briefed by a former *Volksarmee* Lieutenant Colonel (at the time temporarily wearing a West German uniform with the grade of Major) of how the center was used to train senior East German commanders and their Soviet masters how to coordinate the "defense" of East Germany. As I glanced over the center's football field-sized topographical map, I pointed out to the briefer that it was strange that the "defensive" exercises to be played out on this massive exercise map included only about 40 kilometers of East Germany, but showed all of West Germany, much of Denmark, and considerable portions of France. While it was obvious that his "defense" was really an offense, the briefer stubbornly refused to concede the point; his briefing then ended abruptly as he knew I didn't believe him and there was not much else to say other than his propaganda line.

It was important that the Soviets and their Warsaw Pact allies believe that we were a credible threat to their success if they attacked to the West. USAREUR contributed to that belief and its long line of commanders focused on ensuring that we could carry out our missions and make sure that they would have to pay dearly for any incursion. Although the fall of the Wall, German reunification, the withdrawal of the GSFG, and the collapse of the Warsaw Pact and subsequently, the Soviet Union, are certainly attributable to a wide range of complex factors and forces – USAREUR played its role and made a significant contribution.

Role of Intelligence in USAREUR

USAREUR intelligence was fully engaged with the Soviets and the Warsaw Pact during this period. While the combat and logistics elements of the command were involved in constant training and exercises, USAREUR intelligence participated fully with them, while at the same time fighting an "intelligence war" with the enemy. Sometimes it was difficult for us to convince our USAREUR combat arms partners of our double commitment, but we were generally able to manage to accomplish both missions successfully. Often intelligence units in USAREUR spent more time in the field than their combat arms counterparts – everyone wanted additional intelligence resources to add realism to every level of exercise and training; and then "who" was often called to plan and then frequently "play" the opposing forces (OPFOR) – intelligence.

At the same time, at the operational level, USAREUR intelligence was engaged with all aspects of a real-world intelligence cycle: directing the effort, collecting intelligence in all its forms, processing information and data, analyzing and generating a useful intelligence product, and disseminating these products to the appropriate commanders, and addressing questions like is *the enemy preparing to attack? If so, where, when, with what forces? What is his plan? What are his objectives?* In those days we did not have the intelligence systems that are available today for advanced communications, information display, data collection, and intelligence production, and dissemination. We had 64-baud teletypes; plastic overlays; grease pencils; large, smelly machines for making overlays; and stick pins on paper maps. Only in the 1980s did computers start to arrive and begin to give us more modern capabilities.

The variety of our intelligence activity was exhaustive and every opportunity for collection on the enemy was used. Forward Cavalry positions were located on the IGB with guard posts and patrols (both ground and air) to detect border activity. Exotic imagery of every kind from every kind of platform was obtained. Counterintelligence, counter-espionage, and human intelligence were active at every level. Looking back now, we know we probably knew where they were with their major formations all of the time; but, at the time, we never could be sure. Everything was keyed to warning of an impending attack. And we had to be ready for those infrequent times when we weren't quite sure of our analysis or when Soviet exercises could be a ruse for attack preparations.

The Future

So is it over? It is not likely that we will face the same enemy in the same manner in the future and very possible that the Cold War "as we knew it" in USAREUR will never recur. The threat posed by the Soviets remains in the past, but we can look back now and know that we made an important contribution and that USAREUR intelligence was critical to that success. Every "Cold warrior" who served in USAREUR intelligence can be proud of his service and the result.

We can only be absolutely sure of one thing in the future: that the threat will be changing and often "surprise" us. We can only trust that U.S. leadership will ensure that the armed forces and that the intelligence resources fielded to deal with the potential threat are evolved appropriately and sufficiently prepared to agilely and competently respond to it.

Congratulations USAREUR!

U SAREUR personnel: You helped to bring about German Reunification. Be proud of yourself.

German Reunification Day – commissioned by the *News Bulletin for Info & Personnel Security*, and given to author by the artist Marsha Cheney (http://mscheneyprints.com). It depicts symbols of East and West Germany coming together. (Author's collection)

CERTIFICATE OF APPRECIATION

TO THE MEN AND WOMEN OF USAREUR

In gratitude for your service during the period of the Cold War

(2 September 1945 – 26 December 1991)

in advancing peace and stability for this Country

....

A GRATEFUL NATION

Remember Heidelberg:
AUF WIEDERSEHEN

Appendix I

The early days – intelligence training

Photos of Fort Holabird, MD. Fort Holabird is no more. It was in the Dundalk neighborhood, an industrial region of Baltimore, Maryland and many received their basic and advanced intelligence training at this small post. It closed in the early 1970s and Fort Huachuca, Arizona is its current home. These images are historic as the post was bulldozed and no longer exists.

All pictures below are furnished from the archives of the History Office, US Army INSCOM.

Tallmadge Hall, Fort Holabird.

General type classroom in Building 320 (18 June 1963).

Fort Holabird surveillance – downtown Baltimore (circa 1950).

Enlisted barracks, Fort Holabird.

The Golden Sphinx stands watchfully in front of the Headquarters building of the United States Army Intelligence Center, Fort Holabird (15 March 1960).

Fort Holabird Officers' Club.

Appendix II

USAREUR HQ key positions, staff agencies, major units and population

The major leadership positions in the Headquarters in the 1980s were the Command Group consisting of the 4-star Commander-in-Chief (CINC), the 3-star Deputy (DCINC), the 2-star Chief of Staff (CofS), the Colonel - Secretary of the General Staff (SGS) also known as the Gatekeeper (he decided which staff papers went forward to the Generals), the Political Advisor (State Department) and others.

They were all located at the beautiful Keyes Building on Campbell Barracks (the Headquarters of the Headquarters).

The HQ major staff agencies were the DCS (Deputy Chiefs of Staff for...) Personnel, Intelligence, Operations, Logistics, Resource Management, Engineer, and the lawyers – the JAG.

Some of the Major Subordinate Commands combat units scattered around mainly Germany were V Corps (Frankfurt) and VII Corps (Stuttgart) - both Corps with their attendant combat Infantry, Armor and Artillery Groups.

Other important units were 1st PERSCOM, 5th Signal Command, 7th Medical Command, 7th Army Training Command, 7th Army Reserve Command, 18th Engineer Brigade, 21st Support Command, 32d Army Air Defense Command, 56th Field Artillery Brigade, 59th Ordinance Brigade, 66th Military Intelligence (MI) Group (actually under US Army INSCOM – Intelligence and Security Command), Southern European Task Force (SETAF) in Italy and U.S. Command Berlin.

During the Cold War, USAREUR had a working population of about 400,000, which consisted of soldiers, civilians, U.S. and foreign national employees (excluding family members).

Appendix III

Famous US Armed Forces Recreation Center (AFRC)

Alpine hotels formerly belonging to the Nazis and then used by US soldiers

All images in Appendix III are from the author's collection.

Berchtesgadener Hof: This was the crown jewel of the Armed Force Recreation Center Hotels formerly belonging to the Nazis. Top members of the Nazis stayed here such as Goebbels, Rommel, Eva Braun and diplomatic guests like British Prime Minister Neville Chamberlain and the Duke and Duchess of Windsor.

I believe it's featured in the *Band of Brothers* TV series. The US Army occupied the Hof from 1945 until when the Army left, in 1995 and they locked it up. I stayed there in the 1980s – what a view of the Alps! It was destroyed in 2006.

The General Walker Hotel: This hotel was located south of Munich near the Bavaria village of Berchtesgaden, in Obersalzberg. It was an Alpine showplace for Nazi dignitaries and guests and was named the Platterhof. The Platterhof was renamed the General Walker Hotel when the Americans took over in 1952. I stayed there in the '80s and my wife (Charlotte) and I stayed there in the 90s; it was turned back over to the Germans in 1995. It was destroyed in 2000 and is now a parking lot. ☹

Having a drink at
the lounge in the
General Walker Hotel.

Ride the open "train"
underground to the Salt
Mines. Lead couple is
the author and his wife.

And once inside, with
your leather aprons on
you backsides, slide
down to the deeper
regions of the mines!

Chiemsee: Chiemsee Autobahn Rasthaus, located in southern Bavaria, was chosen by Hitler in 1938 to be the first rest house of his autobahn road system. The AFRC took it over as the Lake Hotel after WWII and closed it in 2003. I stayed there in the 1980's and remember it as a summer-type resort.

It is sad that most of these hotels have been destroyed. They were a part of history (theirs and ours) and the German government should have preserved them.

Glossary

Note: This glossary lists expressions from both within the book and from without – but all from the Cold War. It is really a standalone document – a layman's and historian's treasure! It reflects words and definitions of the Cold War era. Some words/definitions have been updated or are no longer in common usage.

11th ACR: A light armored unit, the 11th Armored Cavalry Regiment was positioned on the border between West and East Germany and defended at the Fulda Gap in case Soviet armor invaded the West.

66th MI Group: The 66th Military Intelligence Group was located in Munich, Germany during the Cold War. It belonged to the Intelligence and Security Command and was under the operational control of USAREUR. The Group had several regions primarily in Germany; it was staffed with Special Agents who conducted Counterintelligence Investigations and Operations.

527th MI Battalion: A "strategic" counterintelligence battalion under the command of the 66th MI Group. The headquarters was in Kaiserslautern and the battalion initially had field offices in the Rhineland-Pfalz and Zweibruecken regions in the southwest federal republic. In the 1980's the battalion took command of field offices throughout Germany and the BENELUX. As a strategic battalion, it conducted counterespionage and counterterrorist investigations and reported a variety of threat information to supported commands and installations.

AFN: American Forces Network is the name used by the United States Armed Forces Radio and Television Service (AFRTS) for overseas troop entertainment and command information drives.

AFRC: Armed Forces Recreation Center. They were Rest and Recreation (R&R) Hotel resorts for US Forces taken over from the Nazis at the end of the war. They were located in the towns of Garmisch-Partenkirchen, Berchtesgaden, and Chiemsee – Bavaria, southern Germany. Attractions were the snowy Bavarian Alps, skiing, Chiemsee Lake, the General Walker Hotel, Berchtesgadener Hof, Eibsee Hotel, Zugspitze, the Eagle's Nest (Kehlsteinhaus), cable cars, Lake Konigsee, icy clear rivers, Alpine views and the Casa Carioca Supper Club which presented ice follies, dancing and good meals. The Club burned down in 1970.

AMLM: Allied Military Liaison Missions: French, British, and US Intelligence collectors headquartered in Potsdam, East Germany whose official cover was as liaison officers during the Cold War. See related definition "Tour Officer".

Analysis: In intelligence usage, the conversion of processed information into intelligence through the interpretation of all source data.

Autobahn: Much like the US Interstate network, the autobahn in Germany is known as the *Bundesautobahn* or Federal Motorway. Getting a boost from WWII and Hitler, the autobahn is a multi-lane highway, mostly without speed limits, that now crisscrosses Germany.

B&C: Badge & Credential. These identify the bearer as a duly accredited special agent of U.S. Army Intelligence who is performing official intelligence duties. When a special agent presents these B&C to a person, he/she is enjoined by order of the Secretary of the Army to assist the special agent in the conduct of his/her official investigative mission.

Background Investigation (BI): This is an examination of a person to see if he/she is eligible for access to classified information by interviewing others and checking local and national agencies (NAC) by Special Agents. Other variations are the Special Background Investigation (SBI) and Single Scoped Background Investigation (SSBI). See definition of NAC.

Backstopping: Providing the espionage agent paper ID and human sources to support or back-up his/her false identity. Phone cut-outs may be used. That is, all phone numbers given on false identity documents must be manned by support personnel prepared to back stop or confirm the agent's cover for status (false identity). Backstopping involves: Cover for Status: Who am I, why am I there, what is my occupation? It must be something the agent can live with and be as close to the truth as possible. The fewer lies he has to memorize, the less likely he is to forget his status or get confused.
Cover for Action: Employed when the agent actually conducts an operation. For example, if he's to photograph the newest Soviet tank as it enters or leaves a certain *kaserne*, he must have a credible reason for being near the *kaserne* and for having a camera.

Bellwether Division: The bellwether is the leading sheep of a flock with a bell around its neck. Certain GSFG (defined below) Divisions were known as Bellwether or test divisions. When Chief of the GSFG Section, Order of Battle Branch, Production Division, ODCSINT, detected new equipment entering GSFG Bellwether Divisions, one could predict they would probably spread to other GSFG Divisions.

Beltway Bandit: Interstate 495 surrounds Washington DC and is called the Beltway. The Beltway Bandit term is used to describe private contractors providing services inside the Beltway to the Federal Government. Also affectionally known as "Parkway Patriots" or "Highway Helpers."

Berlin Blockade: The Soviets blocked all railroad and road access to W. Berlin from 24 June 1948 – 12 May 1949 in an effort to supply Berlin's food and fuel needs from Soviet controlled areas (and thus control of all of Berlin). The Americans answered with the Berlin Airlift, also known as Operation Vittles (26 June, 1948 – 30 September, 1949), thought impossible, but successful. Therefore, the Soviets ended the blockade.

Berlin duty train: In the fall of 1945, the U.S. European Commander directed the U. S. Transportation Corps in Europe to establish rail transportation "connections" with Berlin. Commanded by US Military Berlin, the duty train maintained our "Allied Right of Free Access" through Communist East Germany to W. Berlin during the Cold War. It transported US military and civilian personnel and freight both ways between W. Berlin in the East and Frankfurt/Bremerhaven in West Germany.

BMP-2: Soviet-produced *Boyevaya Mashina Pekhoty* or amphibious infantry fighting vehicle.

BRDM: Soviet-produced *Boyevaya Razvedyvatelnaya Dozornaya Mashina* or Combat Reconnaissance Patrol Vehicle, which was a four-wheeled amphibious vehicle.

BTR: Soviet-produced Armor Personnel Carrier with 10 seats for personnel.

Campbell Barracks: *Kaserne* home of HQs USAREUR, Heidelberg, Germany. It was named after Staff Sergeant Charles L. Campbell, 14th Infantry Regiment. He died March 28, 1945 under heroic circumstances while leading a unit near Heidelberg.

Cattle Cars: Colloquial: Two and a half ton military trucks known as "duce and a halfs" that carried soldiers to field training. The earlier meaning of cattle cars was German death trains that carried Jews to extermination camps in WWII.

CCF: The US Army Central Personnel Security Clearance Facility, routinely known as Central Clearance Facility. CCF grants, denies or revokes clearances for Army personnel. It also conducted special screenings such as General Officers' screenings. It initially belonged to the Army's Military Personnel Center (MILPERCEN) and now belongs to the Army Intelligence and Security Command.

Check Point Charlie: During the Cold War, it was the crossing point between W. and E. Berlin for foreigners and Allied Forces.

Chop: Colloquial: A signature of concurrence by another pertinent staff agency on an Information or Decision paper (see listings for each below).

CIA: Central Intelligence Agency. The US civilian government agency formed during WWII to collect and analyze information about foreign governments. It was the successor of OSS (defined below).

CIDC: Criminal Investigation Command. CIDC investigations focus on crimes committed by military members and civilians whenever there is an Army interest in such investigations.

CINC: Commander-in-Chief. In this case, the CINCs were opposing four-star generals or the highest military officers for the US Army and the Soviet Army in Cold War Germany. The American CINC was located in USAREUR, Heidelberg, West Germany and the Soviet CINC was located in Zossen-Wünsdorf, East Germany. The USAREUR CINC commanded US Army Europe.

Class VI: The US Armed Forces divides supplies into ten categories. Alcoholic beverages fall into the Class VI category (personal demand) along with cigarettes and toothpaste. Thus, in Germany during the Cold War, the store that sold drinking alcohol on base was known as the Class VI Store. Alcohol was cheap in the Army overseas due to no tax. Alcohol was rationed (only so much could be bought a month by an individual member of the Forces) via a ration card to prevent black-marketing to Germans at the cheap prices.

Clobbers: Colloquial: Detention of USMLM tour officers by Soviet or E. German soldiers in the GDR.

Cold War: a state of political hostility and tension between countries or factions using means short of armed warfare. In this book, refers to the conflict in Europe from 1945 to the early 1990s between the US and NATO-backed countries and Communism and the Warsaw Pact countries.

Cold War Certificate: An official DOD certificate ("Certificate of Recognition") thanking the 'Cold Warrior' (military or civilian) for his or her service in the Cold War sometime during the period of 2 September 1945 until 26 December 1991. The Secretary of Defense signs it. It is similar to the certificate at the end of this book. Go online if you served to obtain one in your name at https://www.hrc.army.mil/site/active/tagd/coldwar/Apply_for_Certificate.htm.

Combat Arms: Branches of the Army dealing in direct tactical fighting such as the Infantry, Armor or Artillery.

Combat Support: Branches of the Army dealing in support of the Combat Arms. They often find themselves in combat situations. Examples would be Military Police and Military Intelligence.

Combat Service Support: Branches of the Army that sustain the operational Army and whose primary mission is not fighting. Examples would be Chaplain, Quartermaster, Medical, Finance and Adjutant General.

Communism: A social and political structure which practices a classless and stateless society which features common ownership of property and means of production. It does not encourage the entrepreneur.

Compelling Need: Special clearance procedures to:

1) authorize granting a security access before the completion of the required investigation when a Commander declares an emergency situation.

2) waiving certain access standards when a Commander declares an emergency situation.

Compromise or Inadvertent Disclosure: This occurs when someone receives classified information and is not authorized the information. In all cases of a compromise, the question remains, what might the damage be to national security? Investigation may be initiated to determine this. The person who received this unauthorized classified information may be asked to sign an inadvertent non-disclosure statement.

COMSEC: Communications Security. Previously known as CRYPTO, technical security measures to protect telecommunication.

CONUS: This is the technical military term for the 48 Continental states within the United States.

Corps: A large battlefield formation usually commanded by a Lieutenant General and consisting of two or more divisions. Pronounced "Core." See V Corps and VII Corps.

Counterintelligence(CI): Information gathered and activities conducted to protect against espionage, other intelligence activities, sabotage or assassinations conducted for or on behalf of foreign powers, organizations, or persons, or international terrorist activities, but not including personnel, physical, document or communications security programs. Security and CI work hand-in-hand.

Counterintelligence Special Agent(S/A): Generally tries to stop espionage and terrorist activities against the Army and the United States. He or she specifically conducts liaison and operational coordination with foreign and U.S. law enforcement, security, and intelligence agencies. He or she plans and conducts CI investigations of national security crimes. The S/A applies fundamentals of military and civil law. He/she detects, identifies, counters, exploits and neutralizes threats to Army and DoD missions, organizations and personnel. He/she conducts CI collection activities and source operations to include overt collection, surveillance and non-technical operations.

CPO: Civilian Personnel Office. The local base office under the Office of the Deputy Chief of Staff for Personnel (ODCSPER) for hiring and administering civilian members of the Force. It would be known in the civilian world as a human resource office.

CPX: Command Post Exercise. A training exercise for a headquarters not involving subordinate units.

CQ: Charge of Quarters. An enlisted man in administrative charge of a military unit (especially the living quarters or barracks) after hours.

Curb-stoning: A military special agent figuratively sits on a curb side and illegally writes a made-up agent report without actually interviewing the assigned source. Dishonest motivation is laziness or to save time.

Courtesy Letter Program: Letters sent to those who were interviewed to check on the professionalism and dress of the Special Agent conducting the interview and to ensure the agent actually performed the interview (see above definition) and not falsely reported having conducted a Personnel Security Investigation lead.

DAC: Department of the Army Civilian. This is a non-military employee working for the Department of the Army as a civilian. Upon entering civil service for the Army, they take the Oath of Office. Civilians have been an integral part of the U.S. Army since the Revolutionary War. The Board of War and Ordnance was established in 1776 with responsibility to equip and dispatch troops; account for arms, ammunition and equipment; maintain personnel records; and disburse funds. The board was made up of five members of the Continental Congress, clerks and a paid secretary – Richard Peters, the first Army civilian. Civilians were hired by the Continental Army for driving, crafts, carpentry and laborer jobs. Throughout our nation's history, civilians have played a vital role in supporting soldiers. Army civilians have skills that are not readily available in the military, but crucial to support military operations.

DCSINT or DCSI: Deputy Chief of Staff for Intelligence. These were acronyms for the G-2, the most senior intelligence officer in USAREUR. During the Cold War, the billet was usually a two-star Major General. Primary duties were to provide intelligence and counterintelligence support to the Commander in Chief, US Army, Europe, and staff support to Army and joint intelligence commands throughout Europe.

Decision Paper: The medium a staff officer uses to obtain a decision from higher important personnel, usually Generals.

Denied Area: A geographical area controlled by the enemy forces; thereby off limits to friendly forces.

Deutsche Mark **(DM)**: The currency of West Germany during the Cold War and issued by the Allies at the end of WWII, replacing the *Reichsmark*. It was replaced by the Euro in 1999.

Direct Communications Link (DCL): The official name for the Russian Hotline.

DIS: Defense Investigative Service. These DOD Special Agents conduct personnel security investigations for CCF (and other military adjudication agencies) enabling them to make security clearance determinations.

Duty Officer: A junior officer who represents the commander and his military unit after hours.

EAC: Echelons Above Corps. EAC is a higher headquarters above a Corps. They usually have a specific function. USAREUR is an example of an EAC and their primary purpose during the Cold War was to defend against possible Soviet invasion of Western Europe.

Economy: In the Cold War overseas context, it denotes obtaining goods and services in local European stores, e.g., we'll go shopping on the Economy today, instead of the PX and Commissary.

Espionage: The act of obtaining, delivering, transmitting, communicating, or receiving information about the national defense with an intent, or reason to believe, that the information may be used to the injury of the United States or to the advantage of any foreign nation. Espionage is a violation of 18 United States Code 792-798 and Article 106, Uniform Code of Military Justice.

Fallout Shelters: Usually an underground enclosed room to protect the occupants from a nuclear explosion.

False Flag Approach: A method a spy uses to obtain classified information from an individual. The spy convinces the individual to supply information in the mistaken belief that the individual is supplying the information to a country (usually friendly) other than that of the handler (usually Russian or Soviet Bloc during the Cold War).

Field Office: US Counterintelligence personnel were spread across Germany during the Cold War. They were usually assigned to a local (or field) office where they conducted business. Field Offices were staffed with Special Agents to defend US Forces from espionage and terrorist attacks. They conducted counterintelligence threat and countermeasures briefings for US personnel, conducted liaison with military and foreign police and intelligence agencies and conducted a multitude of Counterintelligence and Personnel Security investigations.

FIS (Foreign Intelligence Services): In this case they are the Warsaw Pact clandestine intelligence organizations doing the collection of information against the Allies (See HoIS).

Flag officer: A senior commissioned officer – Admiral or General – who is entitled his or her own flag showing the stars of rank.

Flag Orders: Orders in French, Russian and English that allowed one to ride the Berlin duty train from West Germany to East Germany and Communist-surrounded W. Berlin and vice versa. The Flag Orders were inspected for administrative accuracy by the Soviets at the E./ W. border. Prominent was an American flag at the top/center of the orders, hence the term, Flag Orders.

Flag Note: Small stationary with the General's flag embossed showing his/her number of stars of rank.

Foreign Area Officer(FAO): This is an Army specialty designation for selected Officers. These officers received special training and education in specific foreign area military, economic, cultural, political expertise and foreign language proficiency.

Frocking: An officer authorized to wear a higher rank before actually promoted to the rank. In USAREUR, many officers assigned to the DCSINT billet of Major General were frocked until actually promoted.

Gas Coupons: Gas for one's car is expensive in Germany. The PX (AAFES) sells gas coupons at a reduced (Stateside) rate to DOD personnel. These coupons are given to a German gas station at time of purchase. They are rationed to prevent black-market activity. Gasthaus: Guesthouse. A German-designed inn or tavern with a restaurant noted for serving beer. They are located in Germany, Austria, Switzerland and other European countries. They may have an outdoor beer garden for spring and summer service.

Georgia: In the Cold War case, not the state next to Alabama. It is a Eurasian country between Russia and Asia. Russia is to the north and Turkey is to the southwest. Its population is four million and its capital is Tbilisi.

German Democratic Republic: Known as *Deutsche Demokratische* Republik (DDR) in German and informally East Germany in English. It was the Soviet Zone of Occupation formed at the end of WWII and existed from 1949 to 1990 until German Reunification.

German Reunification Day: On 3 Oct 90 the Federal Republic of Germany (West Germany) and the German Democratic Republic (East Germany) were united and became one country and East/West Berlin became one city.

Glienicke Bridge: A bridge between Berlin and Potsdam that crosses the Havel River. Spies were exchanged there between the Russians and Americans during the Cold War. Therefore, it was often referred to as the Bridge of Spies or Freedom Bridge. Francis Gary Powers was released there in 1962.

GOV: Government Owned Vehicle. The government (Army) bought and owns the car.

Group of Soviet Forces Germany (GSFG): That part of the Soviet army stationed in East Germany during the Cold War. They were the main threat to the West during the Cold War.

GRU: *Glavnoe Razvedovatelnoye Upravleniye* (Main Intelligence Directorate) It was the Red Army's military intelligence organization and continues to be the intelligence arm of the Russian Federation Armed Forces General Staff.

Hauptbahnhof: Main or central train station of a large German city. German trains are known for running on time. The *Hauptbahnhof* may be abbreviated Hbf or HB.

Heidelberg: A city in Baden-Württemberg, Germany, it is the home of HQ USAREUR at Campbell Barracks. The city lies on the Neckar River and covers 42 square miles; with its castle and old bridge, it is a popular tourist city. The population is approximately 140,000.

HoIS: is Hostile Intelligence Service (see FIS)

Hot Line: It was established by a joint agreement between the USA and the USSR. It allows the Presidents of Russia and the United States instant communication in case of crisis. Created in 1963, it is a telex machine and not a phone (at least during the Cold War). It is also known as the Direct Communications Link (DCL) with Moscow and the MOLINK or Moscow Link.

Hot War: Actual fighting between warring countries or factions.

Human Intelligence: The intelligence derived from the intelligence collection discipline that uses human beings as both sources and collectors, and where the human being is the primary collection instrument. It is also called HUMINT.

ID Card: More accurately, the United States Uniformed Services Privilege and Identification Card, it is a laminated identity document issued by the US Department of Defense to its members and dependents. It is used to control access to bases and exclusive stores such as the PX and Commissary.

Imminence of Hostilities: A measurement of the indicators of war made at the Office of the Deputy Chief of Staff, Intelligence, HQ USAREUR, Heidelberg. The indicators would elevate, for example, when the E. German Army or the Soviets in East Germany would move towards the W. German border (hopefully for an exercise and not invasion) or units from the USSR would move into East Germany.

Immobilien: German real estate agency showing immovable properties. They may be rental or owned properties. Civilian members of the forces must live off post and these companies help you find a place to live. One pays their fee and the government reimburses you.

Information Paper: The medium a staff officer uses to provide critical information to higher important personnel, usually Generals.

Intelligence: The product resulting from the collection, processing, integration, evaluation, analysis, and interpretation of available information concerning foreign nations, hostile or potentially hostile forces or elements, or areas of actual or potential operations. We also apply the term to the activity which results in the product and to the organizations engaged in such activity.

Intel 2 Course: Formal course at Vilseck, Germany where all USAREUR security managers were sent to become proficient as security managers.

Iron Curtain: An imaginary and physical border in Europe during the Cold War that separated free NATO-backed countries (US) and Warsaw Pact Communist countries (Soviet Union). Winston Churchill made the term popular in a speech on March 5, 1946 at Westminster College, in Fulton, Missouri.

ISSPM: Information Systems Security Program Manager. The official at a headquarters in charge of Computer Security.

Kaserne: From the German language; barracks, forts or camps where NATO forces in Germany were stationed.

KGB: *Komitet Gosudarstvenoye Bezopasnosti* (Committee for State Security). It was functional from 1954 to 1991 and was the USSR's leading espionage and political police agency. It was a combination of our CIA and FBI. Its mission was the safekeeping of the Communist Party of the USSR.

KP: Kitchen Police. A military enlisted man who performs clean-up duties in the mess or kitchen on a temporary basis. KP may refer to the work or the person. Persons may be assigned to KP duty due to committing a minor military infraction. It can include mopping the kitchen floor, peeling "spuds," washing pots and pans, etc.

LAA: Limited Access Authorization. Granting a non-US citizen access to limited US classified information up to SECRET, based on a Background Investigation and Commander's Statement.

Laredo Leader: Employment screening program for Local and Foreign Nationals hired to work for the US Army in Germany. The program still exists today and is unique to the hiring process in Germany. Belgium and Italy have similar programs that have been tailored after this one but must comply with the Status of Forces Agreement (SOFA) in each country. The program was designed to detect spies, terrorists and other criminal activities which would make them unsuitable for US employment.

Lead: An investigative term referring to any information in an existing case, the investigation of which may show the way to the completion of the case.

Legend: The persona or character assumed by the espionage agent. Involved are learning all facets of this false character such as age, parents' name, birthplace, etc. The nearer to the truth, the better.

MARS: Military Affiliated Radio System. This civilian auxiliary was founded by the Army Signal Corps in 1925 and is operated by licensed amateur radio operators. They assist the military in communications. Although still active today, it plays a lesser role in individual service member communications due to the advent of cell phones, the internet and email. They play a great role in communicating between National Guard units and State agencies and in disasters. They also participate in the testing of new communications technologies.

Military District of Washington (MDW): Located at Fort Lesley J. McNair in Washington, DC, its main mission is ceremonies and special events; i.e.; State Funerals, Presidential Inauguration, burials at Arlington cemetery, guarding the Tomb of the Unknown Soldier, and many more special events. On the Joint side, provides for the defense of our Nation's Capital Region.

MfS: *Ministerium für Staatssicherheit* (Ministry for State Security). It was East Germany's Secret Police or *Stasi*.

MOLINK: Moscow Link or the "Russian Hotline" for communications between the two heads of state in Moscow and Washington, D. C.

Moody Blues: A psychedelic rock band formed in 1967 in Birmingham, England with such mega-hits as *Nights in White Satin* and *Tuesday Afternoon*. Their music captured the look and feel of the Cold War years.

MP: Military Police. They are primarily involved in area security & protection operations and law & order operations. Also known as "White Hats."

National Agency Check (NAC): The NAC is part of every investigation which consists of a check of the Defense Central Index of Investigations (DCII – what investigations on Subject already exist), FBI fingerprint and name checks; the NAC also reveals issues related to financial problems, or encounters with law enforcement that would give advanced notice that problems might be encountered during the investigative process. Other agencies such as State might come into the NAC depending on the nature of the issues uncovered by the FBI checks.

NATIONAL MILITARY COMMAND CENTER (NMCC): Contains the US – Russian Hotline and is the center for command and communications for the National Command Authority, primarily the President. It is located in the Pentagon.

NATO: The North Atlantic Treaty Organization was formed in 1949 in Brussels, Belgium. The original members consisted of the United States and Western European nations. Today NATO consists of 26 independent member countries that include former East bloc countries. In accordance with the Treaty, the fundamental role of NATO is to safeguard the freedom and security of its member countries by political and military means. NATO is playing an increasingly important role in crisis management and peacekeeping.

NCOIC: (Non Commissioned Officer In Charge). A senior enlisted NCO who is responsible for a group/unit of soldiers given a specific job or mission to accomplish. The NCOIC is the conduit for orders and directions to and from the commander of the unit. The NCOIC makes sure that projects are being worked and the progress is satisfactory. They act as a screening element preventing the Division Chief or other Commanding Officer from having to contend with day-to-day minutia. They are also responsible for the continued professional development of all soldiers in the unit, to include running duty rosters, scheduling firing ranges, administrating the semi-annual Physical Fitness Test, and prepping soldiers for their annual Skill Qualification Test (SQT).

NEO: Noncombatant Evacuation Operations: These were government plans to bring family member civilians back to the United States in case of hostilities in Germany during the Cold War.

NIPS: New Bulletin for Information and Personnel Security. This was a monthly security education newsletter produced by USAREUR headquarters and distributed to the US Army and other Defense Agencies, worldwide.

Original Classification Authorities (OCAs): By Executive Order, only certain officials of a major unit may classify new documents.

OCONUS: This is the technical military term for outside the 48 contiguous states within the United States.

Oktoberfest: An annual 16 day beer festival held during late September and early October in Munich, Germany. German beers such as Hacker-Pschorr, Hofbräu, Paulaner and Löwenbräu are served. Annually, 5,000,000 people attend. The first Oktoberfest was held in 1810 to celebrate the marriage of Crown Prince Ludwig. Attendees also eat huge amounts of food and enjoy an assortment of rides.

Open Source Acquisition is the act of gaining possession of, or access to, information available to virtually anyone through readily accessible means such as newspapers, TV and radio news, books, etc. It is synonymous with open source collection. The preferred term is acquisition because by definition, open sources are collected and disseminated by others – open source exploiters acquire previously collected and publicly available information second-hand. Open Source Information can lawfully be obtained by request, purchase or observation.

OPSEC: OPSEC is Operations Security. The purpose of an OPSEC program is to hamper the enemy from obtaining friendly information.

Order of Battle: Consideration of the opposing enemy force. A commander analyzes an enemy's personnel, equipment, tactics, logistics, etc. so he knows what he will face in combat or field operations.

OSS: Office of Strategic Services. A wartime (WWII) intelligence agency formed by President Roosevelt on 13 June 1942; it was the predecessor of the CIA.

Paratrooper: a soldier who is a member of a unit trained to enter combat by jumping from an airplane or helicopter using a parachute. Units of paratroopers are called airborne units.

Plausible Deniability: An intelligence operation executed in such a manner where the operators can disavow any involvement by having a planned explanation of their activities. Also, plausible deniability applies to Governments. This principle means that if an operation is exposed, an enemy counterintelligence service in a denied area must not be able to obtain any credible evidence which would officially tie our government to the operation. For example, when running resident agents within East Germany, they are provided with cameras or other equipment made in East Germany, not West Germany, and absolutely not a Kodak camera. The operation is planned and executed to look like there is no US involvement at all. Even the relationship to the agent is often covered by false flag recruitment (he thinks he is working for a country other than the US).

POC: Point of Contact. The person in an agency responsible for handling a program or action.

POV: Privately Owned Vehicle. An individual person bought and owns the car.

PRA: Permanent Restricted Area. Military areas posted by the host command that USMLM and SMLM tour officers were not supposed to violate.

Propaganda: The distribution of information designed to influence behavior or beliefs of a large group of people.

Ration Card: To prevent black market activity, all overseas DOD personnel are issued a ration card to buy limited monthly amounts of coffee, tobacco and Class VI liquor.

Read – On: Providing an indoctrination briefing to an appropriately cleared individual who requires access to specified classified or sensitive information, based on a need to know, in order to perform a lawful and authorized function. The briefing describes the general nature of the program, procedures for protecting information, and warns of penalties if information is released.

Red Army Faction: Violent left-wing terrorist group (or gang) in Germany during the Cold War. It was also known as the Baader-Meinhof Group in its early days.

Red Brigades: Violent Communist terrorists in Italy during the Cold War. They participated in assassinations and bank robberies. They were also known as *Brigate Rosse*.

REFORGER (Return of Forces to Germany): An annual exercise for war during the Cold War in Germany. Additional combat divisions were delivered to Germany within ten days using division-sets of equipment in POMCUS (Prepositioning of Material Configured in Unit Sets) storage areas. Also, air and sea forces were involved.

Repo Depo: Replacement Depot. In the Cold War, the repo depot at Rhein Main was the processing center for most all of the incoming troops to Germany (USAREUR) who did not have pin-point assignment orders. In time of actual war, it is a staging unit for incoming troops to a theater of operations to replace missing soldiers due to illness, combat wounds, death or normal rotation. Soldiers receive training about the local area and situation before being sent to units.

Road Guards: Military formations have the right-of-way on post. For safety, when a marching or jogging formation crosses an intersection or road, designated soldiers (road guards) from the formation are posted and stop traffic. After the group crosses the intersection, the road guards rejoin the formation.

RTO: Rail Transportation Office. The office in Berlin for the Berlin duty train where passengers boarded and administrative duties were performed. There were also RTOs in Frankfurt, West Germany and Bremerhaven, West Germany. There is no question of the existence of the Berlin and Frankfurt RTOs. Verification of the Bremerhaven RTO: The Bremerhaven Port of Embarkation telephone directory of 1947 indicates there had been a Rail Transportation Office at the Bremerhaven main station. It was housed in a separate building next to the reception building. (Source: Dr. Hartmut Bickelmann, Archivdirektor, Magistrat der Stadt Bremerhaven, Stadtarchiv, Hinrich-Schmalfeldt-Str. -Stadthaus 5-27576 Bremerhaven) .

Ruse: In military deception, a trick of war designed to deceive the adversary, usually involving the deliberate exposure of false information to the adversary's intelligence collection system.

S2 or G2 or J2: is the unit commander's staff section concerned with Intelligence.

Sight Alignment: A term associated with aiming a weapon. While aiming at the target, your aiming vision, rear and front weapon sights and target must all be in a straight line.

Sight Picture: A term associated with aiming a weapon. After obtaining sight alignment and while focusing on the front weapon sight, the front sight appears just below the target (6 o'clock hold) or in the center of the target (center hold).

Security: With respect to classified matters, the condition that prevents unauthorized persons from having access to official information that is safeguarded in the interests of national security.

Security Manager: Official in a military unit responsible for most aspects of security.

SIR: Serious Incident Report. Mandated by Army Regulation 190-40, an MP regulation. All Army Commanders must report serious incidents to the Department of the Army Watch by telephone immediately on discovery, with email or electronic message follow-up. Examples of serious incidents are riots, bombings, terrorist attacks, threats against the President and some other criminal activity.

SMLM: Soviet Military Liaison Mission to the Commander In Chief, Us Army Europe. This mission was composed of Soviet intelligence officers and men located in Frankfurt, West Germany under the provision of the Huebner-Malinin Agreement. Their tasks paralleled those of USMLM (discussed under Tour Officer, below).

SMLM Sighting Card (AE Form 3231 – 1 Aug 77) A card issued to all USAREUR personnel which showed a SMLM car license plate, HQ USAREUR telephone numbers to report seeing a SMLM vehicle, detention instructions and Do's and Do Not's when a USAREUR member (military or civilian) made a detention.

SOFA: Status of Forces Agreement. This is an agreement between countries, i.e. the country which stations military troops in another country and the host recipient country. The agreement covers such issues as where the troops are stationed, access to bases, employment of host country citizens, payments for damage of host country land or facilities, legal jurisdiction, etc.

SOP: Standard (or Standing) Operating Procedures. A set of rules or procedures governing how to react to a certain situation. Usually numbered and titled.

Special Access Program (SAP): A program with special security controls to stop or delay technology transfer.

Special Assistant: A civilian expert assigned to aid the military Division Chief (Colonel) or DCSINT (MG). In addition to helping the DCSINT, this Special Assistant's Office also contained the Civilian Personnel Coordinator and the Civilian Intelligence Oversight Officer.

Spying: espionage in time of war to watch secretly for a hostile purpose and to cause harm against a country.

Staff "Weenies": Colloquial: Soldiers or civilians stationed at a Headquarters who produce staff actions (information papers, research, charts, interpretation of regulations) rather than being in a fighting unit. Also known as Action Officers or Staff Officers.

***Stars and Stripes* Newspaper**: *Stars and Stripes* publishes a daily newspaper for the U.S. military, DoD civilians, contractors, and their families. It operates as a First Amendment newspaper, free of control and censorship. The paper has published continuously in Europe since 1942 and since 1945 in the Pacific and today is also available online. Daily readership is well over 350,000.

Sterile Vehicle: A car devoid of any evidence linking the vehicle to an intelligence agency. Often used in surveillance or collection operations in denied areas.

Stick: Colloquial: The line of paratroopers in a plane who will jump out the same door one after another. There could be a single stick or multiple sticks, depending on the size and configuration of the plane.

Subject: A person or other entity about whom a CI investigation is conducted.

Subversion: Actively encouraging military or DOD civilian personnel to violate laws, disobey lawful orders or regulations, or disrupt military activities, with the willful intent thereby to interfere with, or impair the loyalty, morale, or discipline of US military forces.

Surveillance: From the French: to watch over. There are many types of surveillance, such as camera, mobile foot and vehicular. All aim to uncover the target's actions and associations. Two to three agents usually accomplish foot surveillance in a clandestine manner to avoid discovery by the subject. Vehicular surveillances are usually employed when increased distances are involved and again several vehicles are employed in a clandestine manner to avoid discovery by the subject. A stationary surveillance is known as a stakeout.

Suspense: Time allowed an Action Officer to complete a staff action. It's a due date that is marked on small slip attached to an action.

TOC: Tactical Operation Center. A TOC is a large unit's (battalion or higher) command center in the field. Usually comprised of the commander's special and general staff and activated during exercises and actual combat. The TOC receives battlefield information, analyzes information and issues further orders. Due to sensitivity of operational information and intelligence in the TOC, it may be surrounded by barbed wire and guarded by MPs or by soldiers from the Command's Headquarters Company.

TRA: Temporary Restricted Area. Military areas the USMLM and SMLM tour officers were not supposed to violate. They were usually temporary because of short-term exercises.

Terrorism: The use or threat of force or violence by groups or clandestine state agents in a manner calculated to induce a psychological state, usually fear, in an audience wider than the direct victim, for the claimed purpose of causing some kind of social or political response.

Tour Officer: A term for a liaison officer assigned to the British (BRIXMIS), French (FMLM) or American military liaison mission (USMLM) to the Commander in Chief, Group Soviet Forces in East Germany. They were located in Potsdam, East Germany during the Cold War under the provision of the Huebner-Malinin agreement or similar pact. The unclassified task of the military liaison missions was to provide liaison between WWII allied armies. The secondary, classified (now declassified) task was to collect information about the E. German and Soviet military. Mission officers and NCOs took two-three day car tours around East Germany to gather the information; thus, the term, tour officer. Another term for the liaison teams (coined by the Soviets) was missionary.

Tradecraft: The methodology of espionage.

Train Commander: Usually an Army Transportation Corps Second or First Lieutenant in command of the Berlin duty train (or freight train) as it travelled through Communist East Germany during the Cold War.

Treason: Violation of the allegiance owed to one's sovereign or state; betrayal of one's country.

USAFE: United State Air Forces in Europe. It is the major air force belonging to US European Command. It is located at Ramstein Air Base, Germany.

USAREUR: US Army Europe. It is the major land force belonging to US European Command. It is headquartered on Campbell Barracks in Heidelberg, Germany.

USAREUR's Southern European Task Force (SETAF): Located in Vicenza, Italy. It was an Airborne, rapid response force.

US Constabulary: During the aftermath of WWII, from 1946 to 1952, this organization was comprised of US soldiers who performed policing duties in the Western Occupation Zone of Germany, Berlin and Austria. These first Cold Warriors were referred to by the Germans as the *Blitz-Polizei* or "Lightning Police". Their motto was "Mobility, Vigilance, Justice".

V Corps: 5th Corps or Victory Corps. During the Cold War it was located in Frankfurt, West Germany. Today V Corps is the US Army's only forward-deployed corps. Nowadays, it is headquartered at Campbell Barracks, Heidelberg, Germany in support of CG, USAREUR. The last sentence contains the first mention of CG USAREUR instead of CINC USAREUR. On 24 October 2002, Secretary of Defense Donald H. Rumsfeld announced that in accordance with Title 10 of the US Code (USC), the title of "Commander-in-Chief" would thereafter be reserved for the President, consistent with the terms of Article II of the United States Constitution. Thereafter, the military CINCs would be known as "combatant commanders," as heads of the Unified Combatant Commands. (On 17 February, 2009, this definition was reviewed by the Office of the Chief Public Affairs, Department of the Army, with the comment: "I have no objections.") On 19 October, 2009 a check with the USAREUR Historian revealed the top Army general in USAREUR is now not called the CINC, but rather the Commanding General, United States Army Europe.

VII Corps: 7th Corps. It was the other of two large combat forces belonging to USAREUR. During the Cold war it was located in Stuttgart, Germany. It was deployed to Saudi Arabia in 1990; after that fighting, it was returned to Germany and then was deactivated in 1992.

Vetting: is evaluation of a person for a position. In this case a HoIS determines if the person has good placement for obtaining classified information and any characteristics that could induce him or her to pass information to a foreign power.

Volksarmee: The National People's Army of East Germany during the Cold War.

Volksmarch: German for people's march. It is a non-competitive walked route usually 10K (6.2 miles) in length with refreshments along the way and a medal upon completion.

Walk-In: A person (US or foreign) who reports to a MI Field Office, unexpectedly, to provide information.

Warsaw Pact: Communist countries in Central and Eastern Europe during the Cold War. It was based on a 1955 treaty in Warsaw, Poland. It countered the Western NATO.

World, The: Colloquial: Soldiers referred to the United States as the World when they were returning from an overseas assignment.